SAGE was founded in 1965 by Sara Miller McCune to support the dissemination of usable knowledge by publishing innovative and high-quality research and teaching content. Today, we publish more than 750 journals, including those of more than 300 learned societies, more than 800 new books per year, and a growing range of library products including archives, data, case studies, reports, conference highlights, and video. SAGE remains majority-owned by our founder, and after Sara's lifetime will become owned by a charitable trust that secures our continued independence.

Los Angeles | London | Washington DC | New Delhi | Singapore | Boston

Developing Support Systems for Rural Teachers' Continuing Professional Development

Thank you for choosing a SAGE product! If you have any comment, observation or feedback, I would like to personally hear from you. Please write to me at contactceo@sagepub.in

—Vivek Mehra, Managing Director and CEO, SAGE Publications India Pvt Ltd, New Delhi

Bulk Sales

SAGE India offers special discounts for purchase of books in bulk. We also make available special imprints and excerpts from our books on demand.

For orders and enquiries, write to us at

Marketing Department
SAGE Publications India Pvt Ltd
B1/I-1, Mohan Cooperative Industrial Area
Mathura Road, Post Bag 7
New Delhi 110044, India
E-mail us at marketing@sagepub.in

Get to know more about SAGE, be invited to SAGE events, get on our mailing list. Write today to marketing@sagepub.in

This book is also available as an e-book.

Developing Support Systems for Rural Teachers' Continuing Professional Development

Edited by
Zhao Yuchi
Liu Jing
Awol Endris

 www.sagepublications.com
Los Angeles • London • New Delhi • Singapore • Washington DC • Boston

Copyright © International Research and Training Centre for Rural Education (INRULED), 2015

All rights reserved. No part of this book may be reproduced or utilised in any form or by any means, electronic or mechanical, including photocopying, recording or by any information storage or retrieval system, without permission in writing from the publisher.

First published in 2015 by

 SAGE Publications India Pvt Ltd
B1/I-1 Mohan Cooperative Industrial Area
Mathura Road, New Delhi 110 044, India
www.sagepub.in

SAGE Publications Inc
2455 Teller Road
Thousand Oaks, California 91320, USA

SAGE Publications Ltd
1 Oliver's Yard, 55 City Road
London EC1Y 1SP, United Kingdom

International Research and Training Centre for Rural Education (INRULED)
No. 19 Xinjiekouwai Street
Beijing 100875, China

SAGE Publications Asia-Pacific Pte Ltd
3 Church Street
#10-04 Samsung Hub
Singapore 049483

Published by Vivek Mehra for SAGE Publications India Pvt Ltd, typeset in 10/13 Berkeley by Diligent Typesetter, Delhi, and printed at Chaman Enterprises, New Delhi.

Library of Congress Cataloging-in-Publication Data Available

ISBN: 978-93-515-0120-6 (HB)

The SAGE Team: Rudra Narayan, Sandhya Gola, Guneet Kaur and Nand Kumar Jha

Contents

List of Tables	vii
List of Figures	ix
List of Boxes	xi
Foreword by Dong Qi	xiii
Foreword by Arnold Nhavoto	xv
Acknowledgements	xvii
Executive Summary	xix

CHAPTER 1
An Overall Review of Support for Rural Teachers' Continuing
   Professional Development   1
F. Helen Drinan

CHAPTER 2
Mentoring System for Teachers' Professional Development:
   A Case from Romania   48
Ana Maria Sandi

CHAPTER 3
County Teacher Support System: A Case from China,
   'The Southwest Basic Education Project'   90
Liu Jing

CHAPTER 4
School Cluster System as Support Mechanism for Teachers:
   A Case Study from Cambodia   140
F. Helen Drinan

CHAPTER 5
Pedagogical Workshops as a Rural Teacher Support System
   in Mozambique   182
Ajuda de Desenvolvimento de Povo para Povo (Development Aid from People to People)

CHAPTER 6
Rural Teachers' Continuing Professional Development Support
   System: The Case of Ethiopia   204
Theodros Shewarget Belew

Summary and Policy Recommendations   237
F. Helen Drinan

About the Editors and Contributors   246
Index   250

List of Tables

1.1	UNESCO Strategy on Teachers (2012–2015), Action Line 2	7
1.2	Challenges That Rural Teachers Face and Suggested Teacher Support	11
1.3	Model of Teacher Leadership	40
2.1	Percentage of Observed Lessons in which Differentiated Learning Tasks/Activities Were Organised, by Level of Education (2005/2008)	71
2.2	Distribution of the Observed Lessons According to the Time Allocated to Lecturing, by Time Intervals in 2005 and 2008	72
3.1	Numbers of TLRC Established in Project Provinces	121
3.2	Details of Teacher Training	122
4.1	A Multi-sectoral Classification Scheme for Cluster Functions	161
5.1	Pedagogical Workshop by Province in Mozambique	200
6.1	The Federal Level Administrative Structure	217
6.2	The Regional Level Administrative Structure	217
6.3	The Wereda Level Administrative Structure	218
6.4	Three-year Training Curriculum	221

List of Figures

2.1	Stakeholders Involved in the Mentoring System	66
3.1	Overview of the Five Interventions Conducted by SBEP	96
3.2	The Concept Map of SBEP Rural Teacher Support System	108
3.3	SBEP County Teacher Support System	110
4.1	A Typical, Surface Definition of a School Cluster	153
4.2	Integration of Functions	156
5.1	The Functions of PWs	198
6.1	Detailed Training Structure at Federal Level	219
6.2	Detailed Training Structure at Region Level	220
6.3	Four Objectives of CRCs	226
6.4	The Mathematics and Science Cascading Training Model	229

List of Boxes

1.1	School-based CPD: Guinea, West Africa	14
1.2	School Cluster-based CPD: Uganda	16
1.3	Teacher Development Centres: The Aga Khan Foundation, Global	18
1.4	Innovative Links—School Networks: Australia	19
1.5	Teacher Networks: Singapore	21
1.6	'School That Counts': Brazil	24
1.7	School-based, Distance Learning Teacher Development Programme: SPRED 3, Kenya	25
1.8	CPD through Distance Education and ICT: ABRA, Australia	27
1.9	ICT Projects: Kerala, India	27
1.10	Peer-teaching: Escuela Nueva, Colombia	31
1.11	Peer Observation and Feedback: SBEP, China	32
1.12	Example of CPD Leadership at Local Level	39
1.13	Involving the Community: SIP, Namibia	42
3.1	Feedback from Teachers Trained by SBEP at Hezhang County, Guizhou Province	105

Foreword

Education for All (EFA) is an international initiative that focuses on universal access to quality basic education. As UNESCO's top priority in education, it aims to bring the benefits of education to all children, youth and adults. It is widely acknowledged that teachers are playing a key role in student performance, especially in resource-constrained rural settings where the teacher is often one of the few resources available to the disadvantaged students. Indeed, teachers' continuing professional development is one of the most important elements for the success of education system and stances, particularly those in rural and remote areas, war zones and post conflict situations. A number of education projects worldwide have been conducted as a response to the urgent needs of rural teachers' professional development by setting up local support systems for them. It is of great value to examine the successful practices in this area and identify the common attributes and reform elements that are replicable for rural education elsewhere as they seek relevant support for their teachers to improve education quality.

As a Category II Centre engaged in research and training for rural education in the family of UNESCO, International Research and Training Centre for Rural Education (INRULED) initiates and facilitates exchange and dissemination of experience in international rural education within the EFA framework. To support the UNESCO Strategy on Teachers (2012–2015) and UNESCO Initiative for Teachers Capacity Development in Priority Countries with focus on Africa (2012–2015), INRULED has launched teacher-related projects jointly with the International Institute for Capacity Building in Africa (IICBA) to accomplish the common missions and strategic priorities of both institutions.

In view of IICBA's long-term strategic goal for 2011–2015 planning period in 'developing capacity of African Member States in innovative ways of teacher policy development and management, contributing to the knowledge base on teacher development and management through research and dissemination, and promoting teacher issues through advocacy and partnership' as well as INRULED's expansion of its programme areas to training and professional development of rural teachers, INRULED and IICBA have jointly commissioned, conducted and consolidated research studies in the area of teacher education in/for Africa and China as well as other member states of UNESCO, aiming at capacity building for improved policy-making, standards development, curriculum design and competency-based assessment in teacher education, with particular preference to rural school teachers. The starting cooperation project is 'Developing Support System for Rural Teachers' Continuous Professional Development', which aims to study some good practises on support system for rural teachers in the developing world. According to the project cooperation agreement, IICBA has been in charge of providing three case studies from anglophone, francophone (which was originally written in French and will be published separately) and African Portuguese-speaking countries respectively, and INRULED in charge of collecting case studies from Cambodia, China and Romania.

This publication is one of the outcomes of this joint research project. Offering a valuable cross-country perspective, it shares five innovative practices on teacher support system that have been successfully implemented in different contexts and identifies some key components for an effective teacher support system in rural settings and a range of policy recommendations to help stakeholders provide relevant support to rural school teachers now and build sustainable support system for the future. A training module and a guidance book for policy makers to build up effective support systems for rural teachers based on the findings of this book are under development.

Dong Qi
Director
UNESCO INRULED

Foreword

It is repeatedly said, and for a good reason, that the quality of an education system is as good as the quality of its teachers. An education system needs to have a number of important inputs to provide optimum learning experiences for its learners. Well-built classrooms, good quality textbooks, sufficient supplementary learning materials, well-equipped demonstration and laboratory facilities, etc. are essential resources for an effective learning and teaching to take place in our schools. But, in the absence of a qualified and trained teacher, these resources may not result in student learning. It is believed that a well-trained and qualified teacher may compensate for deficiencies in the inputs mentioned. This is true in most rural settings where resource limitations may make it difficult to have the kind of learning experiences that are obtained in better resourced settings.

However, most teachers in rural areas do not usually have the required level of qualifications and training to be effective teachers. This is so as better qualified and trained teachers usually stay in urban areas. Deploying properly trained teachers in rural areas in sufficient numbers has never been easy. This is a particular challenge in most developing countries where the majority of the population live in rural areas. Unless teachers in these areas are supported both in subject matter knowledge and pedagogy, the teaching and learning in rural schools will suffer tremendously.

It is in recognition of the need to support teachers in rural settings that the two UNESCO institutions—International Institute for Capacity Building in Africa (IICBA) and International and Research Centre for Rural Education (INRULED)—joined hands to gather best practice stories in the various ways and means of supporting rural teachers. It is believed that the case studies can be good resources for in-service training providers as they highlight the various ways of building the capacities of rural teachers and organising support mechanisms for the better utilisation of the limited resources at the disposal of rural teachers.

The joint activities of IICBA and INRULED contribute to the realisation of the goals set out in the UNESCO Teachers Strategy. They also fall within the two global priorities of the organisation, namely Africa and Gender. The organisation has made teachers and issues associated with them its major concern. It also extends greater support to African countries in order to assist them achieve the goals of Education for All (EFA). Moreover, gender issues are mainstreamed in all the activities undertaken by UNESCO.

The five case studies contained in this publication illustrate the multiplicity of contexts and challenges that rural teachers work in, and the kind of support they could be provided. The two case studies from Africa—Ethiopia and Mozambique (they actually are three, with the Niger case written in French)—were coordinated by my institute, IICBA, and the other three—Cambodia, China and Romania—were handled by INRULED. This joint exercise has demonstrated the desirability of pooling resources for better results. In the current resource-scarce situation, collaborative efforts are the way to go, and the experience of IICBA and INRULED can be a good example for other UNESCO entities.

IICBA would like to take this opportunity to renew its commitment to continue working closely with INRULED, and benefit from the experiences of non-African settings, while sharing the lessons it learns from Africa.

Arnold Nhavoto
Director
UNESCO IICBA
Addis Ababa

Acknowledgements

We are grateful to all those who have contributed to the formulation of this publication which is one of the products of the research project on 'Developing Support Systems for Rural Teachers' Continuing Professional Development', especially the writers of each chapter: F. Helen Drinan, Ana Maria Sandi, Liu Jing, Ajuda de Desenvolvimento de Povo para Povo (Development Aid from People to People) and Theodros Shewarget Belew.

The research has gained strong support from the UNESCO International Research and Training Centre for Rural Education (INRULED) and Beijing Normal University, especially Professor Dong Qi, the Director of INRULED and President of Beijing Normal University, and Professor Wang Li, the Deputy Director of INRULED.

This is a publication by INRULED in collaboration with UNESCO International Institute for Capacity Building in Africa (IICBA). Here, we would like to express our sincere appreciation and gratitude to Mr Arnaldo Nhavoto, the Director of IICBA, and Dr Awol Endris, Programme Officer who coordinated the writing of the three case studies from Africa. Though the Niger case study is not included in this publication as it is written in French, our thanks also go to the writer and we are going to publish the case in a separate report.

We are also grateful to Ms Ge Yi, Administration Assistant of INRULED, and Ms Wioleta Kosińska, Intern of INRULED, for their contribution on formatting. A special thanks for the support from the former INRULED's Administration Team headed by Mr Zeng Haijun.

Our sincere thanks also go to the SAGE team including Ms Clare Sun, Mr Rudra Narayan Sharma, Ms Sandhya Gola, Ms Guneet Kaur and Mr Nand Kumar Jha.

Executive Summary

While it is widely known that educational access, quality and equity depend on teachers; parts of the world are facing a shortage of qualified teachers, particularly in remote, rural areas. What do rural school teachers need and how can they be supported in their continuing professional development (CPD)? How can a teacher support system be set up and function in a certain context? What factors would guarantee the success of the system?

These are the type of questions the following chapters set out to answer by taking five case studies from very different contexts and countries: Cambodia, China, Ethiopia, Mozambique and Romania but with a common topic of 'developing teacher support systems in rural areas for their continuing professional development (CPD)'.

Developing support systems for all teachers is pertinent to the quality of teaching and learning that takes place. However teachers working and living in more rural and remote areas often do not have access to the level of support that their urban counterparts enjoy. Therefore this book is devoted to describing teacher support systems from different parts of the world which have succeeded in their context. In this respect they can be considered examples of 'good practise' for their given context. As such it is possible to identify some common themes which can help others in their design and development of similar teacher professional development interventions.

Teacher support systems improve the quality of teaching and learning because it supports the continuing professional development of teachers. This, in turn, provides intrinsic and extrinsic motivation for teachers which benefits, not only the individual teacher, but also the school/institution, staff and students the teacher works with. It also has a wider outreach in that, if done well, and as will be seen in the examples in this book, the support system engages parents and the wider community which can encourage positive partnerships and collaboration.

So what do we mean by a support system for teachers in rural areas? A Teacher Support System could be defined as a support strategy and mechanism for teachers and schools in a given context, particularly in rural areas, which brings together material and human resources to provide continuous, relevant support to teachers' professional development so as to improve the conditions for teaching and learning. For rural areas it ensures the support and resources are available to rural teachers who are normally isolated and have no access to the support they need. Moreover it enables teachers and educators to support each other by providing follow up, sharing good practices and looking for solutions to local or unique issues, such as, large and over-crowded classes, teaching in bilingual or multi-lingual classes, teaching against gender stereotypes, teaching children from extremely poor families, single parent families or orphans. It also differs from a CPD support system in urban areas, which often focus on purely professional development, because a TSS in rural areas also serves the community, as a community learning resource centre to develop literacy and numeracy skills or skills training for rural labourers, so it has a developmental purpose too.

Based on the definition of Teahcer Research Centre summarised by Giordano (2008: 26), we suggest that a support system for rural teachers is characterised by the following elements:

- A group of teachers who serve as a network to exchange of ideas, share good practice and support each other professionally.
- The presence of a group of facilitators (mentor, tutor, trainer or supervisor) who provide ongoing and follow-up support for classroom practice, professional development and in-service courses.
- A space that is called a 'teacher resource centre', which may house meeting facilities, a lending library, reprographic materials and ICT tools (telephone, fax, internet).
- The involvement of wider communities in the TSS, for example, parents, members of the town/village, other professional bodies, local businesses and so on.
- A mechanism put in place for the function, progress, management and monitoring of the support system to ensure accountability and transparency.

Executive Summary   xxi

Therefore the objective of the book as a whole is to identify the fundamental similarities and features of successful rural teacher support systems in different countries, based on these case studies, so that they might be used for the reference or to inform policy and practice of governments of UNESCO member states and other stakeholders.

The book begins with an overall review of support for rural teachers' continuing professional development. Firstly by examining the international context that these systems operate within and secondly by identifying the challenges faced by rural teachers and showing how teacher support systems and activities can build their confidence and professional development. Finally it considers some of the fundamental foundations necessary to make a teacher support system for CPD successful.

The country case studies each follow a similar template in which they describe the background to the context, the organisation and functions of the support system, the effectiveness and outcomes, lessons learnt and what the future might hold.

Ana Maria Sandi in her description of the Mentoring System for Teacher Professional Development in Romania, part of the World Bank funded Rural Education Project, puts forward a clear and decisive argument for mentors as playing a key role in reaching and assisting teachers in rural areas and being essential in school-based professional development systems. She also emphasises that the main condition for the effectiveness of this approach is the continuity of the pedagogical support, which can be guaranteed through formal recognition and institutionalisation of the local support services.

Similarly Liu Jing's description of the Teacher Support System developed on the joint China–UK funded Southwest Basic Education Project is also very convincing. It emphasises that local support systems in which local teachers and local education authorities play a critical role in reaching and assisting teachers in remote areas are able to support them in an effective way. She describes in detail the types of support offered to local teachers, such as, classroom observation and support, mentoring and classroom action research. Key to the system working was building up a shared understanding of the rural teacher support system across the different levels: provincial, county, township, village and teaching points.

In the Cambodian case study Helen Drinan attempts to summarise the extensive work that Bredenberg and Geeves have done on Cluster

School Systems as a support mechanism to teachers in that country. In this case the complexities of the historical, political and socio-economic contexts come into play as do the plans of different international organisations and donors. However some of the positive functions of the Cluster School System are highlighted too, such as, Resource Sharing, Capacity Building and Accountability which provide optimism for the future of professional development for teachers there.

The Mozambican case study describes an innovative support system developed by Ajuda de Desenvolvimento de Povo para Povo (ADPP; Development Aid from People to People) centred around Pedagogical Workshops. The Pedagogical Workshops are part of a process that enables teachers, students and communities to gain life skills that contribute to improving teaching skills and community development. These Pedagogical Workshops have now expanded and developed throughout most of the provinces in Mozambique.

Finally in the case study from Ethiopia Theodros Shewarget Belew introduces a new comprehensive CPD framework and the establishment of Cluster Resource Centres (CRCs). It describes how, as part of the CPD system, the CRCs had to be strengthened to become the focal point for teachers' professional development and training. The system worked by building the capacity of CRC supervisors who are able to provide accountability to the system through reporting, giving guidance and advice and sharing experiences.

It is hoped that the chapters will stimulate further discussion and also raise awareness of the levels of commitment, time and funding needed to support those teachers in the most difficult circumstances. In addition it is equally hoped that the work can be developed further so that in the future quality training and the use of quality training materials will be developed as well as sharing good practices and new approaches at all levels of the education sector.

Reference

Giordano, A. Elizabeth. (2008). *School Clusters and Teacher Resource Centres.* Paris: UNESCO/International Institutes for Education and Planning.

1
An Overall Review of Support for Rural Teachers' Continuing Professional Development

F. Helen Drinan

Contents

List of Abbreviations
Introduction

Section 1: CPD and the International Context
1.1   CPD and Progress towards Education for All (EFA)
1.2   CPD and UNESCO's 'Strategy for Teachers 2012–2015'
1.3   CPD and Paradigm Shifts

Section 2: Why Have Teacher Support Systems?
2.1   Challenges for Rural Teachers
2.2   CPD Systems
2.2.1 School-based Support Systems for Rural Contexts
2.2.2 Cluster-based Support Systems for Rural Contexts
2.2.3 'Teacher Resource Centres' (TRCs) as Rural Teacher Support Systems
2.2.4 School Networks as Support Systems

2.2.5 Teacher Network Systems
2.2.6 Partnership Systems
2.2.7 Distance Education/Learning Systems
2.2.8 Information and Communication Technology (ICT) Systems
2.3 CPD Activities
2.3.1 Peer Coaching and Mentoring
2.3.2 Action Research
2.3.3 Peer Observation and Feedback
2.3.4 Demoing/Modelling
2.3.5 Experiencing and Reflecting

Section 3: Key Components for an Effective Teacher Support System for Rural Teachers
3.1 Meeting Local Needs
3.2 The Role of Leadership in Rural Teacher Support Systems
3.3 Modes, Development and Content of Training
3.4 The Role of the Community in Teacher Support Systems

Concluding Comments

References

List of Abbreviations

AKU	Aga Khan University
CPD	Continuing Professional Development
DFID	Department for International Development
EFA	Education for All
EQUIP	Education Quality Improvement Program
ICF	International Coaching Federation
ICT	Information and Communication Technology
IED	Institute for Education Development
INSET	In-service Training
ITE	Initial Teacher Education
NGOs	Non-Government Organisations
OECD	Organization for Economic Cooperation and Development
PRESET	Pre-service Training
SBEP	Southwest Basic Education Project
SIP	School Improvement Plan

TDC(s)   Teacher Development Centres
TRC(s)   Teacher Resource Centres
UNESCO   United Nations Educational, Scientific and Cultural Organization

Introduction

As the World Teachers' Day slogan suggests, it is time for the international community to recognise and value what teachers contribute to society. This is even more pertinent when we consider teachers who work in difficult circumstances, particularly those in rural and remote areas, war zones and post conflict situations. Providing these teachers with support systems can enable them to continue their professional development and have the confidence to 'take a stand' in society.

Therefore this chapter offers an overall review of support for rural teachers' Continuing Professional Development.[1] It does this in four sections. In Section 1 CPD in general is considered from international contexts. The purpose of contextualising CPD is to identify the drivers for change in CPD policy and planning. The major focus is on the international context but socio-economic, political, historical and cultural contexts are also implied when considering the paradigm shifts in CPD.

Section 2 is brief but essential as it describes some of the challenges faced by teachers, specifically those in rural, remote and difficult contexts.

In Section 3, support for rural teachers' CPD, specifically, is discussed. The common attributes of teacher development support systems and activities, which are relevant to rural contexts, are identified. The sections interlink as the contexts and challenges discussed in Sections 1 and 2 underpin the CPD systems and activities discussed in Section 3. The chapter concludes with Section 4 which looks at desirable foundations for setting up CPD teacher support systems in rural areas.

For the purpose of this chapter, 'CPD for rural teachers', is defined as,

> Continuing Professional Development is an on-going, lifelong process of enhancing the quality of teaching and learning by building the motivation,

---

[1] Continuing Professional Development is referred to as CPD from this point onwards.

commitment, understanding, attitude, skills and knowledge of teachers and other educational staff. It supports career development and progression as well as contributing to pupils' social and academic development.[2]

Section 1: CPD and the International Context

In this section, teachers' CPD is looked at through international contexts but with implied political, socio-economic and cultural perspectives because, more often than not, it is the given context or contexts that determine the success or failure of educational reform. As Guskey (1995) points out, 'because of the enormous variability in educational contexts, there will never be 'one right answer', instead there will be a collection of answers, each specific to a context' and, 'the uniqueness of the educational setting will always be a critical factor in education'. Therefore what works in one setting may not work in another. This is particularly pertinent to rural contexts where the diversity and variability of contexts are enormous.

1.1 CPD and Progress towards Education for All (EFA)

International policy and practice in education has long recognised the importance of the teachers' role in supporting and facilitating quality education. The World Declaration on Education for All (EFA) and its accompanying framework for action, which were developed in 1990 at Jomtien, Thailand, remain key drivers towards improving access to quality teaching and learning globally. In the EFA Framework for Action it states,

> The preeminent role of teachers as well as of other educational personnel in providing quality basic education needs to be recognized and developed to optimize their contribution. This must entail measures to respect teachers' trade union rights and professional freedoms, and to improve their working conditions and status, notably in respect to their recruitment, initial and

---

[2] This definition was given by Eritrean educators with the writer's facilitation in 2010.

in-service training, remuneration and career development possibilities, as well as to allow teachers to fulfil their aspirations, social obligations, and ethical responsibilities. (UNESCO, 1990)

It is important to note that the link between the development of teachers and the provision of quality basic education is made at this stage. Even though the term 'CPD' was not in such wide usage (in 1990) the understanding of the importance of teachers' development throughout their career is evident. Another interesting aspect of the statement is that it recognises 'professional freedoms' which is pertinent specifically when political and socio-economic contexts affect educational reform. The statement also implies that teachers' roles and responsibilities should be viewed in a holistic way, from inside and outside the classroom, as it includes 'aspirations, social obligations, and ethical responsibilities'.

A subsequent UNESCO review on the progress towards EFA in 2011 reiterates the importance of teachers' roles in improving the quality of education and sees the teacher at the core of quality (UNESCO 2011). It states,

> This view is a much more comprehensive and systematic approach to preparing the new- and developing the current- teachers needed to achieve EFA. This begins from the more careful selection of teacher candidates, through better quality initial teacher education, deployment to where good teachers are needed the most, serious induction and probation processes, and continuing professional development. But the success of this process depends on ensuring that teaching is once again seen as a profession of 'first choice' rather than 'last chance', and this requires raising both the status of the profession (e.g., through higher standards of qualification and certification) and teacher salaries and other benefits. (UNESCO, 2011)

In this recent document the term CPD is used and again the development of the teacher is strongly linked to the success of EFA. It implies that unless teachers have access to and are provided with the opportunity to professionally and personally develop, progress to EFA will be limited. As in the 1990 statement it recognises that teacher development begins from the initial teacher education[3] (ITE) stage and continues throughout a teacher's career.

---

[3] Both the terms 'initial teacher education' (ITE) and 'pre-service' (PRESET) will appear in this chapter to describe the start of a teacher's career pathway.

In this statement there is no mention of 'professional freedom' or a holistic view of the teacher as in the 1990 statement, instead there is a request for a 'more comprehensive and systematic' approach which suggests a more structured and collaborative path. Although such an approach is necessary in terms of CPD being, 'systematically planned, supported, funded and researched', (Villegas-Reimers, 2003: 141), one caveat might be that it could be misinterpreted to advocate a more centralised and top-down approach. This would be at odds with the more popular approach to CPD at present which looks at a more devolved, decentralised way of supporting teachers.

The UNESCO 2011 Working Document goes on to emphasise the importance of raising the quality of teachers and recommends that more attention be given to it, by the authors of the post 2015 EFA agenda. Therefore reiterating and highlighting the importance of the role of the teacher in the progress to EFA in the future.

The 1990 and 2011 statements reflect the political and socio-economic contexts of the times. However very importantly, both demand that there be a greater recognition of the role of the teacher in the provision of quality education. Indeed that the profession be regarded seriously and be afforded the status it deserves, in other words, the statements are 'taking a stand for teachers'. In terms of CPD it is significant that both see the support to teachers as:

- a long-term, life-long process;
- impacting on education reform, such as EFA;
- a systematic and comprehensive collaboration.

These themes recur throughout the chapter and are pivotal in the teacher's professional development discourse.

1.2 CPD and UNESCO's 'Strategy for Teachers 2012–2015'

The main emphasis of the current UNESCO Strategy for Teachers (2012–2015), 'is on supporting teachers for quality learning' in order, 'to configure a teaching force that works in an environment that rewards professional improvement and that is committed to improve the opportunities for student learning with well qualified and duly supported teaching practices', (UNESCO, 2012: 1). Here there is clearly a connection between

F. Helen Drinan   7

CPD and the opportunities for student learning. It is significant as it is a current international strategy and, 'the strategy provides an overall framework for a new initiative on teachers, aimed at accelerating progress towards EFA goals'.

Furthermore, it is relevant for teachers in rural areas as one of its key priorities is, 'systematically organizing and disseminating the existing knowledge base about effective teaching, particularly in disadvantaged contexts, and about mechanisms to support teachers and their professional development while removing obstacles to their success', (UNESCO, 2012: 1). In other words, sharing 'best practice' and ensuring there are support systems for professional development of teachers.

Each priority has an action line and activities which if successfully implemented should enable teachers in rural areas to have access to quality CPD. Table 1.1 shows the action line and activities for priority two, 'Improving Teacher Quality'.

Here we see the focus on diversification of strategies and this would align with Guskey's aforementioned diverse educational contexts. Notably ICT is included which is particularly pertinent to rural teacher support systems as is seen later in the chapter. There is recognition of the need to maintain teacher motivation which is even more critical in rural areas where many teachers can feel isolated and 'cut off'. Indeed if CPD is not motivating and relevant to teachers it will not be sustainable.

The sharing of 'best practices' is laudable but a caveat should be raised here as to what is 'best practice' and whose 'best practice'? Johnson, Monk and Hodges (2000) state that, 'Northern/Western ideas about teacher

Table 1.1
UNESCO strategy on teachers (2012–2015), action line 2

Action line: 2. Qualifying teachers and promoting their professional development
Activities:
• Supporting teacher's professional development through diversified strategies including ICT.
• Monitoring, improving and sustaining teacher motivation.
• Clearing house: dissemination of best practices in classroom teaching.
• Teacher evaluation and support.

Source: UNESCO (2012: 2).

change and development are poorly suited to modeling practices and challenges, for those who were historically disadvantaged'. Therefore the decision on what is 'best practice' and what is transferable should be made by those who it actually affects and whose lives it affects, specifically in rural areas.

Most importantly, teacher evaluation and support are included too, as these are too often ignored. Teacher support systems need to include formative evaluation which teachers can understand and use. In this way teachers can support each other without having to rely solely on external 'expertise' or inspectors'/supervisors' evaluation which, more often than not, is summative in nature.

Follow up and ongoing support of CPD activities for teachers is crucial for a robust teacher support system. A teacher support system should be regarded as cyclical so that evaluation and support can be used to inform new developments and change in teacher professional development, making it more organic and flexible.

1.3 CPD and Paradigm Shifts

It is impossible to separate the international context from the diverse global political and socio-economic, historical and cultural contexts, all of which have a direct influence on the education systems of a given country. They can drive policy and reform or, sometimes, do the opposite. There are numerous examples of CPD policy and reform changing direction each time a government changes, so that one government may pursue an 'organisational approach' to CPD, and another switch to an 'individual approach'.

For this reason what is seen during this period of the progress to EFA and even before, are significant paradigm shifts in how CPD is regarded internationally and nationally. There has been a move away from what is termed as the 'deficit model', which Day and Sachs (2009) describe as, 'teachers [needing] to be provided with something (knowledge, skills) which they did not already have', to a more active and 'reflective model', where teachers learn through discovery and active learning. Villegas-Reimers in her extensive literature review on CPD describes the 'Reflective Model' as one which, 'builds on teachers' personal classroom experiences. It requires that the teacher pay attention to daily routine and the events of a regular day, and to reflect on their meaning and effectiveness' (2003: 104).

Since these shifts have occurred, teacher support is less likely to be seen as a process of filling the gaps in teachers' knowledge and skills and more likely to be viewed as a process where teachers are seen as active learners and reflective practitioners, and in turn this is how their students can learn and develop. Moreover CPD is now seen as something that is not short term but long term; a lifelong, ongoing process which takes place in particular, diverse contexts. CPD is now considered a more collaborative process and linked to sustainability and whole-school approaches than it has been in the past.

Additionally what these different contexts show us are the paradoxes of teachers' continuing professional development which make it challenging to set up teacher support systems. Some of the paradoxes currently being discussed are:

- 'marketisation' and/or 'democratisation' of education;
- decentralisation, devolution and bottom-up approaches versus centralisation and top-down approaches;
- managerial versus democratic professionalism;
- autonomy versus central accountability and standards.

These opposite tensions may have common goals and objectives, for example, to improve teacher performance and skills and improve learner outcomes, however it is, 'how they go about doing this and who has control over the process is what distinguishes one from another' (Day and Sachs, 2009: 7).

These contexts, paradigm shifts and paradoxes are necessary to understand in order to consider what makes a successful, relevant and effective teacher support system in rural areas. Section 2 looks at such teacher support systems.

Section 2: Why Have Teacher Support Systems?

As seen from Section 1, internationally CPD is considered an important element in raising the quality of teachers but that more attention needs to be given to teachers and the teaching profession. Therefore raising the quality of teachers needs to be treated, with much more serious attention and more resources devoted to them throughout their career, from recruitment through training to deployment, induction, CPD, and the enhancement of their professional social status and economic rewards. (UNESCO, 2011: 18)

In rural areas this is even more pertinent where the disparities between urban and rural in terms of resources and access are so much greater. In addition students in rural contexts are often from marginalised and disadvantaged groups and these are precisely the target groups the EFA and Millennium Development Goals want to reach. Goal 2 for Universal Primary Education states 'ensuring that by 2015 all children, particularly girls, children in difficult circumstances, and those belonging to ethnic minorities, have access to, and complete, free and compulsory primary education of good quality'. Therefore supporting rural teachers should be a priority to enable them to provide quality education to some of the most disadvantaged children.

2.1 Challenges for Rural Teachers

Firstly it is necessary to consider the generic challenges faced by rural teachers. These can act as indicators to the type of CPD support that is needed. The problems rural teachers face have been well documented in teacher education literature, and while some are common to all teachers (both urban and rural), the issues are often exacerbated in rural areas because of geographic and socio-economic isolation. These problems include poor resources in all aspects, poor access, poor communications, employing the least experienced teachers or untrained teachers, little or no support, low morale and high absenteeism, no incentives, teachers feel they are out of the system, underpaid and are given no professional development. In many countries there is extreme inequity between urban and rural teachers both in the developed and developing world.

Table 1.2 below outlines some of the challenges rural teachers face. Types of teacher support are suggested in order to combat these challenges which often increase the urban–rural divide.

The following points 'unpack' some of these suggestions and discuss them in more detail in terms of their cross cutting themes and common attributes. For ease of reading the teacher support suggestions are divided into:

Table 1.2
Challenges that rural teachers face and suggested teacher support

---

Challenge: Poor resources and poor access/communications due to which teachers feel they are 'out of the system'

Suggested teacher support:

- Develop CPD systems that meet local needs and create local solutions, for example, school-based support systems and School Cluster systems;
- Develop CPD systems that relate to internal rather than external goals and objectives, decentralisation and devolvement;
- Use 'bottom-up' CPD strategies (rather than top-down) that feed into to policy at provincial/central level;
- Involve teachers in identifying professional development needs and being part of the decision making process;
- Use CPD systems that include local leadership to be able to formulate short-, medium- and long-term plans; local implementation of plans;
- Develop plans that consider both institutional and individual CPD needs.

Challenge: Least experienced and/untrained or underqualified teachers

Suggested teacher support:

- Use experienced teachers within the community as coaches and mentors, coaching and mentoring schemes, use of reflective models of CPD;
- Provide incentives to attract more experienced teachers and new teachers;
- Provide relevant professional development training and content;
- Provide 'Bridging Courses' through CPD;
- Recruit more local teachers;
- Recruit more teachers from ethnic minority areas.

Challenge: Little/no support/feeling of isolation/low morale and absenteeism/lack of incentives/underpaid

Suggested teacher support:

- Use peer support systems; collaboration with other teachers and schools; networking beyond the school community, e.g., other institutions, external links;
- Develop learning communities, use of Distance Education and ICT systems;
- Develop School Cluster systems;

(Table 1.2 Continued)

(Table 1.2 Continued)

- Acknowledge teachers' prior experience and knowledge; Incentive schemes;
- Provide systems that offer continuous support, introduce reflective models of CPD;
- Involve parents and community to raise awareness of the importance and relevance of education to bridge socio-economic disparities.

Source: Authors.

- CPD systems which are seen from a wider perspective (the aims, goals) and perhaps could be called the 'why' of CPD;
- CPD activities which are seen in terms of processes, the 'what' and 'how' of CPD.

2.2 CPD Systems

The following CPD systems are discussed and analysed with examples from international practice:

- Whole-school systems
- Cluster-based systems
- Teacher Resource Centres
- School Network systems
- Teacher Network systems
- Partnership systems
- Distance education systems
- ICT systems

These have been chosen because they provide the following:

- Flexibility and the possibility to be 'organic', that is, to grow and develop according to contextual changes that occur;
- 'bottom-up' approaches and also a blend of 'bottom-up' and 'top-down';
- variety within the system so the opportunity to try out different models and activities;
- both individual and organisational approaches to CPD.

In addition they reflect the themes that were identified earlier from international policy on teacher development for quality education, specifically in the progress to EFA. These are:

- a long-term, life-long process;
- impacting on education reform, such as EFA;
- a systematic and comprehensive collaboration.

2.2.1 School-based Support Systems for Rural Contexts

School-based[4] CPD support has been a consistent strategy in various forms and with varying degrees of success (Day and Sachs, 2009) for many years both in urban and rural areas. However extensive research of school-based CPD support has found that when schools commit to supporting CPD they are; more open and supportive and a collaborative culture is instilled across the school; staff has increased levels of self-esteem, self-confidence and enthusiasm. Research has also shown that schools supporting CPD can:

- raise standards of achievement in pupils at all levels;
- help teachers to manage change;
- lead to the personal as well as the professional development of teachers;
- improve the performance of individuals and institutions as a whole;
- increase staff morale and sense of purpose and promote a sense of job satisfaction;
- pull together the school's vision for itself.

These attributes go a long way in solving the challenges of supporting teachers in rural areas shown in Table 1.2, and this is why globally more and more countries are adopting whole school-based systems in both urban and rural areas. In Europe the majority of CPD takes place at school-base and there has been a shift to devolved decision-making.

This is backed internationally by leading teacher education researchers and practitioners that CPD is most effective when it fits existing

---

[4] Also referred to as 'site-based' in some literature.

school culture, is peer-led, collaborative and sustained (beyond one term) (Boyle et al., 2005; Bubb and Earley, 2009; Cordingley et al., 2003, 2005, 2007; Darling Hammond et al., 2009; Goodall et al., 2005; Lord et al., 2008; Timperley et al., 2007). The challenge remains, both in developed and developing countries, in getting teachers to gain access to CPD which embodies these characteristics.

Nevertheless, there are success stories internationally. Schwille, Dembele, Bah et al. (2007) provide a good example of school-based CPD which started small scale but due to its success went national. It is a relevant not only because it is an example from a rural context but also because it has the characteristics of the emerging consensus on good practice in professional development.

Important attributes can be found in the example from Guinea (Box 1.1) with regard to support for rural teachers.

Box 1.1: School-based CPD: Guinea, West Africa

In Guinea, West Africa, a programme was built around small scale grants to provide organisational support and incentives for teams of primary teachers to carry out their own school improvement and professional development projects. In just six years, the programme grew from a pilot in one region to a nation-wide effort reaching isolated rural as well as urban areas. The rationale and underlying philosophy of this programme are described as follows by Dembele and Miaro II: It is based on the premise that if CPD is going to succeed and effective professional development pursued, the teachers need to be engaged and to involve them in a genuine way in determining the content and organisation of the professional development so it is the teachers making decisions and initiating actions based on their perceived needs. This provides an important intrinsic incentive in that it acknowledges teachers' importance as key actors in the improvement of teaching and learning. In practice, in Guinea this has meant: designing an organisational support system that consists of extrinsic and intrinsic incentives, and assistance from a specially qualified support personnel; balancing such a support system with teacher autonomy and self-direction; and having a system to ensure transparency and accountability in terms of student and teacher learning and use of financial resources.

Source: Dembele and Miaro II 2003: 37.

Important attributes can be found in this example from Guinea with regard to support for rural teachers. These are:

Teacher involvement and engagement: The teachers were involved in determining what professional development they needed and were part of the decision-making process.

Intrinsic and extrinsic incentives: By acknowledging teachers as key actors and as people who can contribute to their own development, teachers' intrinsic motivation is tapped into, which provides incentives. Extrinsically incentives were provided by qualified support personnel.

Individual and organisational: Both individual and organisational development is enriched by the experience, through teacher autonomy which is within a system of accountability and transparency.

The Guinea support system provides some useful examples of CPD that appear to be sustainable and transferable as the programme went from pilot to national and was both urban and rural.

2.2.2 Cluster-based Support Systems for Rural Contexts

As an extension of the school-based system, School Clusters provide an opportunity for sharing resources and experience and more importantly can redress the imbalance between schools. Therefore many governments have implemented such systems in both rural and urban areas. The system also allows teachers, principals and schools to deal with institutional change and government education reforms.

School Clusters are eminently suited to areas of limited resources because schools can support and help each other and their fundamental goal is,

> to improve the quality of teaching and learning at the school and classroom levels. Exchanging ideas and information, combating isolation, and fostering co-operation between schools are goals of collaboration among teachers and school directors. School clustering and resource centres also deliver teacher training closer to the school level. (Giordano, 2008: 28)

In addition, as pointed out in the Working Paper 1 under EQUIP 1's Study of School-based Teacher In-service Programs and Clustering of Schools (Mac Neil, 2004), 'This approach includes community participation, ties teacher training curricula to local conditions and school-level goals, and purports to be cost-effective. Pilot activities and innovations, some taken to scale, have proliferated around the world in both developed and developing countries.'

An example of a successful School Cluster-based system can be seen in Box 1.2. The example from Uganda shares key attributes seen in the Guinea programme.

Box 1.2: School Cluster-based CPD: Uganda

A School- and Cluster-Based CPD Programme in Uganda experimented with using the school- and cluster-based approach through the USAID-funded SUPER program (1993–2000). With decentralisation a major part of the country's reform policies, SUPER worked with educators to create a School Cluster system anchored by teacher education colleges, which bring in-service activities to teachers in their schools or clusters. Former teachers, selected for experience and excellence, became 'outreach tutors' based at colleges, each responsible for working with a cluster of about 20 schools. The tutors provide supervision that emphasises teacher support, group facilitation, cooperative, problem solving, and mentoring. They visit classrooms to observe and help teachers improve their practice and help facilitate teacher discussion groups. The tutors also train community mobilisers to encourage parents and other community members to support schools.

Source: Engels, 2001.

Other aspects to consider from this case are:

Decentralisation: In this example educators from teacher education colleges at a more local level (provincial or district) were used not only to build capacity and support teachers in schools but also to engage and mobilise the local community to build a better understanding of what was happening in the schools. As Giordano (2008: 28–29) points out, 'for decentralization ... school clusters increasingly serve a number of administrative purposes through their linking of schools at the sub-district level. At a higher level they are part of the overall education reform'.

Linking with teacher education providers: It is evident from the examples given so far that support systems work when it is based on teachers' needs and is school-based. However CPD also needs to be a part of a comprehensive system for the support to be sustainable. For this reason it is important that INSET and CPD link with other teacher education providers, specifically pre-service training (PRESET) providers, as seen in the Uganda example. In this programme, very importantly, former teachers are selected to be trained as 'outreach tutors' but are linked to the teacher education colleges providing the PRESET.

In this way professional links and dialogues can be developed between institutions in a collaborative process. This might be expertise from teacher education institutes, as in the Ugandan example, providing further in-service or CPD to teachers. However, it would be equally viable for teachers, through their own professional development activities, for example, action research or materials development, to inform teacher education policy and curricula at the teacher education institutes. This reinforces the premise that teacher professional development is lifelong and an ongoing process which starts at PRESET or when an individual makes the decision to enter the teaching profession.

It is essential that there is a collaborative process between pre-service, in-service (in terms of upgrading and recertification of teachers) and CPD. This link is all too often cut after teachers leave their pre-service to start their 'probationary' or induction period in schools. Preparation for induction should begin at pre-service stage so that links and relationships can be built up with local schools.

Introducing sustainable and transferable CPD activities at school-base: In the Ugandan example the following CPD activities were introduced: peer support and collaboration, developing critical and reflective thinking skills, mentoring, observation and feedback. Such CPD activities are effective on many levels; they are relatively inexpensive, they are relatively easy to set up and organise and most importantly they are transferable and adaptable to many contexts, they are organic so there is room for flexibility, teachers can use them at any stage of their development and these are ongoing professional development activities.

2.2.3 'Teacher Resource Centres' (TRCs) as Rural Teacher Support Systems

CPD training activities at school and cluster base often use Teacher Resource Centres (TRCs) which are known by a multitude of names. They are commonly linked to cluster school-based systems (Cluster School Resource Centres) but are not exclusive to this system and they do not all function in the same way. In fact this has been seen as one of the weaknesses of TRCs, a lack of clarity about the function of the centres.

Paradoxically their very multifunctionality has also meant they have been very popular in donor funded projects, for example, English Language Teaching Development Project: Namibia; CRADLE Project: Ecuador; ELTIP and PROMOTE Projects: Bangladesh; RESC Project: Sri Lanka; PEP Project: Swaziland; English Resource Base Project: Zambia; SPRED II Project: Kenya (Ansell, 2000: 1). Box 1.3 shows an example of TRC supported by The Aga Khan Foundation (AKF).

Knamiller in an evaluation of TRCs found that, 'they did not appear to be an effective strategy for improving the quality of teaching and learning in the classroom. Neither did they make a noticeable difference to the availability and use of teaching and learning materials in one classroom'. (Knamiller, 1999: 20). However he later states, 'that the very presence of such centres had a positive impact on teachers' morale and 'feeling of status' and that by providing opportunities for professional interchange were laying the foundation 'for the development of a professional culture'.

TRCs are frequently seen as a base for INSET courses, and Knamiller (1999) also noted that these courses appeared to begin a process of change in teachers by raising awareness and providing ideas and materials that might be experimented within the teachers' own classrooms. Furthermore, such courses at times had knock-on effects on teacher training curricula generally, resulting in the curricula becoming more tuned to the needs of practising teachers.

Box 1.3: Teacher Development Centres: The Aga Khan Foundation, Global

There are several different examples of how TRCs can be designed and used. The Aga Khan Foundation (AKF) provides one such example. It was well ahead of its time in the middle of 1980s as it recognised the importance of the development of teachers and schools and linking it to school-based professional development. In the early 1990s, the Aga Khan University (AKU) linked with primary and secondary education sectors. By the early 2000s, the AKU and Institute of Education Development (IED) had developed Teacher Development Centres (TDCs). The TDCs are used to support local schools and continue to support teachers' professional development at school-base. This system still remains an exemplary one in parts of East Africa and South Asia.

Source: Hopkins, 2002: 293 (in Schwille, Dembele, and Schubert, 2007).

Therefore it could be argued that TRCs could be very useful conduits for CPD at local level but only if the functions and planning of the TRCs are clearly established beforehand. Ansell in his recommendations on the functions of TRCs suggests that the most important thing to do in setting up TRCs is to find out what it should be and do in the given context and concludes by saying, 'that TRCs have a major contribution to make, especially in developing world contexts where provision of resources and materials are inadequate and where funds to facilitate the continuing professional development of teachers are meagre' (Ansell, 2000: 9).

2.2.4 School Networks as Support Systems

Differing from the network of schools in School Cluster systems, school networks cover a much wider geographical area and are often part of a national professional development programme. Box 1.4 gives an example from Australia where school network systems have long been put into practice nationally.

This is a good example of linking CPD to wider issues of educational reform and school restructuring using a comprehensive systematic approach. It also has the common attributes already noted: needs-based, collaborative and it considers both individual and organisational CPD. In

---

Box 1.4: Innovative Links—School Networks: Australia

Australia has a long experience of such network systems, the Innovative Links project is one such project using networks and partnerships to exemplify the themes for successful CPD, such as, relevance and needs identified by the teachers; control of the CPD by the participants; adopting collaborative programme organisation; learning through investigation and practice and critical reflection; focussing on institutional, that is, school reform as well as individual CPD.

Innovative Links was organised through 'Roundtables' in both urban and regional (including rural and remote areas) sites consisting of teachers from affiliated school and teacher educators from participating universities together with employers, unions and National Schools Network representatives. The Roundtables enabled schools to be networked at local level and linked nationally.

Source: Grundy and Robinson, 2009.

addition, as Day and Sachs (2009) point out, the inclusion of employer and unions in the Roundtables provides the industrial relations link to CPD.

2.2.5 Teacher Network Systems

This is perhaps the most natural and organic of CPD support systems. More often than not, and this is particularly true in rural and remote areas, teachers will form support groups because they recognise and understand that learning from peers might be the only professional development they have access to.

The network may take the form of specific subject support groups or across curriculum groups. In many countries, for example, Cambodia, Vietnam and China, teachers in rural areas generally plan lessons and share ideas at the start of a school week. In rural areas teacher networks often remain school-based simply because of logistics, the nearest neighbouring school might be miles away or across mountain ranges.

This type of system can also be regarded, 'as an alternative to government-created and sponsored programmes of in-service development', (Villegas-Reimers, 2003: 80). Indeed in Japan their main purpose has been to 'promote teaching, independent of government control, and a democratic education', (Shimahara, 1995: 183).

Huberman (2001) backs up the importance of such support systems and presents strong arguments for having these networks managed by teachers themselves, so that the networks generate a process by which teachers can communicate, address issues, observe each other's work, bring in people who are experts in other fields, (cited in Villegas-Reimers, 2003: 81). This type of support can alleviate the feeling of isolation often felt by teachers in rural areas and sometimes provide the impetus to broaden the networks.

Indeed there are many examples of teachers forming what has been coined as 'communities of practice' (Palincsar et al., 1998 cited in Villegas-Reimers, 2003: 81) where teachers from more than one school get together to work on their professional development, for example, in Spain. In other countries the teacher network systems are national, for example, in Finland and South America. In South America, 'Each of these national networks is quite active in its own country, and their members have come together in this cross-national network to share experiences, learning opportunities and work activities' (Flores and Arias, 2001).

F. Helen Drinan   21

An interesting example of Teacher Networks comes from the Singaporean example in Box 1.5 where Teacher Networks were developed in late 1997 in order to develop in Singapore schools what Fullan and Hargreaves (1992) called 'interactive professionalism' (Day and Sachs, 2009: 193).

Box 1.5: Teacher Networks: Singapore

The objectives of the professional development activities of the Teacher Networks have sought to: cultivate collaborative inquiry; increase teacher's individual capacity to learn; manage knowledge and value diversity; to increase both individual and organisational capacity to manage continuous improvement (Tripp, 2009: 193).

It does this through six interrelated programmes:

Learning circles: These are the main tool for developing the school's capacity for change through developing more reflective and innovative teachers (Tripp, 2009: 197).

Teacher-led workshops: These are 'by teachers, for teachers', which enable participants to propose alternative views and possibilities and to challenge and clarify their own and others' suggestions (Tripp, 2009: 201).

Teacher Network conferences: To enhance self-esteem and the public image of teachers as well as to inform teachers about the macro issues in society that are driving the changes in the education system which they have to implement (Tripp, 2009: 202).

Well-being programme: 'Runs activities that help teachers cope with emotional, domestic and social demands' (Tang 2011 [in Tripp, 2009: 203]).

Teacher Network website: 'To help develop independent and self-motivated adult learners' (Tang 2011 [in Tripp, 2009: 204]).

Publications: 'Teachers' work is published and this aims to help them clarify their thoughts, it provides local knowledge that can be applied by others', being published is a high-status activity (Tripp, 2009).

There are several key attributes that are transferable from the Singapore experience. The Teacher Network system provides:

Both individual and organisational professional development: At an individual level teachers not only become more reflective and innovative but also more confident and inquiring. At an organisational or school level there is a strong link between how the teachers are learning and how their students learn, that is, developing critical thinking and problem solving skills. In this respect it endorses Barth's (1990) notion of schools as places of learning for teachers as well as pupils (Day and Sachs, 2009: 85).

A link between professional development and wider educational reform: Through the six interrelated programmes, specifically the workshops, conferencing and publications we can see that individual teachers and schools are enabled to understand and translate educational reforms into their own local contexts.

An enhanced image of teachers and improved status: It does this through involving them in what can be called 'higher-level' activities, such as, conferences and publishing their own articles and materials. These are the types of activities that enhance the status of teachers and go a long way to see the profession as 'first choice' rather than 'last chance' as stated in UNESCO's (2011) review of the progress to EFA.

A holistic approach to professional development: The teacher is seen as a whole person and not only as 'a teacher'. Therefore a teacher is allowed to develop both professionally and personally by providing the teacher with pastoral as well as professional and academic support.

Both teacher education and teacher development: In the conferences, teachers learn about other education systems and change and how this can impact them. In the teaching circles they explore and create their own ideas about teaching and learning.

A link between the six: For example, teaching and learning findings from the teaching circles are shared at workshops and conferences and perhaps published or put on the website.

The opportunity for teachers to be involved in the planning and administration: Committees of teachers plan and administer the programmes and thus are developing teacher leadership skills.

2.2.6 Partnership Systems

Partnership systems for CPD can take many forms. However this type of CPD system does not often encompass very rural and remote schools in some countries, specifically in countries where terrain is very harsh and schools might consist of one teacher at a 'teaching point'. Therefore there is even more reason and it is even more pertinent for governments to be aware of this and resolve this type of exclusion. In the following examples we will see how two different contexts have managed such partnerships.

The most common type of partnerships in terms of CPD are school–university partnerships. However there is an ever growing demand, especially as education is being driven more by economics, for schools to build partnerships with the private sector, for example, banks, industry and so on. Furlong et al. (2000: 77–78) suggest a continuum of partnerships, from collaborative partnerships at one end to complementary partnerships at the other. The former, as it suggests, requires the two to work together and share the responsibilities of learning and teaching, whereas in the latter, the two are seen as having separate and complementary responsibilities.

Sugrue (2009) argues that universities are too often side-lined or marginalised from CPD but they have a leading role to play in shaping the role of teachers as public sector intellectuals which indeed would simultaneously raise teachers' status in the eyes of the public. However the partnership must be based on mutual need to be successful.

As was seen from the Innovative Links programme in Australia the partnerships between practising teachers on a whole-school basis and university-based teacher educators was at the centre of the initiative but with the inclusion of employers and unions too.

In Pakistan the Aga Khan University Institute for Educational Development (AGU/IED) offers professional development courses for teachers and other educators. In addition, it offers programmes in cooperation and directly with schools and other partners, such as, local NGOs and public education service providers. They also offer an open learning mode for teachers too. The premise of the institute is that through different partnerships it offers teachers and other educators more choice of when, where and how they continue to professionally develop.

In South America there are numerous examples of partnerships, many between ministries of education and other institutes, primarily universities. The following example in Box 1.6 describes such a state-level initiative with universities and NGOs.

A number of elements in this partnership are worth highlighting. Again we see the use of former schoolteachers being developed into monitors and mentors to work with teachers at school base on the project work. This is important as it is CPD for teachers at different stages of their life (the monitors as well as the teachers). Also by using former teachers there is more chance of relationships bonding quickly and more

> **Box 1.6: 'School That Counts': Brazil**
>
> This is an ongoing programme which was established in 1999 with six municipalities and collaboration of academics from an education centre at the University of Sao Paulo. The programme engages teachers in the development of classroom projects in reading and writing and monitors them using former schoolteachers, who are part of the university centre involved. To stimulate critical analysis of their teaching, participants use narrative accounts and videos to report in their classroom events. During the workshops, teachers get classroom examples similar to their own experience that also serve the purpose of analysis. There is also a distance component consisting of electronic reviews by the regional coordinator of the work done by the teachers (video-clips, narratives and classroom observations). Teachers have access to these communications at a local 'teachers' house' installed by the municipality, which is also a meeting place and resource centre.
>
> Source: Adapted from Avalos, 2009: 130–131.

effectively. Importantly workshops use examples that relate to teachers' real experience, so, are relevant and useful. In addition teachers are able to build useful and necessary skills, such as, critical thinking, through participating in reflective practices such as, narratives and analysing video clips of themselves and others.

2.2.7 Distance Education/Learning Systems

Distance education programmes have been used for CPD in a number of countries for many years. These programmes use different media, for example, radio, television, telephone, written and recorded material and more recently, and rapidly developing, Information and Communication Technologies (ICT), using the internet and online professional development courses.

However in many countries the approach to distance education is still a mixture of media or what is sometimes called a blended approach, that is, there will also be some face-to-face engagement through tutor groups or teacher circles with written and recorded modules. Box 1.7 describes an example from Kenya. This was a distance learning, school-based teacher development programme funded by DFID, which started in the 1990s. Named SPRED 3, it is still regarded as an impressive

> **Box 1.7: School-based, Distance Learning Teacher Development Programme: SPRED 3, Kenya**
>
> One of the key components of SPRED 3 was that it aimed at developing a national system of school-based teacher development through distance learning and tutor-supported methods. Thus one of the key outputs was to the setting up of appropriate structures and modalities for the delivery of a distance education programme for primary schoolteachers. As a consequence a systems framework to deal with CPD has been set up nationally.
>
> The programme also learnt from the previous projects SPRED 1 and 2 and were able further use the TRCs, or Teacher Advisory Centres (TACs), as part of the tutor support system. From each school three teachers were selected and became lead teachers in their subjects, for example, Maths, English, etc. After a five month course they formed school-based subject teams and became mentors for their colleagues.
>
> In addition, it also has the promise and support to move beyond teacher as technician to teacher as reflective practitioner.
>
> Source: Adapted from Christie et al., 2009.

initiative. Some of the attributes mentioned in the evaluations of the programme are:

- It based innovation in the workplace contexts of teachers;
- it aimed at facilitating in-school impact on teaching and learning;
- it used a distance learning mode of delivery to reach rural and remote areas which was tutor supported;
- the training modules used for distance learning were relevant and focused on teachers' classroom experiences and moved them away from didactic and rote methods of teaching and learning to a more active and participatory methodology;
- the modules and other resources reached the stakeholders and were available;
- a monitoring and evaluation procedure is in place that recognises the need for a bottom-up approach, starting with impact at the teaching and learning end. (Adapted from Christie et al., 2009.)

Other factors to consider from this experience are: success was seen and realised only after SPRED 3 developed school-based teacher development with strong policy and strategic planning at the national level. Additionally, the initial training programme took time, at least five months, and the whole thing over many years. Again it is seen that a school-based system within a systematic comprehensive framework and developed over a realistic timeframe proved to have an impact on rural teachers' professional development.

2.2.8 Information and Communication Technology (ICT) Systems

The twenty-first century has seen an increasing growth of ICT programmes and projects in the education sector where it is having a big impact, both positively and negatively. ICT is affecting CPD majorly and according to Grundy and Robison (2009) it is the preferred method of professional development in Australia. They go on to describe 'The Teaching Learning Support Network' (TLSN), in Western Australia as an example of the move towards online professional development: 'The TLSN is an interactive website which has been designed to provide support to teachers undertaking self-directed professional development' (http://www.education.wa.edu.au [accessed on 13 January 2015]). Participation in teachers' networks on the Internet or through local contacts has also been shown to support lasting change in teachers' practice.

In terms of CPD in rural contexts, ICT can be viewed from several aspects, three of which are listed here:

1. Using ICT in distance learning as previously discussed briefly.
2. Using ICT in the classroom as an interactive method for teaching and learning, for example, understanding and using new software.
3. Using ICT on a non-formal, personal level to continue your own professional and personal development.

Examples of these aspects follow. Australia, because of its sheer size and diversity of contexts, is a good example of where distance education for CPD using ICT has been applied. There are numerous examples from Australia but the example in Box 1.8 is relevant because it links ongoing CPD with quality teaching and student outcomes and because the training, 'was built around professional development best practices to address the challenges of providing ongoing training in remote areas

> **Box 1.8: CPD through Distance Education and ICT: ABRA, Australia**
>
> Helmer et al. state that, 'The ABRA training and support strategy was built around ... best practice ... which they highlight in their article as being,' the importance of an ongoing approach that is embedded in teacher practice; is organised around collaborative problem-solving; involves reflection and feedback; and is followed up with support from a range of experts (Guskey, 2003; Hawley and Valli, 1999; Ingvarson et al., 2005; Timperley et al., 2007).
>
> Teachers attended a one-day workshop that trained them in the use of ABRA, and continued learning was reinforced by pairing teachers with a literacy coach. Data were gathered through an implementation fidelity measure, researcher field notes, focus groups, teacher logbooks, and the Early Language and Literacy Classroom Observation tool. The schools involved in ABRA are from all three geo-location classifications in the Northern Territories in Australia, that is, urban, remote and very remote.
>
> Source: Helmer et al., 2011.

(Helmer et al., 2011). In this case it was to train teachers in an interactive computer literacy programme called ABRA (short for ABRACADABRA) for early childhood literacy.

A different approach to using ICT in schools comes from the state of Kerala in India as seen in Box 1.9.

> **Box 1.9: ICT Projects: Kerala, India**
>
> The state of Kerala in India provides a good example of a government being very active in using ICT in different forms. Since 2001 the 'IT@ school projects'[5] have been using computers, camera, video and film animation in an attempt to remodel conventional teaching methodologies in the classroom. It now covers 12,000 schools and has a network of 160 master trainers and 5,600 IT school coordinators who, very importantly, are school teachers themselves statewide. In addition the project also provides specialised training for visually challenged teachers in the state. This is a highly innovative initiative which has made capacity building in ICT training for teachers a priority.
>
> In addition to the training, there are also e-textbooks, animation filming and a range of activities.
>
> Source: www.itschool.gov.in

[5] See www.itschool.gov.in for more information on Kerala State IT Schools.

What is key to bring out in this example of ICT for CPD is that the project is:

- Whole-school: The schools are built on the ethos that ICT is the way forward educationally and involves everyone.
- Focused on capacity building of teachers, so recognising the importance of the role of teachers in facilitating the learning and use of ICT in their students and that training is a priority (teachers are a priority).
- Using teachers from the schools (not external people) as the ICT coordinators, so again recognition of the role of teacher-empowering and enabling them in new technologies.

In reality however many rural teachers, especially those in remote areas but not limited to them, still do not have access to ICT. Therefore, access to technology should be made a priority for these teachers in order for them and their schools not to be left behind.

It is therefore crucial that in terms of CPD, all teachers have at least the basic skills in ICT, that is, to be able to use a computer and the internet. This would avoid what Day and Sachs (2009) describe as, 'eroding the role of the teacher as exclusive holder of expert knowledge', because teachers would be empowered through using ICT. This can be done by using:

- Networks: School Clusters and TRCs if provided with a network of computers provided by governments.
- External providers through partnerships, for example, local business and banks could provide the hardware and software.
- Institutional providers, for example, teacher training colleges, universities could provide hardware, software and capacity building at school–base.

In the next part we look more deeply at how these teacher support systems are applied, that is, what are the common CPD activities and models used that are considered relevant, sustainable and transferable.

2.3 CPD Activities

There are a number of school-based CPD activities which have been tried and tested in many different contexts Kelly (2006) suggests that, 'Site-based professional development activities include peer coaching, mentoring, modeling, observation and providing feedback to others', and states that,

> Practice is most likely to be enhanced in a lasting way when decisions about CPD policy and practice consider the social context of adult learning and allow for richer learning experiences than are usually offered on short course based on a developmental model of skills acquisition.

Missing from this list but equally relevant is 'Action Research' and is included in the following description of activities.

as Apart from CPD activities, teacher education and development literature also refer to CPD models which can be considered as conceptual frameworks. Reference has already been made in this chapter to 'deficit' and 'reflective' models. Kennedy writes extensively on these and other models, such as: 'award-bearing', 'standards-based' and 'transformative' models', (Kennedy, 2005: 2–3). Although this section will not focus on such models, reference will be made to the 'reflective' model because it is well suited to teacher support systems in rural and remote contexts.

2.3.1 Peer Coaching and Mentoring

Mentoring and coaching appear universally accepted as effective tools for effective CPD. However there are subtle differences between the two.

The International Coaching Federation (ICF) defines 'coaching' as 'an ongoing relationship that focuses on clients taking action toward the realisation of their visions, goals, or desires' (Bennet and Martin, 2001: 6). More succinct is Robbins's description of 'peer coaching' which he describes as, 'a confidential process through which two or more professional colleagues work together to reflect on current practices; expand, refine and build skills; share ideas; teach one another; conduct classroom research; or solve problems in the workplace' (Robbins, 1991). From these descriptions it is already possible to see why these activities are well suited to a reflective model of CPD.

'Mentoring' is typically defined as, 'a relationship between an experienced and a less experienced person in which the mentor provides guidance, advice, support, and feedback to the protégé' (Haney, 1997, cited in Quality Improvement Agency), for example, for newly qualified teachers, new teachers arriving at a school or a system. It tends to be short-term rather than long-term and relates to the stages of a teacher's development.

Both 'coaching' and 'mentoring' can be considered part of what has also been termed 'collaborative, peer learning' and 'co-operative or collegial development' by (Glatthorn, 1987) which includes other CPD activities, such as, professional dialogues to discuss professional issues of personal interest; curriculum development where teams of teachers develop curriculum units; action research to collaboratively inquire about a real problem in their teaching; lesson plan sharing. However in order for these collaborative CPD activities to work, the following conditions are necessary:

- a true collaborative school context (and thus, this is not imposed on teachers);
- administrators support the efforts;
- teachers have sufficient time to complete the activities;
- teachers receive some training on how to implement the CPD activities or models effectively. (Adapted from Glatthorn, 1987)

There are numerous examples of how these types of CPD activities and models have been put into practice, for example, teachers developing materials based on new curricula; same subject group teachers developing lesson plans for the semester; different subject teachers sharing experiences of methodology and activities, for example, English language teachers demonstrating more learner-centred approaches to Mathematic teachers.

In Latin America there are many successful examples where it has been an important feature in rural schools for many years. In Chile, as part of a secondary improvement project, teacher professional groups have been established. They started in the 1990s and still continue today without external funding (World Bank funding finished in 2000). These groups are able to meet periodically to share experiences, discuss new methods, create new materials and discuss curriculum reform. Although it is not part of a national policy, the impact on individual teacher's professional development cannot be denied. An external evaluation of the teacher groups in 2001 found them to be successful in terms of teachers being able to develop their own curricular materials (Avalos, 2009).

In Colombia, the well known 'Escuela Nueva' programme provides an excellent example of improving the quality of education in rural areas and also a programme that has been successfully transferred to other similar contexts, for example, in Guatemala. As shown in Box 1.10, it is not only an example of peer teaching but also of the characteristics of quality CPD discussed so far; peer learning and support, teacher networks and use of Teacher Resource Centres.

Box 1.10: Peer-teaching: Escuela Nueva, Colombia

In Colombia, the Escuela Nueva programme (New School Programme), a reform to improve the quality of multi-grade teaching in rural schools in the country, is another example. This programme relies heavily on teacher education and professional development, particularly on peer-teaching, where groups of teachers at the local level take on the responsibility to help one another learn about the new approach and come together periodically (in the 'microcentros rurales') to reflect on the results of their initial attempts to implement change in their classrooms.

Source: Rojas, 1994; Schiefelbein, 1991 [in Villegas-Reimers, 2003: 100–101].

2.3.2 Action Research

As part of the collaborative approach to CPD training, the growth and importance of training teachers in Action Research is pertinent. As a CPD activity it has relevance for the rural context in that it is collaborative and can provide intrinsic and extrinsic motivation for teachers. It does this by giving teachers the opportunity to explore and discover both practical and theoretical aspects of teaching and learning through working with their peers and students, thereby building their confidence and increasing their sense of self esteem as a professional person. It is a good example of both professional development from a personal and organisational perspectives as both can benefit from this. In addition it is an example of how partnerships can develop between schools and other institutes specifically teacher education providers, in that teachers' action research can inform policy at institutional level. O'Hanlon in Villegas-Reimers (2003) describes it as:

> Action research is a process of investigation, reflection and action which deliberately aims to improve, or make an impact on, the quality of the real situation which forms the focus of the investigation. It is a form of inquiry

which involves self-evaluation, critical awareness and contributes to the existing knowledge of the educational community. (O'Hanlon, 1996: 81)

There are three reasons which explain why action research can be an effective model for teachers' professional development: 'it is inquiry-based, and allows teachers to investigate their own worlds; it is aimed at the improvement of teaching and learning in schools; and it leads to deliberate and planned action to improve conditions for teaching and learning' (O'Hanlon, 1996).

A related example of implementing action research as part of rural teachers' professional development comes from Honan et al. (2012) who worked on an Ausaid funded project in rural and remote areas of Papua New Guinea. From this they found that,

> Evidence suggests that 'top-down' approaches to professional learning are not sustainable, so 'organic' local professional learning is required. Our approach may in the long term be more sustainable and useable because of its foundations in a 'grassroots' model, where small groups of teachers are encouraged to spread their knowledge and expertise to other small groups. (Honan et al., 2012)

2.3.3 Peer Observation and Feedback

An example of a project where observation and feedback played a key role in rural teachers' professional development is shown in Box 1.11.

Box 1.11: Peer Observation and Feedback: SBEP, China

Critically it differed from the district school inspection system in that it focused on formative development rather than on evaluating teachers, where the evaluation was more often than not destructive rather than constructive.

Observation forms were designed in a participatory manner and with developmental and research purposes in mind. Thereby developing practice through classroom observation and feedback. Through this observation and feedback system teachers, trainers and head teachers were able to collect qualitative data on how teachers were developing as the project progressed. The observation and feedback were also linked with the participatory training methodology and content that was another activity and part of the teacher support system.

Source: From personal experience on SBEP.

It is the DFID funded Southwest Basic Education Project (SBEP) in China where the aim was to improve teaching and learning for the most disadvantaged children.

This is relevant in that it has and is still being used in some of the most remote areas of South West China providing opportunities for teachers to have professional dialogues about their practice in their classrooms. The purpose of the observations was for trainers, head teachers, key teachers and peers to be able to support teachers in their 'professional development' through observing how teachers:

- develop confidence as teachers;
- put into practice the new methods they have been taught;
- develop these practices in order to improve their teaching;
- develop these practices in order to improve students' learning outcomes;
- show an awareness of gender, cultural and learning differences;
- develop confidence in their relationships with each other and with different colleagues from different institutes.

The purpose of giving oral feedback (as well as written) was for trainers, key teachers, head teachers and peers to support teachers through:

- giving constructive feedback which focuses both on what is positive about the lesson and what needs improving in the teacher's skills and behaviour;
- encouraging a professional dialogue through using the feedback system described in this manual;
- giving teachers time to discuss classroom issues through this feedback system;
- ensuring that no one person dominates the feedback session and that everyone involved in the observation has the opportunity to contribute constructively to the feedback session;

2.3.4 Demoing/Modelling

Another peer learning CPD activity which is used and has been proven effective in improving teachers' skills is the demonstration, or demo, lesson (also referred to as 'modelling'). This is usually done by a more experienced teacher or as part of the cascade training whereby teachers who have undergone training share their experiences in a practical way. The sharing of practice in this way is highly effective if planned and delivered well. This means:

Before the demo lesson
- disseminating the lesson plan for pre-discussion with other teachers;
- disseminating observation and feedback tools to teachers observing the lesson and checking understanding of both the plans and the tools;
- giving guidance in how to observe—this may sound rudimentary but many teachers are unfamiliar with observing others and need to be guided in their observation skills.

During the demo lesson
- observing the lesson using the observation tools and following observation guidelines.

After the demo lesson
- peer feedback, led by the 'demo teacher'—this is an analysis of the lesson with constructive feedback.

As Feiman-Nemser puts it,

> Professional discourse contains rich descriptions of practice, attention to evidence, examination of alternative interpretations and possibilities. As teachers learn to talk about teaching in specific and disciplined ways and to ask hard questions of themselves and others, they create new understandings and build a new professional culture. Over time, they build a stronger sense of themselves as practical intellectuals, contributing members of the profession, and participants in the improvement of teaching and learning. (Feiman-Nemser, 2001: 1042–1043)

2.3.5 Experiencing and Reflecting

'Experiencing and reflecting' can be seen as the umbrella that the above activities come under because they work in synthesis with these CPD activities: observation and feedback, action research, peer learning, mentoring and coaching.

However with the 'reflection' in particular there is an assumption of commitment too: commitment to improving your teaching skills and developing your knowledge in order to provide quality education for your students and doing this through critically reflecting on your own practice. Therefore building and maintaining this commitment should be integral to a support system for rural teachers.

Glazer's et al. (2000) interpretation of 'reflection' would seem a good one to implement, especially for rural contexts because it 'requires that teachers reflect on the daily experiences in the classroom, the changes or experiments that may be implemented in the classroom, and their effect. Once this information is collected, the following steps should be taken: a discussion concerning the information, possibly guided by pre-selected questions; action planning for a modified practice or experiment; readings that can contribute to reflection and discussion; the use of an external facilitator in the reflection process', and again synthesises with the activities already discussed.

In concluding this section some cross cutting concepts emerge from describing the teacher support systems and activities. These can be summarised as:

Decentralisation: Associated with this is devolvement through bottom-up approaches, using school and cluster-based systems which consider local needs and contexts and acknowledges teacher experience and know-how so providing an element of ownership to the support system. It has been seen that bottom-up approaches are more sustainable and effective when they are embedded in national policy and strategy but implemented at grass-roots.

Collaboration: Associated with this are school, teacher, peer networks and activities; through working with communities. It has been seen that forms of collaboration work best when everyone is involved, for example, whole-school or whole-group approaches; when enough time is given to the collaboration and when those involved are trained in the model or activity they are expected to implement.

Institutional and individual: Associated with this are collaborative partnerships, national and regional networks, distance education systems at institutional level and reflective models and using ICT at a more individual, personal level (ICT systems are both institutional and individual). It has been seen that, similar to the theme of collaboration, partnerships work best if mutual needs are met and a comprehensive strategic plan is made with clear roles and responsibilities. Adequate resources, time, funding, quality training and materials are essential for CPD models and activities to be successful and effective.

Lifelong and ongoing: Associated with this theme are the use of CPD models and activities which are School Cluster-based, flexible and organic. It is also linked to a teacher's career pathway: Teacher support systems should not be seen as 'stand alone' but be integrated and part of a teacher's career pathway, starting from when s/he decides to be a teacher until retirement. Therefore links need to be made with other teacher education providers from pre-service onwards. It has been seen that it will depend on the stage of a teacher's professional development and the stage of a particular government's education system as to what CPD models or activities are introduced and implemented. Additionally providing links between different teacher education providers has to be considered.

Reflective and experiential: Associated with this model of CPD are individual, group and institutional professional development which involve CPD activities, such as, peer observation and feedback, demos, action research and mentoring. As with the other caveats this requires resources of time, funding and quality training. Time is particularly pertinent as one of the most common weaknesses in setting up support systems for teachers is not giving them enough time to reflect on their experiences and to share them with other teachers. In addition, as with any CPD system, model or activity design, there must be planned follow up—not just for monitoring and evaluation purposes but as part of the support system.

Section 3: Key Components for an Effective Teacher Support System for Rural Teachers

In this final part of the section, four key components are described that provide foundations for these systems and activities. The components are seen as desirable for an effective teacher support system in rural contexts.

3.1 Meeting Local Needs

A teacher support system that meets local needs with local solutions is more likely to have the commitment of both teachers and administrative staff in schools. Regardless of how effective an intervention may be, without teacher commitment, lasting change will not take place (Berends et al., 2002; Fullan, 2001).

Therefore in rural areas, systems, strategies, models and activities need to be local and 'organic', that is, they address teachers' professional needs in the context of their daily practice … that help them to improve their students' learning outcomes (Honan et al., 2012). This is particularly pertinent to rural areas where access to resources and communications are often poor.

The words 'commitment' and 'organic' are important to note. In educational contexts which are more difficult and challenging, the level of commitment from the whole school staff has to be even higher than normal to ensure quality of teaching and learning take place. So the challenge is how to have a committed staff in contexts which are poorly resourced and supported. The term 'organic' is also of relevance as there is a good deal of evidence that successful CPD initiatives are also those that can move and change according to the changing contexts, whether these are political, socio-economic or cultural. Thus, 'developing systems that are more flexible and context-specific' (UNESCO, 2011) would be prudent when setting up rural teacher support systems.

Ensuring a CPD system meets local needs means moving away from the 'traditional system' of professional development, often referred to as in-service training (INSET), which is frequently centrally controlled and disseminated with external goals and objectives, to a more reflective model where professional development needs are identified by teachers and for teachers and the focus is more on personal classroom experiences. This is not to say that traditional INSET is not still a valid part of teachers' CPD (it has a role in upgrading and certification of teachers) but it is not sufficient, particularly for rural areas because inputs are often short-term and not needs-based or supported through follow up. As Leu points out in her paper on school and cluster-based systems, '[l]ocalized programs often exist side-by-side with traditional centralized inservice programs that often focus on upgrading of qualifications, while localized programs focus on updating with new information and skills' (Leu, 2004).

There is also a strong link between successful educational reform and recognition of local needs as Futrell et al. (1995) discovered in their research, 'truly effective reforms result from local recognition of needs and local solutions. This permits both teachers and administrators to establish a personal commitment to the reform'.

Local needs-based CPD systems, for example school-based and School Cluster-based systems, also mean that rather than goals and objectives for schools, including professional development goals, being set from external sources or 'experts', goals and objectives are set at local level and are needs based with teachers being part of goal setting, decision making process. This is particularly pertinent in rural and remote areas where there might be multi local cultures and languages which differ from the central government, policy and practice.

The more locally needs-based teacher professional development is, the more likely it is to consider the question of culture and language so that design, training and materials can reflect the diverse communities, for example, ensuring local teachers with local languages are recruited through positive drives for recruitment. This in turn may result in devolved pockets of CPD systems within a country. However it can be argued that if it works, that is, if it benefits and facilitates teaching and learning at school-base level, it could be used as a model and scaled-up for similar communities to use.

3.2 The Role of Leadership in Rural Teacher Support Systems

A desirable aspect for a successful teacher support system is the development of local leadership and planning. Supporting school-based, local systems which create opportunities for CPD requires a great level of commitment from not only from teachers but also from school leaders, local education authorities and the community.

It is therefore relevant that a teacher support system for CPD should have a whole-school approach so that there are shared values, knowledge and skills leading to a shared understanding of how they want the school to change and what reforms are necessary. School leaders should not only be involved in their own CPD but also understand what teachers

F. Helen Drinan   39

are doing in terms of professional development. In this way CPD will be seen as a positive intervention rather than a threat. Thus, 'the point is that teacher professional development can be reinforced and institutionalized through the professional development of school administrators and supervisors' (Leu and Ginsburg, EQUIP 1, 2011: 17) and a 'critical mass' of 'change agents' is developed rather than an isolated group who are disempowered as they are seen as a threat.

Box 1.12 provides an international example of how school principals through their own CPD were able to provide guidance and pedagogic support to their teachers. It highlights the need to consider CPD in terms of the whole school as well as in groups or individually.

Box 1.12: Example of CPD Leadership at Local Level

Building Capacity and Commitment for Instructional Leadership in El Salvador

The Excellence in Classroom Education at the Local Level (EXCELL) project in El Salvador focused on improving student performance in 250 rural primary schools. A key component of EXCELL (2003–2005) engaged school directors in cluster-based programmes designed to encourage and help them provide more-effective guidance and pedagogical support for teachers ... Even after the relatively short period of project implementation, there was considerable evidence that directors and teachers became more knowledgeable about and committed to the new pedagogical approaches and that directors devoted more time to instructional leadership.

Source: AIR, AED, & Joseph P. Kennedy Jr. Foundation, 2005. Cited in Leu and Ginsburg EQUIP 1 (2011).

However leadership at local level should not be confined or seen exclusively as the role of the principal or director rather CPD can and is being used, to develop what has been termed 'teacher leadership'. York-Barr and Duke define teacher leadership as: 'the process by which teachers, individually or collectively, influence their colleagues, principals and other members of school communities to improve teaching and learning practices with the aim of increased student learning and achievement' (2004: 287–288). Furthermore as Villegas Reimers points out, 'Knowing how to design, implement and assess professional-development

Table 1.3
Model of teacher leadership

First Level of Analysis: Four Zones	Second Level of Analysis: Six Roles
Zone 1: In the classroom	One: Continuing to teach and improve one's own teaching
Zone 2: Working with other teachers and learners outside the classroom in curricular and extra-curricular activities	Two: Providing curriculum development knowledge Three: Leading in-service education and assisting other teachers Four: Participating in performance evaluation of teachers
Zone 3: Outside the classroom in whole school development	Five: Organising and leading peer reviews of school practice Six: Participating in school level decision-making
Zone 4: Between neighbouring schools in the community	Two: Providing curriculum development knowledge Three: Leading in-service education and assisting other teachers

Source: Grant, 2008: 93.

opportunities is a learned process, and teachers need time and opportunity to learn the necessary skills and knowledge in order to become effective promoters of their own professional development' (2003: 120).

Therefore the role of teacher leaders would be to improve their peers' teaching practice and their students' learning. In essence, teacher leaders are school-based professional developers. Furthermore, Grant's (2008) model of teacher leadership, depicted in Table 1.3 below, provides a clear pathway for teachers' CPD and is suited to school or cluster-based systems.

3.3 Modes, Development and Content of Training

School and cluster-based training as indicated should be needs and school based. This is often in contrast to other modes of CPD training, such as cascade. Cascade training is commonly used, particularly in large scale donor funded projects in developing countries, where large numbers of teachers (often in rural and remote areas) need to be reached.

There has been a lot of criticism of the cascade training method, primarily, because the quality of the training can become diluted by the time it reaches the key stakeholders (teachers) it should be benefitting. However, if it is planned and implemented properly it can be effective in reaching large numbers of teachers and be integrated into a school-based CPD system.

David Hayes (2000: 138) lists the following criteria to be followed if cascade training is to be successful and integrated into other systems: The method of conducting the training must be experiential and reflective rather than transmissive; the training must be open to reinterpretation; rigid adherence to prescribed ways of working should not be expected; expertise must be diffused through the system as widely as possible, not concentrated at the top; a cross-section of stakeholders must be involved in the preparation of training materials; decentralisation of responsibilities within the cascade structure is desirable. In this way school-based systems and cascade training can be synthesised and mutually supportive.

Hayes makes reference to the importance of involving stakeholders in the preparation of training materials. From personal experience it is not only necessary to build capacity in content knowledge and skills but also necessary to have a cadre of educators who are skilled in materials development. This element ensures a degree of sustainability as it gives stakeholders the independence to continue developing courses and materials without external assistance.

However, the content of CPD training and the material should be of good quality, relevant and appropriate for teachers depending on their stage of development. The CPD activities described above, for example, demoing, will only succeed if what the 'trainer' is demoing is useful, practical and teachers have the time and chance to practice the new methods and material before using it in their own classrooms. Taking real examples from teachers' contexts is also another strategy that trainers should use when developing training courses and materials for CPD.

3.4 The Role of the Community in Teacher Support Systems

Knamiller's final point in his evaluation of TRCs is that, 'where TRCs managed to involve the wider community in which they were situated there was raised awareness within the community regarding changes in education and heightened expectations of what education can provide' (Knamiller, 1999: 21).

Indeed when teachers are deployed to rural areas, it is not only the teaching and learning and curriculum they have to 'take on' but also the community. This works better if teachers are recruited from within the community but more often than not teachers are not. In addition in rural areas the community can take on an even more prominent role with regard to school-life, so building relationships is even more pertinent.

Often parents and the wider community do not understand the importance of setting up teacher support systems for professional development. They would prefer funding or budgets spent on new buildings rather than CPD. Therefore, there should be whole-school strategies to involve the community in school planning and reforms. In this way, a shared understanding on why teacher professional development is important to the quality of education could be reached. An example of how this was done is presented in Box 1.13.

Box 1.13: Involving the Community: SIP, Namibia

Involving the Community in School Improvement and Teacher Professional Development in Namibia

Namibia has implemented a nationwide School Improvement Program (SIP), developed with assistance from USAID. This programme brings together teachers, school leaders and community members, with the support of district supervisors, to develop and monitor the progress of yearly school plans that focus on improved quality of teaching and learning. The SIPs include plans for school-based teacher, in-service programmes that promote the effective use of the curriculum that emphasises students' active learning and critical thinking. The strength of this programme is based on the schools' cooperative planning of programmes and monitoring of results with the community. Learning achievement in schools participating in the SIP proved to be stronger than that in non-participating schools.

Source: LeCzel and Liman, 2003.

Concluding Comments

Establishing an effective teacher support system is a complex endeavour in the best of circumstances. Setting up such a system in more difficult contexts, such as rural and remote areas, requires even more of an effort by all those concerned.

This chapter has attempted to describe some of the systems and activities that have proven to be successful in supporting teachers in difficult contexts. In addition it has suggested that four key components make up the foundations for an effective rural teacher support system. In the following chapters educators describe teacher support systems for CPD in very different settings. However, what emerges after reading the chapters are the number of cross cutting themes and commonalities within the different systems.

References

Ansell, S. (2000). Teachers' Resource Centres: 'Concrete and Clay'? Academic Paper published for the University of St. Mark and St. John, Plymouth, UK.
Avalos, B. (2009). *CPD Policies and Practices in the Latin American Region.* In C. Day and J. Sachs (eds), *International Handbook on the Continuing Professional Development of Teachers.* McGraw-Hill Education: Open University Press.
Barth, R. (1990). *Improving Schools from Within: Teachers, Parents and Principals Can Make a Difference.* San Fransico: Jossey-Bass.
Bennett, J.L., and Martin, D.J. (2001). The Next Professional Wave: Consultant/ Coach. *Consulting to Management,* 2 (3), 6–8. The Skills for Life Improvement Programme delivered on behalf of the Quality Improvement Agency by CfBT Education Trust and partners, Reading, UK.
Berends, M., Bodilly, S., and Kirby, S.N. (2002). *Facing the Challenges of Whole School Reform: New American Schools after a Decade.* Santa Monica, CA: RAND.
Boyle, B., Lamprianou, I., and Boyle, T. (2005). A Longitudinal Study of Teacher Change: What Makes Professional Development Effective? Report of the second year of study. *School Effectiveness and School Improvement,* 16(1), 1–27.
Bruns, B., Mingat, A., and Rakotomalala, R. (2003). *Achieving Universal Primary Education by 2015: A Chance for Every Child.* Washington, DC: The World Bank.
Bubb, S., and Earley, P. (2009). Leading Staff Development for School Improvement. *School Leadership and Management,* 29(1), 23–37.
Cordingley, P., Bell, M., Rundell, B., and Evans, D. (2003). *The Impact of Collaborative CPD on Classroom Teaching and Learning: Research Evidence in Education Library.* London: EPPI-Centre, Social Science Research Unit, Institute of Education.
Cordingley, P., Bell, M., Evans, D., and Firth, A. (2005). *The Impact of Collaborative CPD on Classroom Teaching and Learning. Review: What Do Teacher Impact Data Tell Us about Collaborative CPD? Research Evidence in Education Library.* London: EPPI-Centre, Social Science Research Unit, Institute of

Education, University of London. Retrieved from: http://www.eppi.ioe.ac.uk/cms/Default.aspx?tabid=139 (accessed on 20 November 2009).

Cordingley, P., Bell, M., Isham, C., Evans, D., and Firth, A. (2007). *What Do Specialists Do in CPD Programmes for Which There Is Evidence of Positive Outcomes for Pupils and Teachers?* Technical Report. Research Evidence in Education Library. London: EPPI-Centre, Social Science Research Unit, Institute of Education, University of London. Retrieved from: http://www.eppi.ioe.ac.uk/cms/Default.aspx?tabid=2275 (accessed on 8 June 2009).

Christie, P., Harley, K., and Penny, A. (2009). Case Studies from Sub-Saharan Africa. In C. Day and J. Sachs (eds), *International Handbook on the Continuing Professional Development of Teachers*, pp. 167–190. McGraw-Hill Education: Open University Press.

Darling Hammond, L., Chung Wei, R., Andree, A., Richardson, N., and Orphanos, S. (2009). *Professional Learning in the Learning Profession.* A Status Report on Teacher Development in the United States and Abroad National Staff Development Council and The School Redesign Network, Stanford University. Retrieved from: http://www.nsdc.org/news/NSDCstudy2009.pdf (accessed on 20 March 2010).

Day, C., and Sachs, J. (2009). *Professionalism, Performativity and Empowerment: Discourses in the Politics, Policies and Purposes of Continuing Professional Development.* In C. Day and J. Sachs (eds), *International Handbook on the Continuing Professional Development of Teachers*, pp. 3–32. McGraw-Hill Education: Open University Press.

Dembele, M., and Miaro, B.R.II. (2003). Pedagogical Renewal and Teacher Development in Sub-Saharan Africa: A Thematic Synthesis. Paper commissioned for 2003 ADEA Biennial Meeting. Paris: ADEA.

Education For All (EFA). (2005). Global Monitoring Report. Paris: UNESCO.

Engels, John. (2001). *Making Classrooms Talk: Uganda Sustains Its Teacher Improvement and Support System.* Washington, DC: Academy for Educational Development.

Feiman-Nemser, S. (2001). From Preparation to Practice: Designing a Continuum to Strengthen and Sustain Teaching. *Teachers College Record*, 103, 1013–1055.

Flores, A., and Arias, M.D. (2001). Los colectivos escolares que hacen investigación desde su escuela: Informe del II encuentro Iberoamericano. In M.D. Arias, A. Flores, R. and Porlan (eds), Redes de maestros: una alternativa para la transformacion escolar. Sevilla, Spain: Diada Editora. In Villegas-Reimers, E. *Teacher Professional Development: An International Review of the Literature.* UNESCO: International Institute for Educational Planning (www.unesco.org/iiep).

Fullan, M., and Hargreaves, A. (eds) (1992). *Teacher Development and Educational Change.* London: The Falmer Press.

Fullan, M. (2001). *The New Meaning of Educational Change*, 3rd ed. New York: Teachers College Press.

Furlong, J., Barton, L., Miles, S., Whiting, C., and Whitty, G. (2000). *Teacher Education in Transition.* Buckingham: Open University Press.

Futrell, M.H., Holmes, D.H., Christie, J.L., and Cushman, E.J. (1995). Linking Education Reform and Teacher Professional Development: The Efforts of Nine School Districts. Occasional Paper Series. Washington, DC: Center for Policy Studies, Graduate School of Education and Human Development. George Washington University.

Giordano, Elizabeth A. (2008). *School Clusters and Teacher Resource Centres*. UNESCO International Institutes for Education and Planning: Paris.

Goodall, J., Day, C., Lindsay, G., Muijs, D., and Harris, A. (2005). *Evaluating the Impact of Continuing Professional Development (CPD)*. Research Report RR659. The University of Warwick, Department for Education and Skills.

Glatthorn, A. (1987). Teacher Development. In L. Anderson (ed.), *International Encyclopedia of Teaching and Teacher Education*, 2nd ed., p. 41. London: Pergamon Press.

Glazer, C., Abbott, L., and Harris, J. (2000). Overview: The Process for Collaborative Reflection among Teachers, 28 June 2000. Retrieved from: http://ccwf.cc.utexas.edu/~cglazer/reflection-process.html (accessed on 15 April 2009).

Grant, C. (2008). We Did Not Put Our Pieces Together: Exploring a Professional Development Initiative through a Distributed Leadership Lens. *Journal of Education*, 44, 85–107.

Grundy, S., and Robison, J. (2009). Teacher Professional Development: Themes and Trends in the Recent Australian Experience. In C. Day and J. Sachs (eds), *International Handbook on the Continuing Professional Development of Teachers*, pp. 146–166. McGraw-Hill Education: Open University Press

Guskey, T.R. (1995). Professional Development in Education: In Search of the Optimal Mix. In T.R. Guskey and M. Huberman (eds), *Professional Development in Education: New Paradigms and Practices*. New York: Teachers College Press.

———. (2003). The Characteristics of Effective Professional Development: A Synthesis of Lists. Paper presented at the 84th annual meeting of the American Educational Research Association, 21–23 April, Chicago, IL.

Haney, A. (1997). The Role of Mentorship in the Workplace. In M.C. Taylor (ed.), *Workplace Education*, pp. 211–228. Toronto, Ontario: Culture.

Hawley, W.D., and Valli, L. (1999). The Essentials of Effective Professional Development: A New Consensus. In G. Sykes and L. Darling-Hammond (eds), *Teaching as the Learning Profession: Handbook of Policy and Practice*, pp. 127–150. San Francisco, CA: Jossey-Bass.

Hayes, D. (2000). Cascade Training and Teachers' Professional Development. *ELT Journal*, 54(2), 135–145.

Helmer, J., Bartlett, C., Wolgemuth, J.R., and Lea, T. (2011). Coaching (and) Commitment: Linking Ongoing Professional Development, Quality Teaching and Student Outcomes. *Professional Development in Education*, 37(2), 197–211.

Honan, E., Evans, T., Muspratt, S., Paraide, P., Reta, M., and Baroutsis, A. (2012): Implementing a New Model for Teachers' Professional Learning in Papua New Guinea. *Professional Development in Education*, 38(5), 725–740.

Huberman, M. (2001). Networks that Alter Teaching: Conceptualisations, Exchanges, and Experiments. In J. Soler, A. Craft, H. Burgess (eds), *Teacher Development: Exploring our own Practice*, pp. 141–159. London: Paul Chapman Publishing and The Open University.

Ingvarson, L., Meiers, M., and Beavis, A. (2005). Factors Affecting the Impact of Professional Development Programs on Teachers' Knowledge, Practice, Student Outcomes and Efficacy. *Education Policy Analysis*, 13(10), 1–26.

Johnson, S., Monk, M., and Hodges, M. (2000). Teacher Development and Change in South Africa: A Critique of the Appropriateness of Transfer of Northern/Western Practice. *Compare*, 30(2), 179–192.

Kelly, P. (2006). What Is Teacher Learning? A Socio cultural Perspective. *Oxford Review of Education*, 32(4), 505–519.

Kennedy, A. (2005). Models of Continuing Professional Development: A Framework for Analysis. *Journal of In-Service Education*, 31(2), 235–250.

Knamiller, G. (ed.). (1999). *The Effectiveness of Teacher Resource Centre Strategy.* London: Department for International Development.

LeCzel, Donna Kay. (2004). *From Policy to Practice: The Teacher's Role in Policy Implementation in Namibia.* Washington, DC: USAID/EQUIP2 Policy Brief (draft).

LeCzel, Donna Kay, and Liman, Muhammed. (2003). "School Self-Assessment in Namibia: An Adaptation of Critical Inquiry." Paper presented at Comparative and International Education Society Annual Conference in Salt Lake City.

Leu, Elizabeth. (2004). *The Patterns and Purposes of Localized Teacher Professional Development Programs.* Issues Brief #1 under EQUIP1's Study of School-based Teacher In-service Programs and Clustering of Schools.

Leu and Ginsburg EQUIP 1. (2011). *First Principles: Designing Effective Education Programs for In-Service Teacher Professional Development Compendium*, American Institutes for Research in partnership with Academy for Education Development: USAID, Washington.

Lord, P., Atkinson, M., and Mitchell, H. (2008). Mentoring and Coaching for Professionals: A Study of the Research Evidence. Retrieved from: http://www.tda.gov.uk/upload/resources/pdf/m/mentoring_coaching_study2008.pdf (accessed on 16 November 2009).

Mac Neil, J.D. (2004). Working Paper 1 under EQUIP 1's Study of School-based Teacher In-service Programs and Clustering of Schools: USAID, Washington.

O'Hanlon, C. (1996). Why Is Action Research a Valid Basis for Professional Development? In R. McBride (ed.), *Teacher Education Policy: Some Issues Arising from Research and Practice.* London: The Flamer Press.

Palincsar, A.S., Magnusson, S.J., Marano, N., Ford, D., and Brown, N. (1998). Designing a Community of Practice: Principles and Practices of the GisML Community. *Teaching and Teacher Education*, 14(1), 5–19.

Robbins, P. (1991). *How to Plan and Implement a Peer Coaching Program.* Alexandria, VA, USA: Association for Supervision and Curriculum Development.

Rojas, C. (1994). The Escuela Nueva School Programme in Colombia. In P. Dalin (ed.), *How Schools Improve.* London: Cassell Publishing. In Villegas-Reimers,

E. *Teacher Professional Development: An International Review of the Literature.* UNESCO: International Institute for Educational Planning (www.unesco. org/iiep).

Schiefelbein, E., Tedesco, J.C. (1995). *Una nueva oportunidad: el rol de la educación en el desarrollo de América Latina.* In E. Villegas-Reimers (ed.), *Teacher Professional Development: An International Review of the Literature.* UNESCO: International Institute for Educational Planning (www.unesco.org/iiep).

Schwille, J., Dembele, M. in collaboration with Schubert, J. (2007). *Global Perspectives on Teacher Learning: Improving Policy and Practice.* IIEP, Paris: UNESCO.

Schwille, J., Dembele, M., Bah, T.H., Adotevi, J., and Bah, A. (2007). A Nation-Wide Program of Teacher Projects in Guinea: What CanBbe Learned from Comparing the Professional Development Approach with 'Lesson Study' in Japan. Paper presented in Annual Conference of the Comparative and International Education Society, Orlando.

Shimahara, N.K. (1995). Teacher Education Reform in Japan: Ideological and Control Issues. In N.B. Shimahara and I.Z. Holowinsky (eds), *Teacher Education in Industrialized Nations* (Reference Books in International Education, Vol. 3), p. 183. New York: Garland Publishing.

Sugrue, C. (2009). Rhetorics and Realities of CPD across Europe: From Cacophony toward Coherence. In C. Day and J. Sachs (eds), *International Handbook on the Continuing Professional Development of Teachers,* pp. 67–93. McGraw-Hill Education: Open University Press.

Tripp, D. (2009). Teachers' Networks: A New Approach to the Professional Development of Teachers in Singapore. In C. Day and J. Sachs (eds), *International Handbook on the Continuing Professional Development of Teachers,* pp. 191–214. McGraw-Hill Education: Open University Press.

Timperley, H., Wilson, A., Barrar, H., and Fung, I. (2007). *Teacher Professional Learning and Development: Best Evidence Synthesis Iteration (BES).* Retrieved from: http://www.educationcounts.govt.nz/__data/assets/pdf_file/0017/16901/TPLandDBE Sentire.pdf (accessed on 9 March 2009).

UNESCO. (1990). *Education for All: Framework for Action: Meeting Basic Learning Needs,* UNESCO.

———. (2011). *Summary of Progress towards Education for All.* Working document prepared by UNESCO: Tenth Meeting of the High Level Group on Education for All, Jomtien, Thailand. Available at: http://www.unesco.org/new/fileadmin/MULTIMEDIA/HQ/ED/ED_new/pdf/Summary%20of%20progress%20towards%20EFA-colors.pdf (accessed on 20 May 2012).

———. (2012). *Strategy on Teachers (2012–2015).* Paris: UNESCO.

Villegas-Reimers, E. (2003). *Teacher Professional Development: An International Review of the Literature.* UNESCO: International Institute for Educational Planning (www.unesco.org/iiep).

York-Barr, J. and Duke, K. (2004). What Do We Know about Teacher Leadership? Findings from Two Decades of Scholarship. *Review of Educational Research,* 74(3), 255–316.

2

Mentoring System for Teachers' Professional Development: A Case from Romania

Ana Maria Sandi

Contents

List of Abbreviations
Introduction

Section 1: Background of the Initiative

Section 2: The Process of Piloting and Scaling Up
2.1   The Rural Education Project
2.2   The Mentoring Programme in the REP
2.2.1 Development of Mentors' Training Curricula, Training Modules and Teaching/Learning Materials
2.2.2 Mentors' Selection, Training and Recruitment
2.2.3 Setting Up Mobile and Fixed Resource Centres
2.2.4 The Mentoring Process in Rural Schools
2.2.5 Certification Programme
2.2.6 Stakeholders' Involvement
2.2.7 Monitoring and Evaluation

Section 3: Effectiveness and Outcomes
3.1 Problems Solved
3.2 Sustainability
3.3 Cost-effectiveness

Section 4: Lessons Learnt
4.1 Teachers' Continuous Professional Development Cannot Give Results in Isolation
4.2 Grassroots Interventions Need to Be Combined with Nationwide Policies/Actions
4.3 School-based Professional Development Is Useful in Various Contexts
4.4 Solving the Transportation Issue Is Essential for Mentoring Activities in Rural Areas
4.5 The Right Incentives Are an Important Factor for the Success of the Mentoring Programme
4.6 Strong Organisation Is Important for the Success of the Mentoring Programme
4.7 Promotion of New Teaching Methods Takes Time and Follow-up Activities Are Needed
4.8 Quality Assurance through M&E and Impact Analysis Is Important

Section 5: Plans for the Future

Summary

Annexure

References

List of Abbreviations

CPD	Continuous Professional Development
CSI	County School Inspectorates
EFA	Education for All
EU	European Union
GDP	Gross Domestic Product
GoR	Government of Romania
INRULED	UNESCO International Research and Training Centere for Rural Education

M&E	Monitoring and Evaluation
MERYS	Ministry of Education, Research, Youth and Sports
NCITT	National Centere for In-Service Teacher Training
NCITT	National Center for In-Service Teacher Training
PIFMD	Projects with International Financing Management Department
REP	Rural Education Project
TA	Technical Assistance
TH	Teacher's House
US	United States

Introduction

How can rural schoolteachers be supported to engage in continuing professional development? Do certain approaches work better than others on specific topics, or in special contexts? This chapter summarises the lessons learnt from the implementation of a nationwide programme aimed at improving the knowledge and skills of rural schoolteachers in Romania. The key message of the chapter is that school-based professional development in which mentors played the main role is a useful way to reach and assist teachers in rural schools. The training of mentors and solutions for transport problems were critical to the success of the programme. This approach was particularly helpful in making teachers understand the need to shift teaching and learning from rote forms, based on memorisation of facts, to active forms which emphasise critical, analytical and problem-solving skills, as well as in helping them change classroom practices. The main condition for the effectiveness of this approach is continuity of the pedagogical support, which can be guaranteed through formal recognition and institutionalisation of the local support services.

Section 1: Background of the Initiative

The political changes at the end of 1989 found Romania with an education system doing relatively well in terms of access to compulsory education, but with serious quality and relevance problems (Sandi, 1992).

After 1990, the Government of Romania (GoR) embarked on a series of educational reforms. These projects were advancing structural reforms meant to improve education quality, relevance and efficiency. For example, the Education Reform project focused on changing the education curriculum, evaluation, textbooks, finance and management. The curriculum reform in particular introduced new, student-centred teaching approaches, emphasising interactive learning, critical-thinking and problem-solving.

While the general attention and efforts were focused on these reforms, several studies started signalling important equity problems in education. Inequalities of access to good quality education services between urban and rural areas are common to many countries, sometimes even considered unavoidable, but this problem was of considerable scale in Romania, due to the high proportion of the population living in rural areas (almost 45 per cent in the 2002 population census). High discrepancies between urban and rural areas had become a constant feature of the education system (Sandi and Moarcas, 2007).

Great disparities were found between students' achievements in urban and in rural schools. In 2000, only 36 per cent of rural students who took the final examination at the end of compulsory education scored 'very good' compared to 71 per cent of urban students. Rural candidates were eight times more likely to score 'unsatisfactory' in science examination than urban candidates (World Bank, 2003). A census of rural schools (Institute of Educational Sciences, 2002) has also documented the substandard conditions in compulsory education in rural schools.

The Ministry of Education, Research, Youth and Sports (MERYS) took the decision to address the problem through a World Bank supported project, the Rural Education Project (REP). Research conducted in preparation of the REP using a Policy and Human Resource Development grant, identified supply and demand related factors considered responsible for the urban–rural education discrepancies. On the supply side, the low quality of teachers, including the shortage in qualified teachers and the long-term under-investment in rural schools were identified as the main factors. Factors related to teachers included barriers to participation in in-service teacher training, the type of training available and deployment issues (difficulties in recruiting/retaining good teachers particularly in certain teaching fields).The main reasons for the low participation of rural teachers in the conventional in-service teacher training were: isolation, distance to training centres, lack of transportation, costs incurred compared to teachers' salaries, difficulty in finding a replacement teacher during the training period due to the small size of schools. On the demand side, the relative poverty of rural areas (compared to urban areas) was the main factor. Other factors included: weak links between schools and communities and a low capacity to collect education data and information and to use it for policy making (World Bank, 2003).

In-service teacher training became very important in the 1990s. This was due, on one hand, to the low quality of initial teacher training. Universities, known to be conservative institutions, were slow in changing their curriculum in education. They had suffered from a long period of isolation from the ideas in pedagogy and continued to offer outdated information and were out of touch with school realities. For example, courses of initial teacher training did not routinely include active-learning pedagogies. Young teachers graduating universities lacked essential knowledge and skills and were already in need of additional training. Several small-scale projects addressed this issue through in-service teacher training, which familiarised teachers with modern concepts such as: multiple intelligences; student-centred, interactive teaching and learning; critical thinking and problem solving. On the other hand, the education reforms launched after 1990 had to be quickly disseminated to schools and explained to teachers. Large-scale, centralised 'cascade' trainings were used, due to the urgency of the task. The conventional in-service teacher training, which was the main vehicle for the task, was not efficient and didn't reach all the teachers, particularly those from rural schools.

In-service teacher training was outdated in its organisation. Only higher education institutions and regional training institutions called 'Teachers' Houses' (THs) had the right to offer courses and their content did not answer teachers' real needs. In 2001, a ministerial order on compulsory teachers' professional development sought to combine the academic strengths of universities with the practical experience available locally. The order stipulated compulsory in-service teacher training every five years for all teachers. They needed 90 credits of training which had to be earned through 46 credits given by universities and 44 by THs.[1] However, rural teachers had little access to the institutions mentioned in the ministerial order.

In the REP, the basic idea was that through Continuous Professional Development (CPD) rural teachers should improve their teaching, which in turn should enhance student achievement. Two problems were singled out in REP: (1) teachers in rural schools had access to fewer professional development opportunities than teachers in urban schools and (2) a significant number of teachers in rural schools were unqualified. The REP addressed these problems through the support system developed under the project for school-based teacher professional development and through the career development opportunities for unqualified teachers provided by an open distance learning programme. Rural teachers' professional development was not conceived in terms of a one-shot intervention, as in the conventional approach to in-service teacher training, but as a CPD process within the school setting. The re-conceptualisation of teachers' professional development was in line with the new adult learning theories and new cognitive findings.

The REP promoted a new type of training, namely school-based teacher training, which was delivered by mentors[2] instead of being provided by trainers in centrally located training institutions. Mentors would travel to rural schools to bring training to teachers, instead of having all teachers travel to a centrally located institution to get trained. Mentors' access to a solid car, which could travel long distances on difficult roads and in any season, was a key factor in the success of the approach.

Mentors also used a different training approach than the one used by conventional trainers. Mentors didn't lecture, they guided. Teachers

---

[1] At present, in addition to universities and THs, institutions for professional development of educational staff can function on the basis of accreditation granted by the education ministry (MERYS, 2011).

[2] The term 'mentor' comes from Greek. In Greek mythology, Mentor was a friend of Odysseus and a tutor of his son, Telemachus. In time, mentor began to designate a wise person, who shares his/her knowledge and skills with less experienced colleagues.

were not passive receivers of information. They were actively engaged in finding solutions to challenges identified in classrooms. Mentors were collegial, but also untiring in pushing teachers to adopt changes in classroom practices.

There is no single generally accepted definition of mentoring in education, but the qualities of good mentors are always the same: competency in the skills they are expected to share, ability to win peers' respect, ability to share outstanding practices and to guide other teachers.

Mentoring is being used in education for different purposes. One possibility is to mentor student teachers during initial training. In this case, teacher-mentors are used in schools for the practical stage of the initial teacher training programme. Another possibility is to offer newly-qualified teachers a period of support during the first year of their teaching career. In this case, the mentor assigned to a new teacher is called an insertion/induction mentor. In this study, the simple term 'mentor' will be used to designate a CPD mentor, that is, a knowledgeable and skilled person who can provide guidance to their colleagues for the purpose of CPD.

The choice of the mentoring programme was guided by two strategic reasons. The first, already mentioned, was the need to reach teachers in rural schools. The second was related to the content of the mentoring programme. Teachers in rural schools still used rigid teaching methods, which relied heavily on rote learning, placing students in a passive role. The mentoring programme was focused on training teachers new, interactive, teaching/learning methods such as: discovery, group learning, critical thinking, problem solving and conducting differentiated didactical activities.

In other circumstances, the choice of the school-based professional development approach may be due to other reasons, such as the quality of teachers within the context of rapid expansion of enrolment or the shift to more decentralised forms of authority, activity and agency (Leu, 2004; MacNeil, 2004).

From the beginning a decision was taken to first implement a pilot phase of the mentoring programme and test procedures, materials, forms, etc., and to scale up the programme to the main, nationwide phase, only after the necessary revisions were done, based upon the pilot's results and recommendations.

Section 2: The Process of Piloting and Scaling Up

2.1 The Rural Education Project

The overall objective of the REP was 'to have rural school students benefit from improved access to quality education, as evidenced by higher achievement scores and completion and transition rates' (World Bank, 2003).

The objective would be achieved by

- improving teaching and learning through school-based professional development for teachers, providing career development opportunities, and upgrading basic education conditions in schools;
- ensuring rural students' access to basic teaching–learning materials;
- improving school-community partnerships through a school-community grants programme;
- strengthening the analytic capacity at national and local levels of education for policy analysis and formulation, as well as for planning and evaluation.

The project was implemented during 2003–2009. The REP benefitted from the results of a US$ 11.47 million pilot component, which was included in an ongoing project (the Education Reform project) in 2000. The pilot was conceived as an emergency intervention aimed at supporting education in rural schools from eight counties. A National Board for the Development of Rural Education was set up; working groups were established, including education experts, teachers and school inspectors. A rapid needs assessment and the conclusions of national studies on rural education conducted by the Institute of Educational Sciences indicated that the most urgent needs in rural schools were related to the lack of basic educational materials and to the limited knowledge that most teachers and school principals had about the new curriculum requirements introduced by the recent reform. Most teachers and principals did not know how to manage the changing environment. Parents and local authorities did not believe schools had the capacity to provide good quality education. In several rural areas, parents' only motivation for sending children to school was to get the child allowance, which was distributed through schools.

Several school-based activities were conducted during the rural pilot. Of particular success was the grass-roots training delivered to three target groups: (1) school community, including principals, parents, local authorities representatives and school inspectors, aimed at increasing awareness about the content and direction of the education reform, with emphasis on the new curriculum and on the need to get communities involved in school-life and how it operates; (2) school principals, aimed at increasing their capacity to work with the community, improving their understanding of the new curriculum and enhancing their managerial skills to conduct pedagogic supervision and quality control of the teaching process and (3) teachers, aimed at increasing their understanding of the new curriculum and enhancing their capacity to work with the didactic materials provided by the pilot and enhancing their capacity to produce their own didactic materials. While the Education Reform Project was centrally driven, the pilot was implemented at community level and in schools. The excellent feedback received from teachers, parents, community representatives including local authorities, the church, local private sector, etc., led the ministry to engage in a comprehensive project, the REP, meant to assist all rural schools in Romania through grass-roots activities.

The REP performance was assessed based on outcome/impact indicators, which measured changes regarding rural students' achievement scores and completion rates in compulsory education, as well as transition rates to upper secondary and tertiary education. Since increased levels for these indicators in rural areas could have been misleading if levels in urban areas increased as well, the gap between urban and rural areas for these indicators was also measured. The project did well on all six outcome indicators. In addition, progress was measured through output indicators, such as the percentage of rural teachers who were using interactive teaching methods.

The REP Implementation Completion and Results Report (World Bank, 2010) mentions several outcomes:

- In 2009, 10.68 per cent of rural students got high grades (9–10) at the final test of compulsory education, compared to only 2.4 per cent in 2002.

- More than 68 per cent of rural teachers were habitually using interactive teaching methods in the school year 2008–2009, compared to only 30 per cent in the school year 2003–2004.

REP also made a significant contribution to strengthening the education policy making capacity by

- supporting the development and application of national education indicators compatible with international reporting systems;
- the utilisation of a coherent database structure for informed decision making;
- the elaboration of annual national reports on the status of education.

The innovative character of the REP was acknowledged on various occasions, one of them being World Bank's competition 'Improving Lives of People in Europe and Central Asia' in 2008, when the project was one of the winners. In 2007, the mentorship programme was presented to a high level Chinese delegation that came to Romania on a study tour with the purpose of getting information on teachers' school-based professional development. The Chinese education leaders and experts were highly impressed with the effectiveness of the programme and decided to pilot a similar mentoring programme in China.

2.2 The Mentoring Programme in the REP

A school-based teachers' professional development sub-component, further called 'the mentoring program', was developed and implemented in the REP. The aim of the programme was to improve teaching and learning in rural schools by improving rural teachers' abilities, skills and knowledge particularly in the areas of new pedagogical approaches, classroom management and information and communication technologies. Teachers would be encouraged to actively look for modalities of meeting the specific needs of their students. Schools would become communities of learning, where teachers reflect upon their work experience, systematically discuss with colleagues and learn from each other.

At the beginning of REP implementation, the Education 2000+ Center and the British Council Romania were selected to assist the implementation of the mentoring programme. The consultants offered support in:

(1) developing training curriculum, modules and materials; (2) selecting and training mentors; (3) organising and monitoring mentors' fieldwork and (4) ensuring feedback to MERYS.

The basic structure of the rural teacher support system implemented under the mentoring programme is (MERYS, 2006):

1. Development of the mentors' training curricula, training modules and teaching/learning materials
2. Mentors' selection, training and recruitment
3. Setting up mobile and fixed resource centres
4. Mentoring process in schools
5. Certification programme
6. Monitoring and evaluation (M&E)

2.2.1 Development of Mentors' Training Curricula, Training Modules and Teaching/Learning Materials

A group of experts was selected to develop the training curriculum, modules and materials. The experts formed a real team, working in close coordination and cooperation in order to assure the coherence of all the products. The most innovative training materials were the videos of classroom experiences with good and bad examples of lessons. The scripts of all videos were collectively developed in order to assure coherence. The videos were filmed in real rural schools, with teachers and students playing as actors, since no school accepted recording a real classroom lesson.

The draft curriculum, modules and materials were subject to a three steps reviewing process.

1. The draft curriculum was discussed with representatives of the National Centre for In-Service Teacher Training (NCITT), the accreditation institution for all training providers and programmes, in order to get early feedback.
2. Experts (professors from universities delivering initial teacher training and senior education specialists) reviewed the draft curriculum, modules and materials and offered comments and suggestions. In this way, products were improved and also received an academic endorsement.
3. The modules and materials were used in the first round of the mentors' training. Mentors were asked for feedback, based upon

their analysis and their field work. They suggested improvements and got involved in modules development offering examples from their actual experience.

The final curriculum together with ten training modules and four video-scripts were submitted to the NCITT for programme accreditation. After accreditation, the modules were printed and delivered to all School Clusters involved in the national phase of the programme.

The training modules promoted interactive teaching/learning and included tools for assessing student progress using different methods, taking into account various ways of learning. All modules were structured in three parts: (1) the first part offered the theoretical background of the topic, with information presented in a friendly way, easy to be assimilated; (2) the second part facilitated knowledge absorption through group discussions; guiding questions were offered for reflection, discussion among teachers and agreement on the suggested answer; (3) the third part dealt with individual planning and classroom application; guidelines on how to include the topic in the teacher's classroom activity were presented; mentors offered assignments to teachers for applying the new knowledge in their classrooms.

The topics of the ten modules developed under the mentoring programme were:

- interactive student-centred teaching;
- continuous assessment in the classroom;
- learning about student backgrounds;
- adapting the curriculum to the rural environment;
- multi-grade teaching;
- remedial reading (primary level);
- remedial mathematics (gymnasium level);
- Romanian as a second language;
- using computers to teach and learn;
- school leadership and management (for head teachers).

2.2.2 Mentors' Selection, Training and Recruitment

Mentors were selected based on their prior teaching and training experience and knowledge. They were trained in mentoring, adult learning and the ability to identify and communicate best practices. During the training, of great importance was the development of future mentors' interpersonal skills that would be needed for both challenging and supporting teachers.

The mentors' profile that guided selection criteria was:

- senior teacher with substantial, successful teaching experience;
- information communication technology skills;
- qualification as a trainer with training experience in other projects;
- good interpersonal skills;
- ability to work in teams;
- analytic skills and creativity;
- driving license and willingness to drive in difficult conditions.

The selection was publicly announced in order to ensure a transparent process. About 400 shortlisted candidates were asked to send applications. The applications were desk-reviewed by a commission set up by the education ministry and assisted by the technical assistance (TA) providers. In the end, 28 mentors were selected for the pilot phase and 118 mentors for the main phase of the programme. In addition, subject trainers were selected, but in the end they were not used, since schools and teachers did not ask for their support.

The mentors' training and development programme included: (1) direct training, (2) online training and assistance through an e-learning platform and (3) participation in conferences for experience sharing and problem solving.

The 'direct training' lasted for five days. Interactive training sessions were focused on teambuilding, communication, active strategies, flexible approaches, the training modules and their correlation. Participants were provided with the format of a self-development plan aimed at guiding reflection and professional development for the next steps. The plan was structured into: training objectives, selected topics, bibliography used, expected outcomes, modalities of evaluation, and description of activities. The topics addressed during the direct training were:

- how to assume the mentor's role;
- communication skills and building interpersonal relationships;
- how to plan, organise and deliver a training session;

- peer training and coaching;
- simulation activities for self-evaluation;
- needs analyses;
- mentors' portfolio and the mentors' kit;
- training programme management;
- instruments for evaluation, monitoring and reporting.

The 'online training and assistance' was an important channel in the process of continuous learning, communication and counselling. The web-based e-learning platform assured good communication between the project managers, the technical team and the mentors. It also facilitated addressing problems as soon as they occurred. Mentors were invited to virtual meetings to meet each other, share experiences and ask questions.

The e-learning platform had several applications/functions:

- differentiated log-in interface linked to a database;
- real-time chat/forum window/discussion board;
- real-time documents presentation window (power-point, etc.);
- public documents folder (for downloading materials from a library);
- announcements folder;
- tutorials for users on how to use the system;
- application for designing training courses and evaluating participants.

The platform was managed by a system-administrator/facilitator who was also responsible for content design and management. A schedule for online communication and assistance was set up. The access procedures were the usual ones: participants were asked to fill in a registration form in order to obtain a password. Passwords were specific for each category of users: management, trainers, course developers, and mentors. Users could access the chat window and join discussions during the training classes, or ask for assistance. Users could also download documents from the library and follow real-time presentations (with or without discussion) given by a trainer.

The mentors actively used the e-learning platform, which allowed them to interact with the technical team, get answers to their questions and share experience with colleagues.

The training programme for mentors was revised by the experts' team after the completion of the piloting phase. Conceptual, procedural and experiential components were revised taking into account lessons learnt. The training was based on debates, projects, case studies, inquiry and problem solving in a trans-disciplinary approach.

The 'mentors' conferences' offered another opportunity for sharing good practices and for raising the quality of mentorship across all the 41 counties. Conferences for mentors were organised during the pilot and the national phase of the programme. During the pilot phase, the conference focused on what had to be revised in order to optimally start the national phase. During interactive workshops, participants had the possibility to make recommendations, which were taken into account in the final version of the mentoring programme. In order to encourage the inclusion of the new interactive teaching methodologies in the initial teachers training, the conferences were supposed to be held in universities, with university staff participating in discussions and in evaluations of new activities taking place in schools. This stipulation from the initial project design was only partially fulfilled.

The recruitment conditions were: mentors would be detached from their job and work full time; their salary would be higher than the previous normal teacher salary; the REP management office in the MERYS would contract them; when the mentoring tasks were reduced, mentors could return to their initial jobs and perform remaining tasks during holidays or in their free time; after the project closed mentors returned to their initial jobs, unless they continued to be involved full or part time in subsequent projects.

2.2.3 Setting Up Mobile and Fixed Resource Centres

One of the most important features of the mentoring programme was the procurement by the project of robust cars, which were given to mentors. This enabled them to reach remote areas, which otherwise could not have been reached and also gave them independence from the fixed schedules and routes of public transportation. The importance of solving the transportation issue cannot be overemphasised. Without cars at their disposal, mentors could have been trained and willing to engage in mentoring, teachers would have been interested in participating in the programme, but nothing would have happened because mentors would not have been able to reach remote rural schools. In addition, each mentor received a mobile phone to allow permanent contact with experts and management. Training equipment (laptops, video projectors, flipcharts, etc.) were also provided and transported to isolated schools, as well as training materials. This solution was appropriate in the given context (mentors did not have personal cars, rural roads were of poor quality, public transportation was missing, etc.).By the time other projects replicating the mentoring approach were deployed in Romania, the context had changed, roads had improved significantly and the majority of mentors had private cars, which they agreed to use on the condition that gasoline and maintenance be provided by the project.

Procurement of a 4×4 car for each county did not go unnoticed. Procurement of an expensive car in a sector like education, which is always short of funding, may seem an extravagance, unless it is endorsed by the highest education authority and its necessity is communicated to all actors, in order to avoid populist reactions. Several newspaper articles challenged the 'huge expenditure' for 'fancy' cars. With adequate communication, people soon understood why the guaranteed endurance of the car was a key factor in the procurement and why cars were so important.

At the ministry's insistence, 463 fixed resource centres were also established in schools that became hub schools after the consolidation process of schools in rural areas. These centres received equipment (computer, video and TV station, overhead projector, projection screen, copy machine, printer) and supplies (paper, toner cartridges for printers and copiers, etc.). However, for the mentoring process, the most efficient resource centres proved to be the mobile ones.

2.2.4 The Mentoring Process in Rural Schools

Under the programme, rural schools in a commune[3] were grouped in a cluster and direct training was offered to all teachers in the cluster, including those who were not qualified or did not have appropriate qualifications.

A team of mentors was formed for each county. Two mentors were recruited for field work and two substitute mentors were selected and trained to be able to replace the other mentors, if needed. Each group of

---

[3] A commune is an administrative unit in rural Romania comprising of several villages.

mentors received a car and basic equipment and instructional materials. The videotapes with examples of good and bad pedagogical practices were particularly appreciated. In time, videotapes were transposed on digital video disc support, to facilitate the use of these materials by teachers on their laptops. In addition, the mentors developed their own material, which was posted on the e-learning platform.

Before the mentors started work, several activities took place: (1) development of the 'visits map', using an algorithm that optimised the mentors' itineraries; (2) development of the mentors' work plans and (3) organisation of introduction meetings at county level to introduce mentors and their future activity in rural schools.

The mentoring activity was a combination of cluster level direct training and school-based individual and teachers' group activities. The activity was structured in three cycles. During the first cycle, mentors organised direct training schools/cluster schools; the cycle lasted 28 hours spanning over three initial days, followed by two additional days, scheduled after most participants have completed half of their classroom applications. During the second cycle, individual and/or group work was organised in schools; this cycle lasted 16 hours. The third cycle was represented by individual work: classroom applications and reflection; it lasted 52 hours. The mentors' direct training sessions were organised outside the teaching hours, at the end of the school day, on the special methodological day or during holidays.

Teachers' participation in the mentoring programme was free of charge and this contributed to the very high participation rate.

The mentors, assisted by the school principal and school inspector, apprised the teachers who participated in the programme. Following positive results, teachers received 30 professional credits that accounted for the in-service training that all teachers are required to undertake periodically (every five years), according to the education law. After mentors had worked with a cluster for a complete school session, the School Inspectorates were supposed to encourage the continuation of the activity by the teachers in the cluster. Mentors were supposed to continue visiting the cluster, but on a much less frequent basis, to help sustain teachers' work.

The mentor activity involved a combination of structured and less structured activities, such as observing classroom practice, asking questions and giving advice. A detailed record of activities was undertaken.

2.2.5 Certification Programme

Certification was an important incentive for teachers' participation in the mentoring programme. A system of formal recognition of successful participation in the mentoring programme was implemented. The NCITT established the procedure and documentation needed for issuing diplomas certifying the achievement of 30 credits by graduating teachers. Formal diplomas issued by NCITT were awarded to all teachers who participated in the programme.

2.2.6 Stakeholders' Involvement

The stakeholders involved in the mentoring system and their relationships are presented in Figure 2.1. MERYS initiated the REP and assured overall project overseeing. MERYS' management department for projects with international financing was responsible with general project management. The department assured the coordination with other ministry departments and institutions subordinated to the ministry. It was also responsible with selecting and hiring the TA, hiring the mentors and organising their training, monitoring and evaluation and all other managerial tasks. The NCITT authorised the training programme and issued the certificates to graduating teachers. The County School Inspectorates (CSI) hosted the county project management units and closely cooperated with them for implementing the REP. School inspectors coordinated with mentors on scheduling school visits, joined mentors whenever possible, assured coordination with the local Teacher Houses activities and organised follow up activities. The TA designed the training programme and the teaching/learning materials, in close cooperation with selected teachers, inspectors and ministry experts. It was also responsible for training mentors and monitoring and evaluating their work. Mentors implemented the school-based teacher training programme and evaluated participating teachers. Teachers participated in training activities and organised themselves for continuing training activities at school level.

2.2.7 Monitoring and Evaluation

M&E was performed through a sophisticated system of monitoring visits and reporting. In particular, portfolios proved to offer useful information regarding the activities conducted by teachers and mentors.

During monitoring visits, several activities took place: interviews with school principals, discussions with teachers, observation of training

Figure 2.1
Stakeholders involved in the mentoring system

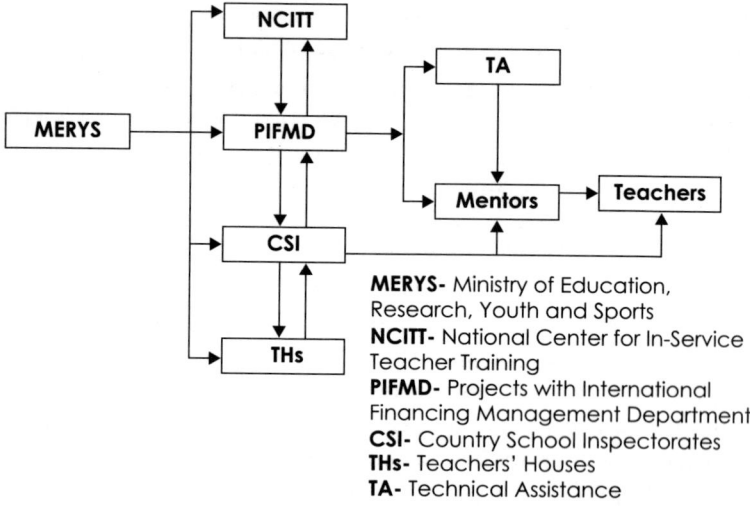

MERYS- Ministry of Education, Research, Youth and Sports
NCITT- National Center for In-Service Teacher Training
PIFMD- Projects with International Financing Management Department
CSI- Country School Inspectorates
THs- Teachers' Houses
TA- Technical Assistance

Source: Author.

sessions delivered by mentors and review of the mentors and teachers' portfolios. Portfolios were an important source of information on the extent and quality of work in schools, since they collected evidence regarding the training sessions, lessons plans, training needs analyses, memos of the professional discussions between teachers and mentors, individual professional development plans, progress record reports for each teacher, teacher and mentor joint reports on the level of professional development that has been achieved and an evaluation sheet for each teacher.

For such a large-scale activity, with many persons involved in parallel in various activities, reports proved to be an efficient monitoring tool. All reports were prepared in a standardised format, which was developed before the piloting phase and was improved after it. The reports described in detail the daily activity of the mentor: when, where and with whom did the mentor work and what they did. Official documents signed by school principals confirming the mentor's presence in the School Cluster and the time spent were also regularly collected.

Reports with teachers' feedback on the training sessions and on the other activities were also regularly produced. Questionnaires collected specific information on how the mentors conducted their activities. More than 80 per cent of the total number of respondents to questionnaires rated the performance of mentors as very good or good, with more than 60 per cent of the respondents rating the mentors' activity as very good in all respects. The monitoring activity certified the mentors' professionalism, their capacity to work in difficult conditions, travelling to distant places, adjusting to unexpected situations, such as adverse natural events (floods, heavy snowfalls, storms, etc.), epidemics or even teachers' strikes.

Reports allowed the project management to constantly monitor progress towards the achievement of the intended targets in terms of number of clusters visited, schools and teachers benefiting from mentoring, etc. Remedial measures could be immediately taken when targets were not reached on time.

The Pilot Phase of the Mentoring Programme: When the REP was designed, the school-based teachers' professional development was not used in Romania as an alternative to the conventional centralised training. The piloting phase of the mentoring programme was very important for preparing the main phase, by testing and further refining plans, instruments, procedures and materials.

The number of schools involved in the pilot phase had to be sufficiently large to prove the validity of the approach in a variety of settings. It had also to be sufficiently small to allow close monitoring and analysis. Consequently, rural schools in six of Romania's 41 counties were included in the pilot. During the pilot phase, 1,067 teachers attended the mentoring programme. This represented 93 per cent of the total number of primary and lower secondary teachers in the six pilot counties.

After the successful completion of the pilot phase, a conference was organised, attended by mentors who had already worked in pilot schools and the newly recruited mentors needed for the nationwide scaling up of the programme. The mentors from pilot counties presented their experience and shared with the new mentors examples of good practice. Discussions were organised in order to review tools used in the programme and to make improvement recommendations.

Preliminary activities undertaken before the initiation of the mentoring activities in pilot schools included development of the Mentor's Kit and development of instruments and baseline study for the M&E mechanism.

The Mentor's Kit included the Guide of Mentoring in Rural Schools, as well as instruments to be used in schools: questionnaires, outline of the school report, forms for teachers and school self-assessment. The Guide was written in a user-friendly manner and allowed for the independent use of materials by mentors and teachers in the field. The draft Mentor's Kit was ready before the first mentors training seminar and its content was analysed and tested throughout the first round of the mentors' training. The instruments were also tested during the first school visits by the mentors. The Mentors' Kit was reviewed after the piloting phase and was distributed to the mentors to be used in the main phase of the project.

During the piloting phase, learning materials were also tested and improved. The training materials distributed to participants included, among other things, theoretical summaries, easily accessible for memory refreshment, brief descriptions of teaching techniques and instruments for frequent assessment of students' progress. The majority of trained teachers (97 per cent) declared they had benefitted from the printed learning materials and they had access to other bibliographical materials (RomEuro Consult, 2008).

The M&E mechanism included: (1) initial, intermediary and final evaluations and (2) periodic monitoring and reporting.

A baseline study was prepared at the beginning of the piloting phase. Data and information on teaching methods, teachers' attitudes, teaching resources, etc., were collected and analysed in order to allow for future comparisons with data and information collected at an intermediary stage and at the end of the project.

Pilot mentors were closely monitored by means of desk reviews and field activities. Mentors were asked to regularly fill in specific forms and send them to the experts group who carefully reviewed them and sent feedback to the mentors. The experts group also performed field visits. The set of monitoring and reporting procedures included:

- mentors report after each school visit and training session;
- school reports after each semester of training;

- quarterly reports to the REP management on the work of the mentors, the subject trainers, the response of rural teachers and the effectiveness of the training given;
- synthetic reports on feedback from stakeholders on the training process;
- reporting to the project management following supervision visits to selected schools, with suggestions for improvement of the mentoring process.

Section 3: Effectiveness and Outcomes

3.1 Problems Solved

In education it is difficult to assess effectiveness during the life of a project, since real outcomes, at the level of students' learning, are noticeable only after a longer period of time, which usually goes beyond the project closure. It is also difficult to identify the effect of a single change factor upon students' learning. Therefore, it was difficult to answer the questions implied by the project performance indicators: 'did the mentoring programme contribute to solving the problem of rural students' low learning achievements' or 'did the mentoring programme contribute to solving the problem of the gap between rural students and urban students' learning achievements'? Learning achievements, as measured by national tests indicated an improvement, but one can only guess that part of it was due to teachers' upgraded knowledge and skills. The Implementation Completion and Results Report (World Bank, 2010) mentions several outcomes and impacts of the mentoring programme.

It is somehow easier to assess the problems that were solved at the level of education output. In quantitative terms, almost all rural teachers were trained. Out of the total number of rural teachers, 87 per cent, that is, 62,604 teachers received official credit awards, certifying their successful participation in the mentoring programme. The remaining 13 per cent of the teachers, who could not attend the REP's mentoring programme due to various reasons (medical or maternity leave of absence during the mentor's school visits, teaching job acquired after the mentoring period, etc.) were included in a replication mentoring programme supported by the GoR. Mentoring was conducted in clusters with teachers coming from about 8,400 rural schools.

There were 146 mentors who were recruited and trained. The group of mentors was acknowledged as a professional group and the professionalism gained from the opportunity to mentor during the REP implementation was of great use in subsequent projects, which relied on mentoring programmes.

Mentors were able to travel to distant places with the cars procured for each of the 41 counties. Cars became real mobile resource centres, as a result of the equipment and materials they carried. In addition, 463 fixed resource centres were established and equipped. In this way, the training of rural teachers was facilitated and even those from the most remote areas could benefit from various learning materials.

The school-based professional development/mentoring programme represented a major shift from the conventional, inefficient, centrally organised teacher training programmes. The mentoring programme promoted innovative learning, a type of learning characterised by anticipation and participation, as opposed to the mechanical maintenance learning, characterised by the acquisition of fixed outlooks, methods and rules (Botkin et al., 1979). The innovative learning is more appropriate in times of change, when it can bring renewal, restructuring and problem reformulation. If anticipation may be best understood by contrasting it to adaptation, participation is more than the formal involvement; it is an attitude characterised by cooperation, dialogue and empathy. Rural teachers had the opportunity to participate in interactive learning sessions, which promoted conceptual and practical changes in their classrooms. They were also encouraged to engage in experiential learning, which is learning through reflection on what you are doing. An important achievement of the mentoring programme was the appearance of communities of practice in schools. Thus schools start becoming a place where passionate and concerned teachers continuously learn how to improve teaching and learning, while regularly interacting.

Monitoring and evaluation activities performed under the final Longitudinal Study, including classroom observations, confirmed the efficiency of the professional development programme (RomEuro Consult, 2008). The observations indicated that most rural teachers were using interactive teaching methods, thus meeting the output indicator target of about 70 per cent of rural teachers using the new methods. In about two thirds of the observed lessons of the final study teachers had organised group work with students, while in the baseline study the value was two times smaller. An interesting finding was that in the baseline study a high percentage of the teachers declared they could use group work with their students, while actual classroom observations indicated that in fact the method was not used in more than 70 per cent of the lessons. In the final study, the reverse was the case. Although the percentage of lessons in which group work was observed had increased, teachers were more cautious in assessing their capacity to use the method and the percentage was lower. A possible explanation is that through the programme, the level of awareness and responsibility of teachers has increased.

A significant increase was found in the percentage of lessons with differentiated tasks/activities. While in the 2005 baseline study differentiated tasks/activities were organised in 42.4 per cent of the observed lessons, in the 2008 final study the percentage increased to 72.3 as shown in Table 2.1.

The time allocated to lecturing has also decreased. If in the 2005 baseline study only 7.1 per cent of the observed lessons didn't have lectures, in 2008 the percentage increased to 15.9. Likewise, if in the baseline study 22.5 per cent of the observed lessons allocated more than 30 minutes to lecturing, in 2008 the percentage was reduced to 2.3 as given in Table 2.2.

Table 2.1
Percentage of observed lessons in which differentiated learning tasks/activities were organised, by level of education (2005/2008)

	Primary Education		Gymnasium		Total	
	2005	2008	2005	2008	2005	2008
Percentage of lessons in which differentiated tasks/activities were organised very frequently and frequently	41.6	66.4	50.0	78.7	42.4	72.3

Source: RomEuro Consult (2008).

Table 2.2
Distribution of the observed lessons according to the time allocated to lecturing, by time intervals in 2005 and 2008

	Year	No Lecture	1–15 Minutes	15–30 Minutes	More Than 30 Minutes
Percentage of lessons by time allocated to lecturing	2005	7.1%	52.0%	18.2%	22.5%
	2008	15.9%	75.1%	9.1%	2.3%

Source: RomEuro Consult (2008).

Excerpts from the answers provided by teachers during the beneficiary assessment conducted under the Longitudinal Study also confirm the effectiveness of the training programme (RomEuroConsult, 2008):

> We are far away from the city and therefore it was much better to get training in the school.
>
> We need to be trained, to introduce changes ... In this way parents' trust in the school increases ... In this way the school is going on a good path ... When you use in the classroom the things learned, pupils are reacting, they are happy to do new things.
>
> The training was interesting, we learned new teaching techniques: snowball, cube, clustering, brainstorming, gallery walk. I use them in the classroom and they help me. I could apply some of them, I used less other.

REP contributed also, at least to some extent, to the resolution of a more general problem, namely, the low capacity of policy makers to monitor education issues, such as multifaceted inequities and consequently, to produce evidence-informed policies. In particular, the rural–urban disparities were not adequately monitored and analysed. After the REP implementation, the analytic capacity at national and local education levels was strengthened. The education system has reliable indicators and databases accessible at various decisions making levels, which can be used in analyses, evaluations and planning. This does not mean that the situation of rural students is now highly improved. First, the mentoring programme was not properly institutionalised, as will be discussed later. Second, other supply and demand factors continued or started influencing the situation of rural schools, of which the most important one is under-financing.

3.2 Sustainability

The sustainability of the mentoring programme can be addressed at the school, the county and the national level.

At the school level, the main recommendation at REP's closure was to continue activities in order to strengthen the initial results of the mentoring programme. A teacher or a group of teachers was to be appointed in each rural school to be in charge of the further adoption and development of new teaching practices. They would be accountable to the school principal for this activity. Another recommendation was for the principals to be more involved in driving/supporting the change processes after the mentor's visits in the schools. In the absence of follow-up studies, it is difficult to assess whether these recommendations were put in practice. What is known is that no formal official measure was taken to endorse these recommendations. However, a change in the 'culture' of many rural schools was noticed and mentioned on several occasions.

At the county level, the recommendation for local authorities (School Inspectorates and THs) was to take the appropriate measures for further development and continuation of the mentoring programme. For a while, School Inspectorates recruited mentors who worked under the REP and assigned them mentoring responsibilities. Meanwhile, the new National Education Law (MERYS, 2011) included specific provisions regarding mentors.

At the national level, sustainability issues can be discussed in terms of: (1) institutionalisation and (2) replication of the mentoring programme.

In terms of institutionalisation of the mentoring system for teachers' professional development, two problems had to be solved. First, mentors had to be acknowledged as a distinct category of education staff. Second, accreditation of the mentoring programmes had to be possible, in order to encourage teachers to attend activities in view of receiving the associated training credits.

The first problem was addressed through the new National Education Law (Romania's Official Gazette, 2011).Three categories of mentors are mentioned by the law: teacher–mentor, professional insertion/induction mentor and mentor for CPD. The first category is represented by teacher–mentors who coordinate in a school the practical stage of a teacher student during their initial training.[4] The second category is represented by mentors who are assigned to a new teacher to help and advise them during the first year of profession. The last category is represented by mentors similar to the ones created through the mentoring programme, who support teachers' CPD. The function of a CPD mentor is mentioned only in the frame of THs (Art. 247–i). In schools, only mentors for initial teacher training and for professional insertion are mentioned (Art. 247–1).

A special legal provision regards teachers who have obtained the highest didactic degree and have exceptional didactic and managerial results. These teachers can earn the title of 'teacher-emeritus'. Alongside this title, the teacher automatically receives the quality of CPD mentor (Art. 243–2).

Another type of institutionalisation took place when several mentors established a professional association, the Romanian Association of Mentors,[5] which for the time being is focused on mentoring student teachers (practical stage of the initial teachers training) and mentoring beginner teachers.

According to the National Education Law (MERYS, 2011), the continuous teacher training includes professional development and career advancement (Art. 242–1). Continuous teacher training is described as a right and as an obligation (Art. 245–1).

The second problem is solved through the accreditation process created under the NCITT. The council has already accredited several mentoring programmes. The semi-autonomous council was recently transformed into a department of the MERYS and has the same functions as the council. The accreditation and the periodic evaluation of the providers of continuous training and of the programmes they are offering are done by the MERYS, through its specialised departments (Art. 244–3). The same departments are in charge of the development of the methodological framework for organising and implementing teachers' continuous training.

---

[4] Initial teacher training includes in Romania: (1) specialised theoretical initial training in a university; (2) master in didactics (2 years) in a university and (3) a one-year-practical stage in a school under the coordination of a teacher– mentor (Art. 236–1 of the National Education Law).

[5] http://asmero.ro/?language=en

In terms of replication, after REP's closure the mentoring programme was immediately taken over by MERYS and was included in two projects: (1) the CPD of Pre-university Education Staff Project (2006–2009), financed by the GoR, which supported mentoring for the CPD of all upper secondary schools teachers and (2) the Early Childhood Reform Project (2006–2011), financed by the Council of Europe Development Bank and the GoR, which supported mentoring for the CPD of about 48,000 pre-school staff: teachers, kindergarten managers and auxiliary staff. After Romania's accession to the European Union (EU), three additional projects, which included mentoring for teachers' CPD, were developed and financed under the EU financed 'Sectorial Operational Programme Development of Human Resources 2007–2013': (1) Teachers' Professional Development through Mentoring Activities (2008–2011), aimed at rural teachers and teachers from schools in disadvantaged cities; (2) Innovation and Performance in the Urban Teachers' Professional Development (2010–2013), aimed at developing a standardised CPD for teachers in big cities, including mentoring activities and(3) Professional Development of Rural Teachers through Mentoring Activities (2010–2013), a continuation of the REP mentoring programme, which is implemented in five counties, following the recommendation of the final Longitudinal Study for mentoring activities to be continued in rural schools (see the annexure).

The content of the new mentoring programmes was improved, updated and adapted to new contexts. For example, in the mentoring programmes for teachers in urban schools, the module on 'curriculum adaptation to the rural context' was replaced by modules dealing with violence in schools. However, the main principles of the programmes remained the same as in the REP.

3.3 Cost-effectiveness

Was the mentoring programme for rural teachers a more cost-effective alternative to conventional in-service teacher training? The answer to this question will be structured in two parts: (1) the cost-efficiency of the programme and (2) its effectiveness.

Simple calculations can prove that the mentoring programme was more efficient than other centralised teacher training activities. It was estimated that a regular in-service teacher training programme offered by a TH in Romania costs RON 800–1,200 (about Euro 200) per trainee.

Additional costs are incurred by the teacher's transportation to the TH and their accommodation, if needed. The cost per teacher trained under the mentoring programme was of about RON 3, with no additional costs.[6] In replication mentoring programmes, costs were slightly different, but continued to be relatively low for the mentoring programme. The fee paid to a mentor had to be increased, following a general increase in teachers' salaries. In urban areas, mentors used public transportation and in rural areas personal cars were used, the gasoline and maintenance costs being covered by the project.[7]

Pursuing efficiency at any cost can be dangerous. Savings-driven managers may be inclined to include in programmes as many teachers as possible, disregarding the quality of their training. The fact that the mentoring model is more efficient than the conventional teacher training does not mean that savings should be an absolute guiding principle. A sufficient number of mentors are needed. Time and resources to train them are required. A budget to cover the costs of frequent trips to rural schools and the cost of training materials and equipment is needed.

Cost-effectiveness is usually preferred to efficiency, but is more difficult to quantify. It is questionable whether it makes sense to estimate the economic return of the mentoring programme, because its objective, like the REP's objective, has an equity dimension, rather than an economic return one. Although increased equity may have some economic benefits, it cannot be measured because the techniques for estimating the income effects of improved education quality are not well developed. What is important is the fact that the project's objectives were correctly defined and its activities represented the least-cost way of attaining the objectives.

The main outcomes expected from the mentoring programme are non-monetary, involving improved access to quality education in rural areas. As indicated by the REP's M&E plan, the development outcomes were measured through performance indicators, such as improved rural school completion rates, improved rural teacher qualifications and improved results in the assessment of learning achievement of rural students.

---

[6] Estimation communicated by the head of the MERYS department for foreign supported projects.

[7] At the end of the mentoring programme under the REP the 41 cars were given to county School Inspectorates to be used for further local needs.

The REP's effectiveness was measured during implementation with a sophisticated tool, the Longitudinal Study, which monitored a large range of indicators and provided quantitative and qualitative information. The final study provided detailed data and information indicating that the REP, including the mentoring programme, has attained its objectives.

Section 4: Lessons Learnt

There are many lessons that can be drawn from the design and implementation of the mentoring programme for rural teachers' professional development in Romania. They range from general lessons, derived from the role of the REP, the project in which the school-based teachers' professional development approach was included, to detailed lessons derived from particular activities carried out in the mentoring programme. The aim of presenting these lessons is to identify those elements that may be replicable elsewhere.

4.1 Teachers' Continuous Professional Development Cannot Give Results in Isolation

Teachers' CPD is a very important measure aimed at increasing education quality. However, unless it is embedded in a broader set of education policies, it may not have the desired results. For example, in the case of the mentoring programme, which promoted interactive-learning methods, it was difficult to implement these methods in a context in which high-stakes graduation exams privileged memorisation over critical thinking and problem solving. Insufficient incentives may discourage teachers from making the effort needed for changing their teaching methods and vice versa, correct incentives may work favourably. In addition, a contradiction between principals and school inspectors' evaluation criteria and teachers' changed and improved classroom practice might further discourage teachers from working hard towards bringing changes in their schools. The solution is for principals and inspectors to also be trained, before or together with teachers and to be committed to support the implementation of changes.

4.2 Grassroots Interventions Need to Be Combined with Nationwide Policies/Actions

REP focused on a range of grassroots activities, one of them being the school-based professional development. At the same time, it supported the work that led to the definition of the national education indicators, the development of the education data base and the initiation of the annual education reports presented to the Parliament by the minister for education. In this way, the foundation for informed policy making was created, leading to the accurate assessment of equity issues and enabling timely adoption of measures to correct them. More was needed. As mentioned above, because school inspections and teachers' evaluations were not reformed, principals and inspectors were left behind rural teachers in many respects. Teachers were introducing new teaching methods that were unknown to those assigned to review their work. Instances of negative feedback from principals led to the compulsory inclusion of principals in the school-based professional development activities. The situation of school inspectors was more uneven. Some succeeded to get aligned with the new methodologies, others continued to resist changes.

4.3 School-based Professional Development Is Useful in Various Contexts

The mentoring scheme implemented in rural schools was highly successful. The new, alternative approach to teacher training was used for reaching teachers in distant rural areas. However, it was also initiated to better reflect new teaching and learning methods that emphasise interactive, student-centred teaching. This alternative approach to the conventional teacher training is characterised by significant differences. While the conventional teacher training relies on one-time, centralised initiatives, school-based professional development is based on iterative activities assisted by the mentors and continuous collaborative and reflective actions. Individual teachers are benefitting, while the school as a whole evolves into a community of practice/professional learning. The success of the rural programme and the lack of comparable development opportunities in urban areas led to the design of similar school-based professional development for teachers in urban schools. The approach proved to be useful in training all teachers, irrespective of their school environment (rural/urban, disadvantaged/affluent). Therefore, the mentoring system developed under the REP should not be understood as an approach valid exclusively for educating teachers in disadvantaged rural schools.

4.4 Solving the Transportation Issue Is Essential for Mentoring Activities in Rural Areas

Geographic constraints (isolation, flooding, poor infrastructure) and lack of transportation lead to the isolation of rural teachers from a variety of professional development opportunities accessible to their urban schools colleagues. Once mentors could use a car, they could travel and reach remote rural schools.

4.5 The Right Incentives Are an Important Factor for the Success of the Mentoring Programme

Incentives are important both for mentors and for teachers. The type and level of incentives offered to mentors needs to be appropriate; otherwise, they will leave the programme once they begin to encounter difficulties. Mentors' salaries/fees need to be significantly higher than the salary of a regular teacher, who does not need to leave home and travel to distant places. Incentives are also important to encourage teachers to participate in CPD. Incentives, such as teachers' certification by means of training credits that count for career advancement were highly appreciated in REP. Accreditation institutions need to be involved early in the mentoring programme design process and informed about new approaches supported by the programme. Otherwise, unknowledgeable staff can block and delay programme accreditation and/or approval of the certification scheme.

4.6 Strong Organisation Is Important for the Success of the Mentoring Programme

The prior training of mentors was essential for the programme's success. Mentors knew well the topics of training and also were able to easily gain the respect and collaboration of teachers. The supply of quality support materials such as teaching materials and forms for certifying teachers for attendance were other important factors. Finding the right time for the training sessions and other mentoring activities is challenging. It is easy to retain teachers after school, but they may be already tired after the hours they have spent teaching. Teachers may not agree to use their holidays for training. Officials may need to agree to the use of the periodical pedagogical meetings for mentoring purposes, if time for such meetings is legally allocated.

4.7 Promotion of New Teaching Methods Takes Time and Follow-up Activities Are Needed

There is a need for persistence and stimulation to modernise teaching practices by means of the mentoring process. In particular, the use of new, student-oriented teaching methods takes time and cannot be implemented without the long-term involvement of various actors. In the case of the REP, the following actions were recommended, but only partially achieved.

- Appointment of a teacher/group of teachers in charge with the development of new teaching practices and accountable to the school principal in each school
- Higher involvement of school principals in follow-up activities after the mentor's visits and in supporting the continuation of activities
- Involvement of school inspectors and methodologists in mentoring follow-up activities
- Using teachers' pedagogical meetings to refresh the knowledge and skills acquired through the mentoring programme

Follow-up activities need to be developed in schools to assure continuing progress in the activities undertaken. School Inspectorates need to be involved in the programme from the beginning. It is known that the teachers' CPD gives good results when it is long-term, school-based and collaborative, actively involving all teachers, focused on students' learning.

4.8 Quality Assurance through M&E and Impact Analysis Is Important

Monitoring should be focused both on quantitative and on qualitative issues. Although collecting quantitative data is easier, its relevance is limited unless it is complemented with qualitative information such as: the impact of teachers' participation in the programme on their skills and competencies; the teachers' perception of the quality and relevance of training modules and materials; teachers' appraisal of various elements of the mentors' activity (delivery of training, mentoring, coaching, tutoring).

Section 5: Plans for the Future

The plans for the future can be discussed in terms of Romania's plans for further use and development of the mentoring system for teachers' professional development and in broader terms related to the future of the approach of school-based CPD based on mentoring.

Ever since Romania joined the EU in January 2007, all its policies are in one way or another influenced by this membership. Although in education there is no compulsory EU legislation, the EU is interested in improving the quality and the equity of its members' education systems. The open method of coordination is used by member states to learn from each other by sharing data and information and by comparing activities. The European Commission encourages the adoption of best practices and the coordination of education policies. Member states are helped to modernise their education and training policies, through the Education and Training 2020 Work Programme's exchange of information, data and good practice, mutual learning and peer review. In particular, teachers' CPD is considered an important vehicle for improving the quality of education.

In terms of education quality,

> three of the teacher characteristics deserve particular attention. The first is pedagogical content knowledge, a very promising source of teacher competence which integrates knowledge of the subject matter and knowing how to teach it. The second concerns teacher preference for either a more direct, structured approach to teaching or a constructivist approach. Third, the concept of teachers' sense of self-efficacy is an interesting factor. Most studies have found a positive relationship between teachers' beliefs about their efficacy and student achievements in core academic outcomes. (European Commission, 2010)

Policies in the area of teachers' professional development take into account the 'changing world of teaching' in which, teachers strive to equip learners with a wide range of skills that they will require to take their place in a world that is in constant evolution; this hastens the need for the development of more competence-centered approaches to teaching, together with greater emphasis on learning outcomes. Pupils are increasingly expected to become more autonomous learners and to take responsibility for their own learning. The learners in any class may come from an increasingly wide range of backgrounds and may have a very broad range of abilities. In this context, even initial teacher education of the highest quality cannot provide teachers with the knowledge and skills necessary for a lifetime of teaching. Teachers are called upon not only to acquire new knowledge and skills but also to develop them continuously. (European Commission, 2010)

In the context of decentralisation, with schools assuming more autonomy, the school-based professional development is considered as a promising approach to CPD in the EU.

In Romania, teachers' participation in CPD is considered a professional duty. The legal requirement, as mentioned in the National Education Law, is for each teacher to acquire 90 credits of in-service teacher training/professional development during five consecutive years. School-based professional development is not yet officially acknowledged as an alternative to the conventional teacher training approach. This approach is relatively new and was used only in the framework of projects, usually developed with international donors. The MERYS's high level leadership agreed to formally acknowledge the new professional development approach, but failed to do so in the new education law. The professional development mentor is mentioned as a function only in THs (Art. 247–i). In schools, teacher–mentors for initial teacher training and mentors for professional insertion/induction are mentioned (Art 247–l). No requirements are listed, while for all other categories of education staff, clear requirements are listed. The idea is probably that the mentor stationed at the TH will provide professional development assistance to schools served by that TH, although such an explanation is not provided. Secondary legislation dealing with teacher education will need to be more specific in this respect.

Mentoring programmes such as the one developed under the REP can be deployed in order to address emergency issues or for the rapid diffusion of reform measures, which otherwise would take a much longer

Ana Maria Sandi   83

time to be known. The mentoring programmes can also be developed as an alternative to the conventional in-service teacher training, particularly when initial teacher training is lagging behind and the centralised in-service teacher training does not reach teachers in remote rural areas. However, the most efficient use of the mentoring model is in CPD, if it is institutionalised, that is, if mentors are recognised as a distinct category of education staff and mentoring programmes are accredited in order to allow the certification of attending teachers.

There is also a need for sufficient resources to be available

> to enable them to offer regular institutionalized training to teachers wishing to claim access to such professional needs.... these conditions require some form of state institutionalized teacher education and training service. No amount of small scale ad hoc provision by well-intentioned non-governmental organization providers can ensure national CPD will be accessible to all who need/want it. At the moment, the nation state is the only agency with the responsibility. (Yates, 2007)

The way in which the category of mentors was institutionalised in Romania leads to several challenges. The fact that a teacher 'emeritus' is automatically given the mentor status is problematic for the CPD mentors. Good teachers are not necessarily qualified as CPD mentors. They need specialised training and certification. It would be preferable if a legal provision specified the conditions under which a person can become a mentor for teachers' CPD. These conditions should include specific training and an accreditation procedure.

The school-based teacher professional development approach used in the REP was intensely used in projects financed with EU structural funds that actually replicated the mentoring programme. The fact that the approach was not yet institutionalised in Romania may have several explanations. One is the financial situation. The Romanian education system has been struggling for years from under financing. In all education laws, 6 per cent of the Gross Domestic Product (GDP) is mentioned as the compulsory allocation to education, but this amount was never reached. Successive governments have allocated only 3–4 per cent of GDP to education,[8] but the actual spending at year end is closer to

---

[8] The allocation in 2012 is of 3.6 per cent of GDP.

2.5–3 per cent, which is very low, compared to 5 per cent of GDP, the average European allocation to education. Training is costly and under tight budgetary constraints imposed by the economic crisis, education budgets and teacher training suffer. School consolidation and low teacher salaries have worsened the situation of rural students. External resources, such as the EU funds, are a useful source of funding, used to compensate the absence of sufficient internal resources; in this situation, there is no official reluctance to this alternative type of training, but there is no pressing need to institutionalise it. Another explanation is resistance to change on the side of the conventional training providers. The power of the actors interested in conventional teacher training, that is, universities, may explain why the new approach was not formally mentioned in the new education law. Projects, which are more independent endeavours, may be an easier framework to courageously promote new modern approaches. In this case, the 'project effect' can also mask the unwillingness of the government to allocate funds to mentoring systems for teachers' CPD.

Preserving the group of qualified mentors is a challenge. Unless further opportunities for work are created and decent incentives are offered, the group of trained and experienced mentors will disappear. If opportunities for work exist, the group will also need additional opportunities for its own CPD.

The conclusions of this chapter are highly context-dependent. In other contexts, conclusions regarding the mentoring approach may be drastically different. For example, the mentoring system for teachers' professional development was highly valued by Romanian rural teachers, while rural teachers in the United States (US) didn't value to the same extent the mentoring format (Glover and Nugent, 2011). In fact, in the US, non-rural teachers valued higher the mentoring format than rural teachers. This may be the case because the context in the US is such that despite perceptions about limitations in access to professional development in rural areas, rural teachers are not seriously disadvantaged in their receipt of professional development. The mentoring system needs to be adapted to actual contexts and needs: 'the school-based and cluster approach to teacher in-service development, however, is new and is not amenable to the imposition of models. Approaches will and should grow differently in different locations according to local conditions and needs (Leu, 2004).

However, the advantages of this approach make it highly recommendable in the most diverse contexts. A recent study on teachers for rural schools in Sub-Saharan Africa focused on teachers' deployment, utilisation and management. The study identified one of the reasons for the deployment problems in the region as being the limited opportunities for professional advancement in rural areas, which discourage teachers to go to rural schools.

> Urban areas offer teachers easier access to further education and training, while rural areas offer limited opportunities to engage in developmental activities such as national consultations, including those with representative organizations. Teachers in rural areas may even find it more difficult to secure their entitlement to professional development from regional educational administrations and must overcome many obstacles, including corruption by officials. (World Bank, 2008)

Distant schools present challenges for teacher support. While teachers need continuing professional support, provision is hampered by logistical difficulties.

Diverse situations compel countries to turn to local systems of CPD to ensure adequate support. Countries are also trying to strengthen in-school support. For example, the above mentioned study cites various local support services, designed to provide pedagogical support for teachers: network of coordinating centre tutors (Uganda); ward education coordinators and local teacher resource centres (Tanzania); School Cluster coordinators (Mozambique); district resource teachers (Lesotho). However, insufficient transport often hampers the activity of these persons (World Bank, 2008).

A final remark concerns the importance of the work of international researchers, since

> it is perhaps by working to better understand, critique, use and where feasible integrate the different discourses, research and the evaluative frameworks available to us, that policymakers working in the field of teacher education for EFA [Education for All] will come to devise better policies and achieve improved Global Social Justice. (Yates, 2007)

Summary

How can rural schools teachers be supported to engage in continuing professional development? Do certain approaches work better than others on specific topics, or in special contexts? This chaper summarises the lessons learnt from the implementation of a nationwide programme aimed at improving the knowledge and skills of rural schools teachers in Romania. The key message of the chapter is that school-based professional development in which mentors played the main role is a useful way to reach and assist teachers in rural schools. The training of mentors and solutions for transport problems were critical to the success of the programme. This approach was particularly helpful in making teachers understand the need to shift teaching and learning from rote forms, based on memorisation of facts, to active forms which emphasise critical, analytical and problem-solving skills, as well as in helping them change classroom practices. The main condition for the effectiveness of this approach is continuity of the pedagogical support, which can be guaranteed through formal recognition and institutionalisation of the local support services.

Annexure

Projects implemented or under implementation in Romania by the management unit for projects with foreign financing, which have mentoring as the main objective

No.	Title	Period of Implementation	Objectives	Expected Results
1	Professional Development of Rural Teachers through Mentoring Activities[a]	01.12.2010–30.11.2013	Assuring access to quality education for students in rural areas, by improving the CPD of compulsory education teachers, providing them with a significant assistance in career development	6,000 education staff trained (1,500 from primary education, 4,500 from lower secondary), out of which 4,500 women; 5,400 participants certificated, out of which 4,000 women; 12 mentors trained; 1 mentoring program accredited; 1,100 users registered on the project portal.
2	Innovation and Performance in the Professional Development of Teachers from Urban Areas[b]	01.12.2010–30.11.2013	Development and implementation of a complex, standardized professional development program for teachers in big urban centres, which will include training, mentoring, development-research, debates, workshops, career reflection, teachers' evaluation	1,800 education staff trained (300 primary education, 200 vocational education, 650 lower secondary education, 650 upper secondary education), out of which 1,260 women; 90% participants certificated; 32 mentors, career counselors and local coordinators trained; 2,400 users registered on the project portal.

(Annexure Continued)

(Annexure Continued)

No.	Title	Period of Implementation	Objectives	Expected Results
3	Professional Development of Teachers through Mentoring Activities	01.12.2008–30.11.2011	Assuring access to quality education for students in disadvantaged areas through the CPD of teachers in compulsory education	Training curriculum and 8 training modules accredited; 29,000 teachers (9,000 urban, 20,000 rural) participate in mentoring program; at least 90% of participants get transferable professional credits; 50 mentors trained.
4	Early Education Reform Project[c]	01.01.2007–30.12.2013	Improvement of the quality of infrastructure and responding to the actual needs of children through better services, which are favoring the achievement of the maximum potential of each child, using international education standards.	Professional development of staff working with pre-school children (about 35,000 teachers and 13,000 auxiliary staff); professional development of about 2,500 kindergarten managers; supporting parents in understanding the importance of early childhood education and their role; training modules developed and accredited.

[a] http://mentoratrural.pmu.ro/?q=content/prezentare-proiect
[b] http://mentoraturban.pmu.ro/
[c] http://proiecte.pmu.ro/web/guest/pret/

References

Botkin, J., Elmandjra, M., and Malitza, M. (1979). *No Limits to Learning, Bridging the Human Gap*. Elmsford, New York: Pergamon Press.

European Commission. (2010). Teachers' Professional Development—Europe in International Comparison—An Analysis of Teachers' Professional Development based on the OECD's Teaching and Learning International Survey (TALIS), Luxemburg.

Glover, T., and Nugent, G. (2011). *A National Study of Rural Teachers' Professional Development, Instructional Knowledge, and Classroom Practice*, National Center for Research on Rural Education.

Institute of Educational Sciences. (2002). *Rural Education in Romania* (in Romanian): Bucharest.

Leu, E. (2004). The Patterns and Purposes of School-based and Cluster Teacher Professional Development Programs. Working Paper #1 under EQUIP1's Study of School-based Teacher In-Service Programs and Clustering of Schools, USAID.

MacNeil, D.J. (2004). School- and Cluster-based Teacher Professional Development: Bringing Teacher Learning to the Schools. Working Paper #1 under EQUIP1's Study of School-based Teacher In-Service Programs and Clustering of Schools, USAID.

MERYS. (2006). Rural Education Project Mid-Term Review Report, Bucharest.

———. (2011). Order no. 5.564/2011 for the approval of the Accreditation and Periodical Evaluation of the Continuous Training Providers and of the Training Programs Offered by them (in Romanian).

Romania's Official Gazette. (2011). The National Education Law.

RomEuro Consult. (2008). Implementation of the Methodology and Tools for M&E in REP. The Third Longitudinal Study (in Romanian), Bucharest.

Sandi, A.M. (1992). 'Why is it so Difficult? Misconceptions about Eastern European Education in Transition', *International Review of Education*, 38(6): 629–639.

Sandi, A.M., and Moarcas, M. (2007). Romania Education Policy Note, World Bank.

World Bank. (2003). Project Appraisal Document on a Proposed Loan in the Amount of US$60 Million to Romania for a Rural Education Project.

———. (2008). *Teachers for Rural Schools: Experiences in Lesotho, Malawi, Mozambique, Tanzania, and Uganda*, Africa Human Development Series.

———. (2010). Implementation, Completion and Results Report (IBRD-46910) on a Loan in the Amount of US$60 Million to Romania for a Rural Education Project.

Yates, C. (2007). Teacher Education Policy: International Development Discourses and the Development of Teacher Education, Paper prepared for the 'Teacher Policy Forum for Sub-Saharan Africa', 6–9 November 2007, UNESCO, Paris.

3

County Teacher Support System: A Case from China, 'The Southwest Basic Education Project'

Liu Jing

Contents

List of Abbreviations
Introduction

Section 1: Background to the Southwest Basic Education Project (SBEP)
1.1   Understanding the Context: A Brief Background to Basic Education in China
1.2   A Generic Description of SBEP
1.3   An Overview of SBEP Output 2

Section 2: Support to Rural Teachers' CPD before SBEP
2.1   The Existing Policies on Teacher Support Pre-SBEP
2.2   The Existing Support to Rural Teachers in the Inception Stage of SBEP
2.2.1   The Major Providers of Teachers' Professional Development
2.2.2   Types of Support Offered to Local Teachers
2.3   Developing a TSS as a Response to Teachers' Needs in the SBEP

Section 3: Process of Developing and Implementing a Teacher Support System

3.1 Develop a Shared Understanding and Framework for Function
3.2 Get CEB's Approval and Support
3.3 Set up and Institutionalise the Township TLRCs
3.4 Capacity Building of County Trainers
3.5 Identify Support and Embed Good Practice to Sustain the System
3.5.1 Teacher Training through INSET
3.5.2 Observation and Feedback
3.5.3 Mentoring
3.5.4 Classroom Action Research
3.5.5 Additional Activities Initiated by Township TLRCs
3.6 Develop and Manage Resources
3.7 Monitoring and Evaluation of the TSS

Section 4: Effectiveness and Outcomes

4.1 County TSS Was Strengthened
4.2 All Teachers Received Training through County TSS
4.3 Capacity Was Developed
4.4 Continuous Support Was Provided to Teachers
4.5 More Resources Were Available to and Used by Teachers
4.6 Positive Changes in Teaching and Learning

Section 5: Lessons Learnt

5.1 Matching Government Policies Is a Key to the Success of TSS
5.2 A Shared Understanding and Adequate Support
5.3 Needs-based TSS Initiatives
5.4 Ensure Adequate Conditions for County Trainers
5.5 Reliable Funding
5.6 Quality Assurance through Monitoring and Evaluation

Section 6: Sustainability of the Initiative

6.1 Individuals and Institutions Became More Capable
6.2 SBEP Teacher Training Modules Have Been Used in Government INSET
6.3 Pre-service Teacher Education Influenced by SBEP Experiences

Summary

Annexure

References

List of Abbreviations

CAR	Classroom Action Research
CEB	County Education Bureau
CPD	Continuous Professional Development
DE	Distance Education
DFID	Department for International Development
EOP	End-of-Project Review
INSET	In-service Training
JMS	Junior Middle School
MoE	Ministry of Education
MTR	Mid-term Review
NPMO	National Project Management Office
NST	National Support Team
NYCE	Nine-Year Compulsory Education
SBEP	China–UK Southwest Basic Education Project
SDP	School Development Planning
TLRC	Teacher Learning Resource Centre
TOT	Training of Trainers
TRO	Teaching Research Office
TSS	Teacher Support System

Introduction

This chapter presents a case study from Southwest China with a focus on setting up a support system for rural teachers based on the existing education administration system. The key point of this chapter is that a local support system, in which local teacher training institutions and local education authorities play a critical role in reaching and assisting teachers in remote areas, is able to support rural teachers in an effective way. The commitment of the actors involved in the system, the relevance of the training and support delivered to teachers through the system and the capacity building of local teacher supporters are the key to the success of the support system.

The chapter is divided into six sections. It begins with an introduction of basic education in China and the background of the Southwest Basic Education Project. The second section reviews the existing policies and practices for teacher support in rural areas and presents the challenges to professional development for rural teachers. The process of developing and implementing the County Support System and the effectiveness and outcomes of this initiative are illustrated in Sections 3 and 4. Section 5 discusses the lessons learnt and addresses some conditions of the effectiveness of this approach. The challenges to sustain and institutionalise the initiative are discussed in Section 6.

Section 1: Background to the Southwest Basic Education Project (SBEP)

1.1 Understanding the Context: A Brief Background to Basic Education in China

Since the Dakar Conference in 2000, China has made great progress and achievement in the Education for All international policy. In 2004,

> 2,576 counties (cities and prefectures) were accepted as having fulfilled the 9-year compulsory education, increasing the coverage rate of 'two basics' (namely, nine-year compulsory education was basically universalized; illiteracy was basically eliminated among the young and middle-aged groups) from 85% in 2000 to 93.6% in 2004. The total enrollment of primary school students nationwide reached 112 million with a net enrollment rate of school-age children of 98.95%. The total enrollment of junior secondary school students reached 65.28 million with a net enrollment rate of 94.1%. (MoE, 2005)

In light of this success, the Government was turning its attention to access for marginal groups in the poorest counties, with the aim of ensuring that all counties achieve Nine-Year Compulsory Education by 2010. The Government was also paying increasing attention to improving the quality of basic education. Southwest Basic Education Project was introduced in 2006 with the aim to support the Government in addressing these two challenges, focusing in particular on the poorest counties in Yunnan, Sichuan, Guizhou provinces and Guangxi Zhuang Autonomous Region.

Although official enrolment and transition rates in China are high, these mask significant local disparities. Children from poor families, often from ethnic minorities, face substantial barriers in accessing quality basic education.

> Although the net primary enrolment rate is often quoted at 98.95%, in some of the project counties this figure is as low as 70%. In some parts, enrolment for girls was as low as one third of this county average. Disparities in completion rates at primary school are also significant with average rates across the 27 project counties of 78.2% for girls and 79.5% for boys. Transition rates to junior middle school are usually much lower than completion rates in these counties, especially from primary schools in remote areas to junior middle schools. (DFID, 2006)

The overriding reason for this low enrolment and transition is poverty. Within this, there are a range of complex and interlinked factors. Although costs for schooling are reducing due to a recently introduced fee exemption and subsidy programme, they still represent a significant portion of a family's disposable income. Opportunity costs have to be weighed against the perceived relevance of schooling and the distance that children have to travel to school. Additional factors for girls are the tradition of early marriage and the shortage of female teachers and role models. In many communities the added difficulty of learning in Mandarin without the aid of bilingual teaching methods and materials is a further challenge. Choices become even more difficult at junior middle school, where costs are higher and many children have to board because of the distances involved. This added cost of boarding is often prohibitive.

The government has already begun to address issues of quality through the introduction of a new national curriculum in 2001. It stresses the need to change the practice of emphasising too much on knowledge impartment and calls for the creation of supportive environments for students' all-round development. However, for schools in the project counties furthest away from the townships, children were not able to benefit fully from the new curriculum. In many cases, teachers teach for the examination as this is how their performance is judged. Rote learning is the norm. There is little to encourage pupil interaction or encourage problem solving skills and creativity.

Official figures for 2004 show,

> the proportion of full-time teachers with adequate academic qualifications in primary and secondary schools in rural areas increased rapidly. The proportion of qualified full-time teachers in rural primary schools rose to 98%.

The proportion of qualified full-time teachers in regular junior secondary schools reached 93%. (MoE, 2005)

However, this doesn't necessarily guarantee high quality of education. Many of the teacher training institutions have little direct contact with rural schools and courses are academic. Pedagogical training is largely theoretical. As a result, many teachers are poorly prepared for the conditions they face when they start teaching. In-service training (INSET) is largely through workshops and not reinforced by support for the teacher on return to their school. There was some kind of teacher support but no system was in place. Due to a lack of coordination and resources this cannot yet provide the support to enable training to bring about sustainable change to education quality.

1.2 A Generic Description of SBEP

SBEP was a bi-lateral development project between the Chinese Government and the Government of the United Kingdom. The main purpose of the project was to support the Government of China to achieve its goals in basic education, by increasing government capacity to implement effective programmes that increased equitable access, completion and achievement for the disadvantaged boys and girls. The project covered 27 rural and remote counties which are considered some of the poorest in China. The 27 counties are spread over the four provinces (or autonomous region) of Yunnan, Guizhou, Sichuan and Guangxi. The total budget for the project was £23.6 million and each province provided 10 per cent of the amount as local funding of the project. The project was officially launched in November 2006 and was completed by the end of March 2011, its duration was almost five years.

The approach adopted by the project was multi-faceted and systematic. The major interventions conducted by the project are illustrated in Figure 3.1.

SBEP addressed the challenges facing Chinese Basic Education by focusing on three main problems: low student enrolment and retention rates, particularly at junior middle school level, poor quality of education and weak educational management. The expected outcomes of SBEP were described as follows:

Output 1: Improved equitable access for disadvantaged children, especially junior middle school girls, to Nine-Year Compulsory Education.

Figure 3.1
Overview of the five interventions conducted by SBEP

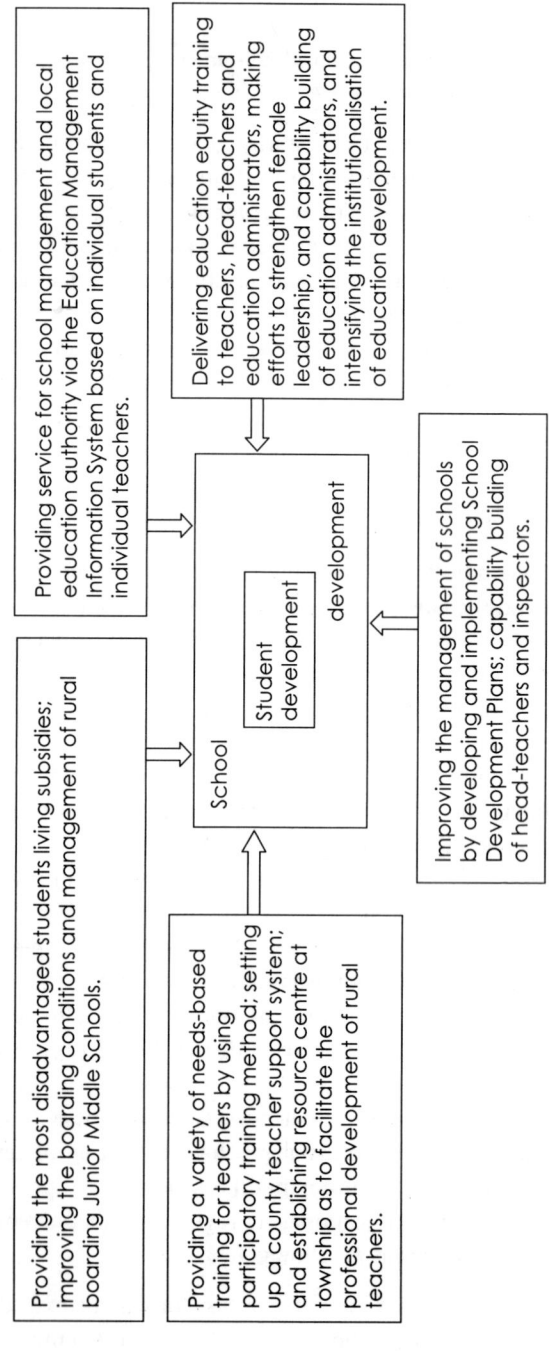

Output 2: Improved teaching and learning outcomes through strengthened capacity of teacher development systems to reach the most disadvantaged girls and boys.

Output 3: Improved systems of school management that promote the interests of the most disadvantaged girls and boys.

Output 4: Improved capacity of monitoring and evaluation systems to orient policy and practice in favour of the most disadvantaged girls and boys.

Output 5: Improved capacity of the education system to better meet the needs of the most disadvantaged girls and boys.

1.3 An Overview of SBEP Output 2

The objective of SBEP Output 2 was to improve the effects of teaching and learning so as to benefit the most disadvantaged girls and boys through strengthening the capacity of the teacher development systems (SBEP NPMO, 2008). The expected outcomes of SBEP Output 2 were listed as follows:

- At least five needs based training modules, appropriate for disadvantaged teachers, to support new national curriculum and distance learning project developed and in use by Mid-term Review (MTR).
- By the end of the project, integrated systems for teacher development will be strengthened at county level to establish and improve the operation of teacher learning resource centres in the 50 per cent poorest townships to provide effective support to disadvantaged schools in their district.
- By the end of the project at least 90 per cent of teachers in the project counties (according to design phase figures) will have received needs based training.
- By the end of the project all teaching points and village schools will have an increased range of appropriate teaching and learning materials available to them and will make effective use of them.
- By the MTR, the time spent on whole class teaching will be reduced from 90per cent to 75 per cent; by the end of project, the proportion

will be reduced to less than 60 per cent and teachers will have a wider range of skills to give better attention to students with different learning needs.
• By the MTR, the time spent in students' active participation in lessons will be increased from 20 per cent to 35 per cent and by the end of the project, this proportion will be raised to over 40 per cent.
• By the end of the project, experience contributes to development of national policies in pre- and in-service teacher training for more effective implementation of new national curriculum in rural areas.

The designers of the project focused on two main strands of improving the capability of teachers in implementing the new curriculum—through training and through establishing a teacher support system which could facilitate the sustained development of teachers' professionalism.

In the case of teacher training, a survey was carried out and, on the basis of the findings of the survey, seven teacher training modules were developed giving support to the implementation of the new curriculum. Four of them were Core Modules which included:

• Participatory Teaching[1]
• Education Equity
• Participatory Chinese Language Teaching
• Participatory Mathematics Teaching

Three of the seven modules were designed as elective modules:

• Development and Utilisation of Local Teaching Resources
• Multi-grade Teaching through Participatory Approach
• Teaching Strategies in a Bilingual Context

Training was delivered to teachers in project counties in a cascade mode. In each project province, a provincial trainer team and a county

---

[1] Participatory Teaching refers to a learner-centred approach in teaching which advocates active involvement of learners in learning. This training module intends to update teachers with methods and techniques that will help them best cater to the needs of their learners.

trainer team were identified and built up. Provincial trainers were staff selected from provincial Normal University,[2] Teachers College and provincial Teacher Training School. County trainers were selected mainly from Teaching Research Office (TRO) in County Education Bureau (CEB), county Teacher Training School and most importantly local outstanding school teachers were chosen as part of the team.

National training of trainers was conducted for provincial trainers and some county trainers; provincial training was delivered to county trainers which prepared them both for the content of the training modules and the methodology of training. Teacher training was planned and conducted at county town and mainly at township centre schools.

In the case of the Teacher Support System (TSS), county Teacher Learning Resource Centres (TLRC) and township TLRCs were set up so as to deliver the support and service to local teachers. The system had three components:

- To establish township-level TLRC as the entity which aims to promote the sustained development of teachers' professionalism
- To promote the existing school-based system in project counties, townships and schools which is characterised by regular study of teaching theories, joint lesson planning and research in teaching practice

---

[2] Normal Universities refer to Teachers University. In China, pre-service teacher education is mainly provided by four types of institutions, namely secondary normal school, teachers college, normal university and comprehensive university. Secondary normal schools take junior secondary school graduates with the aim of preparing them to teach in kindergartens or primary schools. Teachers colleges normally provide three-year programmes for senior secondary school graduates to teach in junior secondary schools. Normal universities provide four-year programmes that grant degrees in teacher education to prepare senior secondary teachers. Comprehensive universities also provide pre-service teacher education programmes. Since the structure adjustment of teacher education institutions in 1999, this three-level pre-service teacher education system gradually has transformed into a two-level system (including four-year Normal Universities and three-year Teachers Colleges). Most secondary normal schools have been abolished, upgraded or merged into higher teacher education institutions. Only a few of them are kept in the central and western provinces.

- To embed a variety of activities such as classroom observation and feedback, mentoring systems and classroom action research so as to give follow up support to classroom teachers after face to face training was delivered

Section 2: Support to Rural Teachers' CPD before SBEP

2.1 The Existing Policies on Teacher Support Pre-SBEP

In rural China, the teacher support system falls on both county and school levels, support provided from county level plays a major role in teacher training and Continuing Professional Development (CPD). Teacher training and teachers' continuing education are conducted mainly by the Teacher Training School at county level. Other institutions such as the TRO and the County Center for Education Technology also organise and conduct teacher training programmes. The overlap and mixture of roles and functions of these county teacher training institutions often leads to problems of repetition of training themes and conflicts over timing, venue and personnel. In response to this challenge, a formal document entitled 'Guidelines on Capacity Building of County Level Teacher Training Schools' was issued by Chinese MoE in 2002. It suggests that all institutions in charge of teacher training at county level should merge to integrate and distribute their resources in a more effective and efficient manner. However, the progress of integration was much slower than expected. Research found that 85 per cent of administrative districts and counties in China have set up teacher training centres but less than 25 per cent of them successfully merged with the TRO and the County Center for Education Technology by the end of 2005 (Zheng and Huang, 2007). In the SBEP context, very few cases were found that teacher training institutes at county level successfully merged and worked efficiently due to the absence of commitment of local government and poor financial capacity.

2.2 The Existing Support to Rural Teachers in the Inception Stage of SBEP

The following summarises the professional support to classroom teachers provided in counties and townships at the inception stage of SBEP.

2.2.1 The Major Providers of Teachers' Professional Development

Teaching Research Office in County Education Bureau: In China, the main responsibilities of the TRO are: monitoring the teaching quality in all schools of that county; providing technical assistance to teachers; doing research, surveys, collecting data; delivering demo lessons, providing teacher training in subject content and facilitating the implementation of the new national curriculum.

An SBEP field visit report found that all the TROs interviewed complained that they were short staffed and under resourced so were not able to support all the schools in their area. Many members of the staff are administrators rather than education professionals. Most TROs only supported the nearest township centre schools because most teaching points[3] were logistically very difficult to get to and time spent travelling to these remote spots was not cost effective.

Teacher Training School: County level Teacher Training Schools play an important role in the provision of continuing education for primary and secondary school teachers in China. In 2002, the MoE issued 'Guidelines on the Capacity Building of County Level Teacher Training Schools', which argued that the focus of in-service teacher education has been transformed from compensatory education aiming at updating the level of teachers' qualification to continuing education

---

[3] In China, primary education in rural area is delivered by three types of schools: centre school located at township; village schools located in the villages under a township; and teaching point scattered in the very remote and disadvantaged contexts. Teaching Points are small sized with one or two teachers working with 20–30 students. Normally these schools provide basic education from grade 1 to 3 through multi-grade teaching approach. 'In 2008, the total number of rural primary school was 253,041, within it 77,519 were teaching points which accounted for 30.63% of the total' (MoE, 2009).

aiming at enhancing teachers' professional capacity and ability. Teacher Training Schools were required to relocate their functions in order to meet the new challenges in continuing education and thus providing continuous support for the reform and development of basic education in the county.

Therefore, both the TRO and the county Teacher Training School are in charge of teacher's professional development but with slightly different foci, for example, the Teacher Training Schools on upgrading teachers and teachers' continuous education and TROs on research in classroom teaching and support to teachers in the field.

Key Teachers[4]: Defining a key teacher is difficult. A key teacher can be a head teacher, subject head teacher, director of teaching, or an excellent teacher. Key teachers are identified as role models for other teachers and most of them are based at schools in the county towns rather than remote areas. In SBEP context, key teachers were organised by the TRO to give demo lessons at township centre school to all the teachers in a township including teachers from village schools and teaching points. Some of the key teachers were appointed as assistants of the TRO to provide support to remote village schools and teaching points. There was no payment for their demo lessons but their contribution was recorded for the annual work review in some of the counties.

County Education Bureau: The CEB's role in the TSS is administrative rather than professional. Some CEB members of staff work as SBEP county trainers but they tend to be the organisers rather than the implementers of the training.

2.2.2 Types of Support Offered to Local Teachers

Generally speaking most people in the project counties equated TSS with INSET. The concept of Teachers' CPD or a system for teachers to develop professionally was not yet fully realised.

---

[4] Key Teacher could be a formal title for teachers who are chosen by Provincial Department of Education or County Education Bureau against some assessment criteria. It often goes with a certificate and a certain award. In the context of SBEP counties, Key Teacher is an informal term which refers to the outstanding teachers who are good at their job and chosen as role models for others.

INSET: Ministry of Education, China (1999) issued 'Regulation on Continuous Education of Primary and Secondary Teachers'. It required that all teachers should complete at least 240 hours' in-service training within five consecutive years in order to better meet the needs of the teaching position.

Most INSET was organised by the TRO, Teacher Training School, or Continuous Education Office of the CEB through a cascade mechanism. The major arrangement of the training was to select a few key teachers from county town schools and centre schools to receive training at provincial or prefecture capital city. The key teachers were trained by prefecture or provincial experts. Few teachers in Village Schools and Teaching Points got the chance to be trained outside their county. Most INSET for the majority of centre school teachers, Village School and Teaching Point teachers was at township level or school-based which was conducted by the key teachers who received the training at prefecture or county. In general, the quality of such training was poor because of the loss of information and absence of quality control measurements.

Classroom Observation and Feedback: The Staff of TRO conducted observation and feedback sessions for teachers but mostly at township centre schools. Some TROs did this systematically but the norm was that the schools nearest to the county town got visited, others did not. Some schools had set up internal classroom observation and feedback system and integrated it into their school plans and sent end of year reports to the TRO. However these efforts seemed to depend on individuals involved rather than there being a sustainable system in place. Additionally again the Teaching Point teachers did not have time for observation and feedback on their lessons as they were always teaching.

Distance Education (DE): In 2003, the Modern Distance Education Project was launched with the aim to provide education resources to teachers and students in rural areas by equipping rural schools with television and DVD, satellite TV receiver system or computer classroom with internet access. The DE system in China relates to the hardware and materials sent from national level to rural and remote schools. There is a website for the DE material so if teachers have access to computers they can download guidelines on how to use the material. The way the DE materials were organised and used varied greatly from one county to another. However the overriding feeling of local teachers was that the material, although appreciated, was not relevant to the rural areas. This was particularly pertinent for teachers from teaching points and village schools. In some cases, teachers were reluctant to use DE materials because they were afraid to be held financially responsible in case of loss or damage.

The existing teacher support at the inception stage of SBEP was too weak to meet teachers' needs in professional development. The major challenges at that time could be summarised as follows (SBEP NPMO, 2007):

- The training or support provided to teachers in remote areas was ad hoc and often just 'one offs' as the TROs, in all counties, were overstretched and under resourced. A well-structured and sustainable teacher support system needed to be set up.
- Lecture was the dominating teacher training approach. Teachers had little chance to have a say or share their experiences. The mechanism for interaction or feedback between teachers and their supporters was weak or absent.
- The provision given by teacher supporters was irrelevant to local teachers as most of the training content were copies from provincial or prefecture level training with little adaption according to local context. Therefore training did not help teachers meet the challenges in their practice such as teaching large classes, teaching in bilingual or multi-grade or both contexts.
- The capacity of the teacher support provider needed to be strengthened. There was no policy, plan or financial support for the professional development of TRO staff at county level. Teacher educators and supporters needed to update their ideas, knowledge and skills about teaching and learning, particularly in the process of the national new curriculum reform.
- The teachers working in village schools and teaching points in the remote areas couldn't be reached by the current system due to lack of human resources, difficult terrain, complicated logistics and lack of funds.
- Teachers in project counties had never heard of a TLRC or any other forms of resource centres for teachers. There was a strong

need to develop and use relevant distance education resources and local teaching resources.

2.3 Developing a TSS as a Response to Teachers' Needs in the SBEP

One of the main goals of the SBEP was to improve the quality of teaching and learning in the most disadvantaged areas of Southwest China. Key to improving quality is to build teachers' capacity. This could be done through quality training using relevant, quality materials and methodology. However training alone is not enough. The training needs to be put into practice, monitored and followed up. Most capacity development projects for teachers implement the training but neglect the follow up support. The latter is the essential ingredient for teachers to be able to develop professionally (and personally) and to impact on the quality of teaching and learning in schools. Monitoring and follow up of training and support to teachers' professional development were essential parts of SBEP teachers' support system. These elements were pertinent in the SBEP context where teachers work in extremely remote and challenging situations with few or poor resources and little access to other teachers or teaching/learning materials.

Through establishing a support system on the project, SBEP teachers began to build confidence in developing their teaching skills and practising new methods. The quotes in Box 3.1 give an indication of the importance teachers put on their training and support.

Box 3.1: Feedback from Teachers Trained by SBEP at Hezhang County, Guizhou Province

- 'I find the training and support very useful because we learn through experience which helps us understand and internalise.'
- 'Being supported gives us plenty of chances to share opinions and practice new methods.'
- 'The content and approach to the training and support gives me inspiration to my teaching.'
- 'I find the training and support equal, harmonious and democratic, it is "real worthy learning".'

Source: Drinan and Liu, 2008.

Section 3: Process of Developing and Implementing a Teacher Support System

Based on the study on the current situation of teacher support in project counties, SBEP National Support Team[5] (NST) worked closely with the provincial and county Output 2 teams to develop and implement a TSS. The basic procedures of setting up and running the rural teacher support system under SBEP Output 2 included:

- Building up a shared understanding of TSS and develop a framework for function
- Getting CEB's approval through policy-making and support in administrative management of the TSS
- Setting up and institutionalise the township TLRCs
- Capacity building of county trainers
- Identifying county and township level support to sustain the system and embed good practice through TLRCs
- Developing and managing resources for teaching and learning at township TLRCs
- Monitoring and evaluation of the TSS.

3.1 Develop a Shared Understanding and Framework for Function

At the incipient stage of the project, the work on TSS mainly focused on embedding classroom observation and feedback systems into schools since there was no shared comprehensive understanding about rural teacher support system. A cross provincial workshop was conducted in October 2009. It was attended by a group of 32 provincial and county OP2 coordinators from the four provinces and 27 counties on the SBEP. Each province presented their progress in teacher training and setting up a teacher support system which aimed to build on TSS activities through

---

[5] National Support Team (NST) here refers to a group experts made up of international and national consultants who provided technique support to SBEP output 2 from its design to implementation and evaluation. By way of public bidding, Cambridge Education (CE) and the British Council were chosen to form the National Support Team to provide consultancy to SBEP.

sharing systems that had worked. NST introduced the concept of a TLRC and how it worked for supporting teachers in challenging contexts. It was suggested to set up county TLRCs and township TLRCs given the policy condition of China and the responsibilities of the township centre schools to their neighboring village schools and teaching points. Provinces and counties discussed the possibilities and feasible approaches of a TSS in the SBEP context. The agreed points were as follows:

- 'Within the SBEP the key goals for the TSS were to: (1) support the professional development of teachers in remote and rural areas, (2) improve teachers' teaching skills, (3) expand teachers' professional knowledge, (4) improve students' learning and enjoyment in the classroom for the most disadvantaged girls and boys, (5) contribute to the development of INSET in rural areas, (6) improve ways of working, (7)improve links with the parents and the wider community' (SBEP NPMO, 2010).
- A shared definition of a TLRC. A TLRC can be seen as the 'hub' for the teacher support activities. The definition and shared understanding of the TLRC, as defined by the provincial and county coordinators for Output 2 on the SBEP, was as follows:

    An institution or organization which is based in a township centre school where the resources and personnel from divisions in the CEB, such as, Teaching Research Office, Distance Education Office, Teacher Training School and township Centre School, work cooperatively to provide continuous professional development and support for teachers in rural areas. (SBEP NPMO, 2010)

    In the SBEP context, the township TLRC served as a place for: (1) all teachers at township level to train in professional knowledge and skills; (2) teachers to share and exchange information; (3) teachers and educationalists to conduct research or surveys on issues in education, especially classroom teaching and learning; (4) teachers to conduct demo lessons, classroom observations and feedback; (5) teachers, especially those from teaching points and village schools, can seek professional support; (6) county educationalists to learn more about teachers' needs and offer relevant support. (SBEP NPMO, 2010)

A concept map of the SBEP rural teacher support system was developed as given in Figure 3.2.

Figure 3.2
The concept map of SBEP rural teacher support system

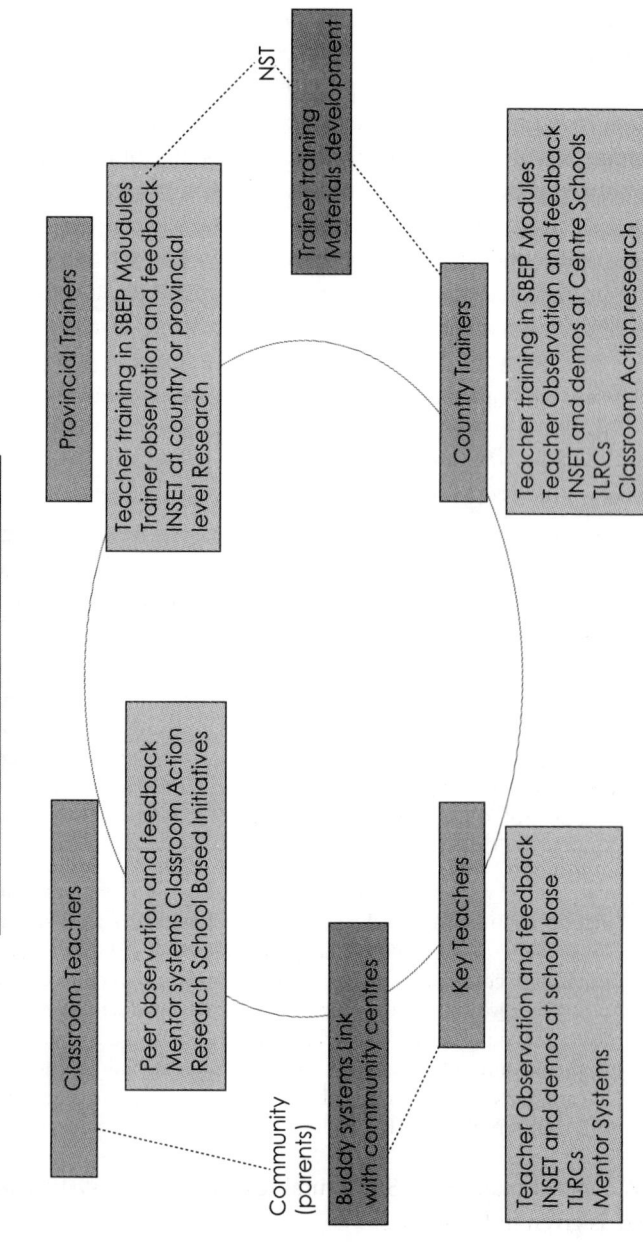

Source: SBEP NPMO, 2010.

The diagram depicts the system as a cycle because each group ultimately supports the other. The provincial trainers need information from the classroom to do research on teaching and learning, likewise classroom teachers need the support of the county and provincial trainers' knowledge and skills. Thinking of the system as cyclical and interdependent helps to break down hierarchical relationships which so often hinder learning and development in teachers' professional growth.

The diagram clearly depicts the activities the trainers and teachers are involved in and how they link to each other.

Figure 3.3 shows which institutions are involved in the support system and how the institutions supporting teachers at county and township level are linked to and interact with the teachers working in remote village schools and teaching points.

A framework of SBEP TSS was developed which clearly presents activities, time and frequency of activities, responsible person and outcomes. See the annexure for detailed framework.

3.2 Get CEB's Approval and Support

Research indicates that support systems for teachers are most likely to succeed when local education bureau administrators are committed to and exercise leadership in establishing and implementing any type of support activity. Without the direction and support of the leader, even the best intentions can fall short of expectations.

In China, CEBs play a critical role in the success of teacher support system because they take the responsibilities for teacher recruitment, INSET and providing support for teachers CPD and assessing the performance of their teachers. The CEB's leadership in the TSS is essential in developing and achieving support system goals. In the SBEP context where most of the current teacher support systems were weak, the CEB's acknowledgement of the importance of the TSS provides a sense of direction to the townships and schools. It plays an important role in the process of clarifying the roles and responsibilities of the different institutes involved in teacher support system and in communicating their importance to experienced and newly qualified personnel.

Within SBEP, the commitment and leadership of CEB in the TSS means: (1) to issue formal documents to state the policy and to take actions to merge Teacher Training School, TRO and Education Technology Centre

Figure 3.3
SBEP county teacher support system

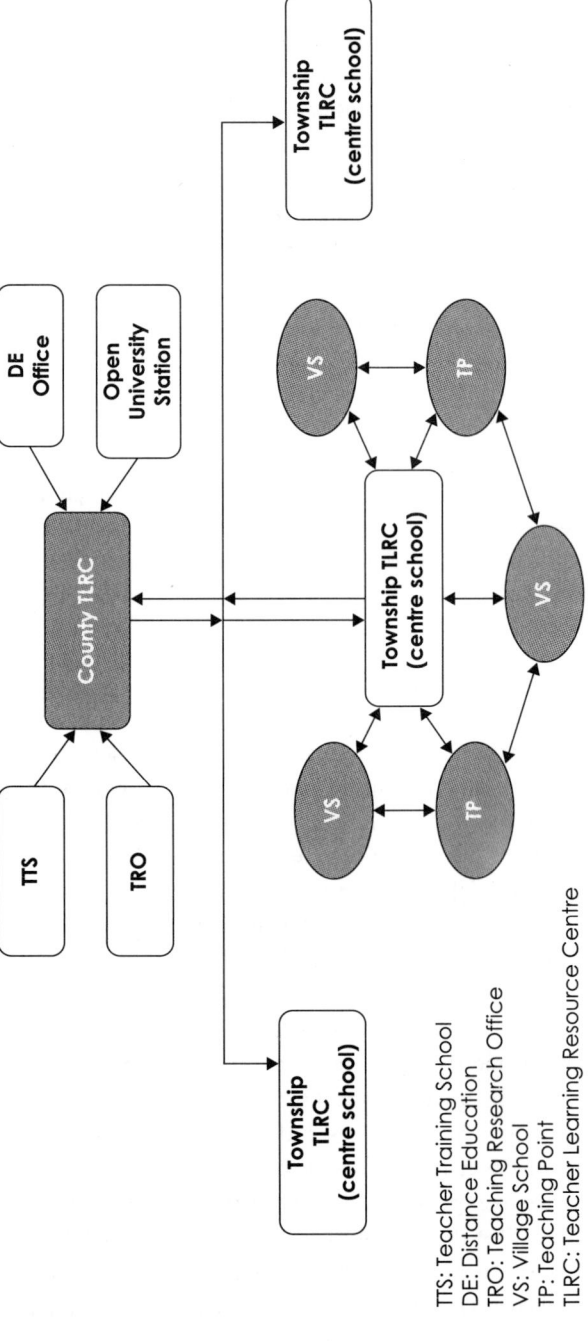

TTS: Teacher Training School
DE: Distance Education
TRO: Teaching Research Office
VS: Village School
TP: Teaching Point
TLRC: Teacher Learning Resource Centre

into one institution (it could be called as County TLRC); (2) to set up and institutionalise the Township TLRC.

With the efforts from SBEP Output 2, a few project counties managed to make the policy of merging existing teacher training institutions into a County TLRC and issued formal documents describing the function, roles and responsibilities of the centre and its management mechanism. However, due to the difficulty and complexity of merging institutes, many counties only managed to issue documents to encourage the collaboration of the institutions rather than taking actions to merge them. Most TLRCs were established at township level and based in township centre schools.

3.3 Set up and Institutionalise the Township TLRCs

In China, township centre schools were set up in 2001. As one of the units in the Chinese educational management system, the centre schools have been authorised the role and responsibility of the management and support of the village schools and teaching points in the area. Before SBEP, centre schools had been playing the role of supporting teacher's professional development though there was not a consensus of what to do and how to do it. To set up and strengthen the existing TSS needed to build up the TLRC in the township centre school. As the SBEP emphasised capacity building, to build up a TLRC means not to construct a real building but to name and authorise the centre school as an official organisation for providing continuous support to teachers and to set up a mechanism to operate the TSS.

In order to set up and operate the township TLRCs, CEBs made a series of efforts which included:

- Developing the township TLRC policy documents and identifying the administrative status of the township TLRC
- Deciding on the roles and responsibilities within the township TLRCs
- Setting the selection criteria for the township TLRC staff
- Giving the authorisation to staff from county TLRC (if there was one) or staff from county institutions such as TRO, Teacher Training School or DE Office to provide support to township TLRCs
- Identifying the activities conducted by TLRCs

The project counties started to set up and operate township TLRCs in 2008. More township TLRCs were set up and operated in 2009 and 2010 though project counties did it at varied pace according to the budget and other resources at hand. All of the counties started the township TLRC initiatives in their poorest townships where the School Development Planning (SDP) Programme under SBEP Output 3 was also implemented from 2008. This whole-township and whole-school approach not only targeted all teachers working in the poorest area, but also integrated teachers' CPD into a more holistic school development process.

3.4 Capacity Building of County Trainers

To ensure the goals of the support system were met, all support providers needed to be properly selected and trained. These support providers were called county trainers in SBEP and a series of training were delivered to them to teach and work with adults. In the SBEP, personnel were organised so that the following teams exist:

- Management and Technical Assistance Teams at county level: CEB director, staff from divisions in CEB such as TRO, Distance Education Office or Continuing Education Office; staff from Teacher Training School and key teachers from schools in the County town.
- Personnel in the TLRC at township level: Head-teachers from centre school and village schools, directors of teaching affairs in schools, a group of key teachers.

The selection of county trainers focused upon the experienced teachers who met the following criteria and exhibited a desire to share personal and professional knowledge and experience to help other teachers grow in the profession. In general, the SBEP project counties chose those who

- are respected by both peers and administrations as a role model in the profession;
- have strong interpersonal relationships or skills;
- are able to develop a trusting, respectful and confidential relationship;
- demonstrate curiosity and an eagerness to learn;
- have relevant experiences of teaching in very remote areas.

It was essential that teams were prepared and trained before running the TSS through the TLRCs. In the SBEP a series of training and workshops were organised and delivered to the county trainers. Specifically, these trainings included:

Background and Concept about TSS in the SBEP and County Trainers' Role in it: Information about the SBEP background, the relevant data in the baseline studies and the SBEP Teacher Needs Assessment Report were shared with county trainers in order to ensure they understood their responsibilities with the teachers they were about to support and project expectations. The TSS framework were printed and shared with county trainers, schools and teachers.

Skills to Conduct and Manage Teachers Training: A national Training of Trainers (TOT) was provided to a group of key county trainers by NST. The TOT at province level and county level was delivered to local county trainers to ensure each one of them master the basic skills for conducting participatory teacher training.

Topics of the TOT included the difference between children learning and adult learning; the cycle of teacher training; how to adapt or develop proper teacher training materials; skills for managing a training session; skills for instruction, questioning and feedback in a training session; and data collection for further training.

Effective Classroom Observation and Feedback: The best form of in-service support would be that which helps all types of teachers to share experiences so that those who exemplify good practice can show how they teach and how they talk about teaching. Observation and feedback would be at the core of the teacher support system because only in a real context could the issues come alive and be relevant to teachers. Therefore, skills of classroom observation and giving constructive feedback are two of the most important skills for the county trainers. A four-day national workshop on this topic was provided to key province and county trainers from 27 project counties. Similar training on this topic was conducted at province and county level to ensure all the county trainers were able to practice classroom observation and feedback in a professional way.

Mentoring Skills: Ideas of mentoring and skills for being a mentor were introduced to SBEP county trainers. Topics such as models of mentoring, roles and responsibilities of mentors, skills of a mentor were covered in the training workshop.

Classroom Action Research: The teachers' own experience of survival in the classroom, especially those working in harsh conditions should be valued and shared. Typically in the SBEP context, most teachers have to meet the challenges of teaching large classes, multi-grade teaching and teaching children in bilingual contexts. They have to find local solutions to solve local problems. The teachers themselves need to be able to articulate their own experience and be helped to identify what is innovative and can be shared with colleagues. Learning to conduct classroom action research could enable teachers to do this. A training course on classroom action research was provided to county trainers by NST. As most of the county trainers are classroom teachers, they were expected to support teachers to do classroom action research in their own context.

3.5 Identify Support and Embed Good Practice to Sustain the System

Four major CPD activities were identified and implemented through the TSS. Gradually, they were being integrated into school daily life. In addition, some school-based initiatives were carried out in some counties.

3.5.1 Teacher Training through INSET

INSET courses were implemented in different ways in the TSS. Here are three examples of how they were organised.

INSET through the Township TLRCs: The TLRCs were based at centre schools in townships. Teachers from village schools and teaching points in that township were invited to attend INSET at the TLRC. The INSET was conducted by county trainers. Examples of INSET activities that were provided are:

- SBEP modules not covered in the 15 days training set down by the project
- Units from SBEP modules
- Model/demo lessons relevant for rural contexts

- Micro-teaching
- New topics that county trainers have learnt and practised from other training
- Professional discussions on new topics or on classroom issues raised by teachers

INSET at School-base: This INSET was initiated by key teachers in the school whether it was a centre school, village school or teaching point. Key teachers with the support of the head teachers run the INSET. A typical activity was observation and feedback, either by a senior, more experienced teacher or by peers. Other forms of school-based INSET were demo lessons for less experienced teachers or sharing skills learnt from external training.

External INSET: The third type of INSET occurred at an external venue either at county or provincial level, for example, rural teachers visiting a provincial (city) primary school. This was the responsibility of the county TLRC to organise through the township TLRCs with the support from the province team. It provided teachers with two or three INSET days a year where they were introduced to the latest pedagogic developments and resources. The provincial trainers were responsible for organising the content and training.

3.5.2 Observation and Feedback

The observation and feedback focused on the formative development of teachers not the evaluation of teachers. Therefore teachers were not graded or evaluated during their observations. They were given constructive feedback after their observations which focused on improving for their next lesson.

An observation and feedback handbook was designed for developmental and research purposes. Thereby developing practice through classroom observation and feedback. Through this observation and feedback county trainers or mentors were able to collect qualitative data on how a teacher was developing as the project progressed. School teachers were trained on how to conduct classroom observation and give feedback to their peers. The observation and feedback linked with SBEP teacher training/INSET in that the focus was on the methods and teaching strategies used in their lessons. A record of classroom observation and feedback was kept in the hands of teachers and their supporters, which informed the further development needs of the teachers.

3.5.3 Mentoring

County trainers were identified as mentors and appointed to provide support to the township TLRC and a certain number of village schools. Normally mentors worked in pairs and worked with one township TLRC. A number of teachers in the neighbouring village schools were identified and built up relationship with these mentors. Mentors made their plan of visiting schools and teachers every school year and kept record of their work. The Mentoring models adopted in SBEP TSS included:

Mentoring for Induction: Mentors were the county trainers who either were experienced teachers or TRO staff with rich teaching experience with a supportive and encouraging attitude. The mentees were the new teachers or less experienced ones to the school. Experienced and inexperienced teachers were paired so that new teachers were supported professionally in their induction year.

Mentoring for Progression: This model was used to support professionals who may have been teaching for a long time but now have more responsibilities or new challenges, for example, new curriculum and new methodologies. So the mentoring helped teacher to respond to the demands of their new role, to understand the responsibilities it brings and the values it implies.

3.5.4 Classroom Action Research

Classroom action research in this context referred to a practical way for teachers to look at their own work and to check it is as they would like it to be. The benefit of this type of action research was it helps a teacher to formalise their learning and give a clear and justified account of their work, not on a one-off basis, but as a continuing regular feature of their practice. Teachers in a school were grouped according to the subject or grade they were teaching. Each group or individual made their classroom research plan. The topics the teachers studied were the challenges teachers were facing in their real life, such as how to improve the oral communication competence of ethnic minority students in Chinese, how to motivate students to study mathematics and how to support students' learning through a meaningful way, etc. County trainers provided technique assistance to the research groups or individual teachers by phone calls and their field visit to schools.

3.5.5 Additional Activities Initiated by Township TLRCs

SBEP township TLRCs were encouraged to have their own initiatives in addition to the four activities mentioned above, as long as the activities were consistent with the SBEP TSS aims and objectives and were operated from a clearly defined vision. The initiatives carried on schools in some counties included:

Joint Lesson Planning: Township TLRCs encouraged teachers from the neighbouring schools to meet periodically to do lesson planning together based on their working schedule. Teachers shared ideas, experiences and resources with a focus on instruction through learner-centred approaches. They developed lesson plans for the coming units with fresh ideas, new techniques or resources.

Classroom Open Week: One week in the school year calendar was set as an Open Week. During the Open Week, teachers, parents and other community members were invited to walk into any classroom they were interested in and gave feedback to the teacher and students they observed. This created an opportunity for teachers to learn from each other and learn more about their students in different learning contexts. Parents and community members also had a chance to get involved in school life.

Reading Club: Teachers were grouped based on their reading interest and met once a month to share and discuss books they read. Each seminar had one teacher as a host who made presentation on the book she or he had read and organised a discussion on the topics in the book. Teachers developed professionally and personally through sharing ideas, knowledge and experiences.

Delivering Demo Lessons to Teaching Points: To ensure the effectiveness of the support provided to the teachers in village schools and teaching points in the very remote areas, an interactive system was built up which allowed village schools and teaching points to report to township TLRC their needs at the end of a semester and the township TLRC responded to it by making a schedule of supporting activities for the coming semester. The major support was delivering demo lessons in the village schools and teaching points. It offered a chance to the only teacher in that teaching point to observe and discuss demo lessons in her or his own class. This approach ensured the support was needs-based and cost effective.

Teaching Competition: Project counties organised classroom teaching competition annually or biennially. Teachers were encouraged to try new ideas and practice new methods or techniques introduced by the SBEP teacher training modules. Outstanding teachers were awarded a prize by the CEB to make role models. Their lessons were recorded and made into discs as a learning resource distributed to township TLRCs for further training to teachers.

3.6 Develop and Manage Resources

Resources were given to township TLRCs so as to facilitate sustainability after the end of the project. The materials were produced through a variety of project activities conducted by SBEP Output 2 teams. These resources included:

- Seven teacher training modules developed by SBEP
- Toolkit for multi-grade teaching
- DVDs of Classroom Teaching in project schools which present good practice of student-centred activities, using of local resources or skills used in multi-grade teaching

Each project province developed and provided resources to their TLRCs according to the local needs and provincial budget. For example, in Yunnan province, each township TLRC was distributed a package of learning resources which included: books on topics such as Educational Psychology, Learning Theory, Learning Assessment; a collection of excellent lesson plans made by project school teachers; four DVDs which were supportive resource for new national curriculum and distance education; DVDs of good lessons recorded in Yunnan provincial teaching competition.

Township TLRCs collected resources for teaching and learning made by local teachers. These resources mainly were: copies of lesson plans; teaching aids such as pictures, cards and hand-made tools; classroom action research papers written by teachers and book reviews. These resources were supportive to classroom teaching and learning in project context. Teachers learnt to develop and adapt resources into their practice and made the learning more enjoyable and relevant to local life.

A staff of TLRC was appointed as resource manager and rules to borrow and use the resources were developed with the purpose to make these resources available to teachers and support their teaching.

3.7 Monitoring and Evaluation of the TSS

Given the huge scope of the project in terms of the population of teachers and students covered and the wide geographic location of the project counties, it was crucial to have a quality assurance system in place to ensure the consistency and standard of project activities in different counties. The SBEP national and provincial support teams conducted field visits periodically during the life of the project. The purpose of the visits was to monitor the progress of the TSS at county, township and school levels and to see what impact the TSS has had on teaching and learning. The NST and province teams observed and participated in the classroom observation and feedback sessions run by the county and township TLRCs to teachers in village schools and teaching points. Misunderstandings were corrected, confusions were clarified and good practices were collected and disseminated through the regular visits.

A series of guidelines and handbooks were developed and shared with all stakeholders. These materials not only brought coherence to the Teacher Training, TOT and CPD activities, but also provided standardisation and quality across the provinces and counties.

Guidelines for Implementing Teacher Training and Quality Standards Framework for Teacher Training: The Guidelines for Teacher Training and the Quality Standards Framework for Teacher Training were a set of standards which presents the expectations for the training at each stage (before, during and after training). A series of indicators were developed and presented in the guidelines in terms of training: Planning and Preparation, Organisation and Arrangement of the Trainers and Participants, Using and Management of the Resources,

Learner-centred Training Approaches, Monitoring and Support to the Training and Record Keeping.

SBEP Classroom Observation and Feedback Manual: The observation and feedback system for teachers in remote and rural areas was valued most by these teachers for their CPD. To embed and institutionalise classroom observation and feedback system was the priority of TSS. This system differs from the inspection observation system in which the focus is on the formative rather than the evaluative. A manual was developed for teachers and county trainers to conduct classroom observation and feedback in a well-structured manner.

SBEP Handbook for a Teacher Support System in Rural Areas: A handbook for a Teacher Support System in Rural Areas was developed for the project, which provided guidelines to the organisation and implementation of TSS. It was divided into two parts: A description of TSS explains the concept, rationale and the organisation of the TSS; Tools for the TSS. The handbook was shared by other stakeholders such as CEB staff, head-teachers and inspectors. It ensured a shared understanding of TSS and a consistency of implementing the TSS across the provinces and counties.

In addition to these handbooks and manuals, conferences on the TSS were organised by NPMO annually. These conferences offered opportunities for sharing good practices and for ensuring consistency and raising quality across project regions.

Section 4: Effectiveness and Outcomes

4.1 County TSS Was Strengthened

After the MTR in 2009, a TSS was established in most of the SBEP counties. The system had three components: (1) Township TLRCs which promoted and sustained the development of teachers' professionalism for all teachers in the township; (2) school-based systems which supported teaching and learning; (3) a variety of activities focused on classroom observation and feedback, classroom teaching action research and mentoring had been tried and embedded in some project counties and schools. The establishment of TLRC in each project province is shown in Table 3.1:

Table 3.1
Numbers of TLRC established in project provinces

Province	Number of Project Counties	Number of Townships	Number of Township TLRC
Guizhou	6	128	106
Guangxi	6	78	42
Sichuan	9	260	24
Yunnan	6	72	77 (including 5 county TLRCs)
Total	27	538	249

Source: Yanqing and Davison (2011); China–UK Southwest Basic Education Project: End-of-project review; Quantitative Survey Report, SBEP NPMO.

4.2 All Teachers Received Training through County TSS

Most of SBEP teacher training courses were conducted at county and township TLRCs. Therefore teacher training and other CPD activities had been made accessible to teachers in the very remote schools who were normally neglected before because of the geographic isolation and limited logistic resources.

The training provided was substantial and by the end of 2010, the targets set at the beginning of the project were either over or basically achieved as shown in Table 3.2.

4.3 Capacity Was Developed

The SBEP is a project with a clear emphasis on capacity building. It means to strengthen both individual and institutional capacity. Capacity at the individual level refers to the will and ability of an individual to set objectives and to achieve them using one's own knowledge and skills (Matachi, 2006). With the establishment of the TLRCs and the implementation of county TSS, the provincial trainers, county trainers and the TLRCs staff had received a series of training courses on a variety of topics. Their knowledge about teacher education, adult learning and CPD got updated, their skills to plan teacher training programme, develop CPD activities and deliver actual teacher training were strengthened and

Table 3.2
Details of teacher training[a]

Province	Teachers to Be Trained	Teachers Receiving Participatory Teaching and Percentage	Teachers Receiving Education Equity and Percentage	Teachers Receiving Participatory Language and Mathematics Teaching and Percentage	Teachers Receiving Local Resources Development and Utilisation	Teachers Receiving Multi-Grade Teaching	Teachers Receiving Teaching Strategy in a Bilingual Environment
Guangxi	16,450	15,096 92%	15,096 92%	6,163 37%	48	769	295
Sichuan	5,571	5,028 90%	5,028 90%	5,028 90%	70	0	0
Yunnan	13,933	18,967 136%	12,485 90%	24,443 175%	474	40	0
Guizhou	18,311	22,190 125%	22,190 125%	16,399 90%	17,194	562	1,016
Total	54,265	61,971 114%	55,489 102%	52,033 96%	17,786	1,371	1,511

Source: Yanqing and Davison (2011); China–UK Southwest Basic Education Project: End-of-Project Review; Quantitative Survey Report, SBEP NPMO.

[a] The table does not include data on training of county and township trainers.

reinforced. Moreover, their attitude toward teachers and teaching in disadvantaged contexts had fundamentally changed and their awareness about professional development had been raised and renewed.

These individuals not only created a backbone team in each project county in teacher training and teaching research, but also guaranteed the quality of the future training. The words from the director of continuous education office in Zhenxiong CEB proved this point as he reported:

> A professional county trainer team has been set up and strengthened since the implementation of the SBEP. Each of our 10 project townships has 3 to 4 county trainers who provide support to the schools there. They serve as seeds of student-centered teaching approach and will continue to play a supportive role to further improve our education quality even after SBEP. (SBEP NPMO, 2011a)

Capacity at the institution level refers to anything that will influence an organisation's performance and includes human resource, planning, process management, communication and inner-institutional linkage, organisational culture and leadership. (Matachi, 2006) In the case of the SBEP, teacher education institutes at provincial level and county level, such as Teacher Training School, Teachers College and TRO of CBE were assigned to be responsible for Output 2 activities. The capacity of these institutes had been improved in terms of work planning, process management, mobilising human and physical resources, communication, inter-institutional linkage and organisational culture. They became more capable and confident to conduct needs analysis, design and manage needs-based teacher CPD programmes, assess the impact and make proposals for new initiatives. Improvement of institutional capacity was believed to assure the sustainable development of the project experiences.

4.4 Continuous Support Was Provided to Teachers

'There is strong evidence that an effective TSS is in place and integrated into the daily practice of the county Teacher Training School and township TLRCs thereby making it sustainable for the future' (Drinan and Jing, 2010). An example of this was Huimin township centre school, which as one of the 20 TLRCs of Langcang County in Yunnan Province. It sent their key teachers to five village schools and one teaching point in its area every semester to conduct demo lessons or classroom observation and school-based training. This was timetabled at the start of each new term and shared with the neighbour schools so that both sides were aware of the coming school-based activities. Huimin Centre School also had an 'open week' where they invited the neighbour schools to come and observe and discuss lessons. It was emphasised that they combined their routine jobs with the TSS, that is, it was integrated and systematised.

At county level each TLRC was asked to send their TSS plans to county support team which was normally under the management of TRO in CEB or county Teacher Training School. County trainers put timetables together and were grouped to implement the planned activities in different townships. This was not seen as extra work but as part of their TSS system.

This pattern was adopted in most township TLRCs in SBEP. Township TLRC grouped its key teachers to support the teachers in the remote area regularly. Teachers in the very remote area got access to training opportunities and better resources without leaving their workplace.

4.5 More Resources Were Available to and Used by Teachers

A certain amount of teaching and learning materials had been made available to all teaching points and village primary schools and a special training module on how to use and develop local teaching resources had been developed and delivered to TLRCs. Teachers' awareness of using local resources in the classroom was raised and they were more capable to use teaching and learning materials effectively. The End-of-Project (EOP) quantitative review found that 'the use of both standard and self made materials in primary schools at both the MTR and EOP review is substantially higher than at the Baseline which made strongly support the learning of the children' (Yanqing and Davison, 2011).

4.6 Positive Changes in Teaching and Learning

The training delivered by the project had been very well received by the teachers and had facilitated effective implementation of the new curriculum. The follow-up support provided to teachers after the training gave teachers the chance to reflect and internalise what they learnt in the training courses, to practice new methods or techniques in their classroom, to share their experience with colleagues and to correct misunderstanding or clarify confusion with their mentors. A more student-centred teaching approach had been introduced to and developed in the classrooms in the disadvantaged schools. Classroom observations found that

> both teaching and learning is improving; students are more active as are teachers; teachers are growing in confidence as are students; the teaching/learning process is more interactive and teachers are able to elicit from students and encourage them to be more creative, questioning and be able to problem solve. (Drinan and Jing, 2010)

The following findings of SBEP EOP quantitative survey proved again the positive changes in teaching and learning:

- Teacher training through the SBEP County TSS was found very helpful or helpful by the vast majority (more than 80 per cent of primary teachers found it very useful, nearly 70 per cent of Junior Middle School (JMS) teachers found it useful) according to the EOP survey.
- Decline in 'whole class teaching' went from nearly 90 per cent to a level of 68 per cent (at primary level) and to 72.2 per cent (JMS level) according to the MTR and continued to decrease to below two-thirds by the EOP (64.4 per cent and 65.0 per cent at primary and JMS level respectively).
- Substantial increase by teachers in the use of open questions and open dialogue since the baseline study.
- Students spend much more time in groups in comparison with the baseline.
- Teaching and learning in classrooms has become more active, the percentage of students who had participated in two or more activities in the two weeks prior to the EOP survey surpassed 45 per cent.

Section 5: Lessons Learnt

5.1 Matching Government Policies Is a Key to the Success of TSS

'One of the most important best practices to come from the successful implementation of the project design is that of choosing to support government programmes and policies in the expansion of quality basic education in poor and disadvantaged counties' (Beemer and Halsey, 2011). The design factors of participatory teaching and a teacher support system matched those of the evolving MoE's policies and practices and SBEP gave the ministry opportunities to examine well managed and carefully monitored pilot activities in four provinces.

The County TSS initiated through Output 2 of the SBEP was aligned with the policies issued by the MoE and Provincial Department of Education which require the establishment of an integrated entity at county level to better serve local teachers' CPD and eventually improve the learning outcomes. It ensured the legitimacy and status of the TSS in project counties and promised the sustainability of it.

In those counties where the TSS was set up, equipped and functioned successfully, they had converted the project TSS framework into a series of detailed documents to outline the roles and responsibilities of the different parties involved in the TSS. It also meant resource and personnel allocation and management were considered and arranged so as to ensure the success of the TSS operation. In the case of SBEP, all teacher training courses delivered through the TSS got accreditation from the local education management system and credited into teacher's continuous education programme. This contributed to teachers' motivation and active participation in the TLRC-based training or school-based professional development initiatives.

5.2 A Shared Understanding and Adequate Support

The TSS is not only about teaching, learning and training, but also involves assessment of teachers, student achievements and school evaluation. In SBEP County TSS, head teachers, inspectors and CEB officials played very important roles in it.

Based on the needs assessment, a series of training was developed and delivered to head teachers, inspectors and CEB officials in SBEP in order to improve accountability and increase their capacity to practice instructional leadership to teachers. In counties where their support system ran smoothly, the receptiveness and participation in teacher support activities of CEB officials and head teachers was of capital importance to the success of the TSS in improving education quality.

Only with the strong support from local education administration, could the TSS activities and locally-generated innovations got sanctioned and supported through financing and resourcing. Successful TSS in the SBEP showed that the more informed the CEB leaders and inspectors were about the project's aspirations and activities of the TSS, the better it was for continuing support.

5.3 Needs-based TSS Initiatives

It is known that the teachers' CPD leads to good results when it is needs-based, actively involving all teachers and focusing on learning outcomes. In addition to the baseline investigation, a survey focusing on teachers' needs was conducted in project counties. Based on these findings, realistic objectives were identified in the logical framework of SBEP and its TSS framework. It brought the teachers, administrators, teacher supporters together to focus on common objectives and work collectively toward the goals. It also gave the individual teachers a sense of direction and built up the ownership for their development personally and professionally.

The activities carried out through the TSS and the support provided to teachers was accepted well. The training content and modules provided through the SBEP showed a deep understanding of the teachers' working context. Therefore teachers were keen to learn and explore knowledge, skills and techniques to tackle barriers hampering their children's learning.

The new national curriculum reform in China since 2001 encourages teachers to use child-centred approaches in the classroom rather the traditional 'chalk and talk' method while most teacher training was delivered in a trainer-centred way. Therefore teachers had a difficult time accepting the new participatory, constructivist methods. The training sessions, workshops and in-class support activities in the SBEP TSS were planned and conducted using a participatory approach which provided a demonstration of learner-centred methods and opportunities for teachers to practice these methods, share their experiences and provide local solutions. Teachers felt respected and valued by participating in discussions and sharing ideas and gradually incorporated the pedagogical reforms and curricular aspects into their teaching.

5.4 Ensure Adequate Conditions for County Trainers

The function of the township TLRCs relies heavily on external supporters from county town and key teachers in township centre schools. Several reports from the SBEP counties suggested that an insufficient number of support staff had hampered programme effectiveness and progress. In the context of SBEP, most county trainers were often senior teachers on secondment, who were never appointed on a permanent basis. Their workload increased a lot when they served both as a teacher in their own school and a supporter for one of the township TLRCs. TLRCs staff encountered the similar challenge, working as normal teacher or staff in the township centre school and making time for TLRC's activities such as in class observation and feedback in a very remote village school or teaching point. In those project counties where the TSS functioned well, adequate conditions were ensured for county trainers to play their role:

- First, adequate time to perform duty was allocated for teacher supporters.
- Second, cost of transportation, food and accommodation during the remote school visit was reimbursed to teacher supporters. If the financial situation allowed, compensation or finance incentives were offered.
- Third, the work and performance of teacher supporters were recorded and assessed for their future professional advancement.

5.5 Reliable Funding

Support systems for rural teachers require reliable funding to carry out even the most basic activities. In the case of the SBEP, the TSS in project counties relied on grants during the project life. It was expected that the county CEB could take over the responsibility of running the TSS by arranging government allocation for it. However, due to the lack of financial resources available to the CEB for funding TSS, TLRCs at both county and township levels found it hard to function satisfactorily.

The shortage of funds for TSS initiatives led to the following consequences: First, the TLRCs at county and township levels could only manage to function to a certain degree. School-based training and classroom observation and feedback system were embedded into school daily routine while other initiatives like the mentoring system and classroom action research which needed sufficient staff and financial resources were not able to be carried out. Second, while classroom follow-up of teacher trainees maybe put into an action plan, it was often too big a task, requiring the county trainers to visit too many classrooms that were far apart. Therefore, because of distance and accessibility, the most remote and disadvantaged schools and teachers were left unreached and neglected.

5.6 Quality Assurance through Monitoring and Evaluation

It is important for national and provincial technical support teams to monitor the progress of the TSS in the project counties in order to identify strength and weakness in the implementation of TSS initiatives and more importantly to provide relevant support to county support teams. The SBEP had project evaluation teams focusing on both quantitative and qualitative issues, which produced reports annually with suggestions for action plans for the next year.

The SBEP concentrated on building capacity locally in the hope of sustaining the project and its impact. This meant training key personnel involved in the TSS such as county trainers, head teachers, inspectors and CEB officials, as well as providing continuous technical assistance to county and township TLRCs.

However, it took time and needed the long-term commitment of various actors involved in the TSS to help teachers adopt the new curriculum and more student-centred methodologies confidently and effectively. The TLRCs set up in the poorest townships functioned well when they received intensive support from county teams and when they were regularly monitored and assisted by the provincial team. Teachers and their local trainers got motivated and actively participated in the school or TLRC-based activities. When funding came to an end, technical support from province level and in-class support from the county trainers reduced remarkably. Some of the TLRCs and teachers there were not ready for self-reliance financially and technically. All of these factors lead to the lack of motivation and eventually cessation of activities.

Section 6: Sustainability of the Initiative

With the success of access to education, the government began to take measures to reach a balanced development between urban and rural education. Teachers have been recognised as the most critical factor to ensure a high quality of rural education. The State Council of China issued the 'National Medium and Long-term Educational Reform and Development Programme (2010–2020)' in July 2010. It calls for the promotion of the professionalism of teachers and the improvement of the teacher training system. Particularly, it requires putting teachers in rural areas as the priority of this effort. (State Council of China, 2010) The MoE in its document of 'Guidelines on Enhancing the Training of Primary and Secondary Teachers' issued in 2011, proposed to promote the capacity building of teacher training institutes and to proceed with the reform at county and district teachers training institutions which encourages the integration and unity of the county teacher training school with other institutes providing relevant service in teachers' development.

It's no doubt that these policies on teachers' continuing education and teachers' support systems provide a high level of political support to the continuation of rural teacher support system. It is believed that the successful practice of County TSS in the SBEP will have sustained development based on the evidences as follows.

6.1 Individuals and Institutions Became More Capable

Evidence showed the capacity and confidence level of the institutions and individuals supporting teachers increased dramatically which laid a strong foundation for them to sustain the successful practices and initiate new programmes. For example, in Sichuan province, the general coordinator of the SBEP and the coordinator of Output 2 were appointed as the chief consultants of the National Teacher Training Programme[6] of Sichuan. In Guizhou Province, the Guizhou Teacher Training School, which was

---

[6] National Teacher Training Programme is an important measure taken by Chinese government to improve the overall quality of teachers, especially those from rural primary and secondary schools. It started from 2010 and includes two major projects: Project of Exemplary Teacher Training and Project of Rural Key Teacher Training in central and western China

the major institute which implemented the SBEP Output 2 initiatives, won the bidding of a provincial government supported project entitled 'The Quality-Upgrading Project for Rural School Teachers' in 2008. Its experience of needs-based teacher training with a focus on the most disadvantaged group and providing follow-up support ensured the success of the project.

6.2 SBEP Teacher Training Modules Have Been Used in Government INSET

The training modules developed by the SBEP and the learner-centred methodology were very well received because of the positive impact on teaching and learning. The content of the modules and the participatory approach of conducting training sessions have been fully incorporated into the implementation of the National Teacher Training Programme of Guangxi and Guizhou and Sichuan. The Quality-Upgrading Project for Rural School Teachers in Guizhou adopted SBEP training modules and its ways of organising and managing teacher training, which disseminated the SBEP experiences to rural teachers in non-project counties of that region.

6.3 Pre-service Teacher Education Influenced by SBEP Experiences

The experiences of teacher training and support delivery have been disseminated into the pre-service teacher education programme. In 2009, the SBEP supported the action research sponsored by Southwest University. This meant the 14 Normal Universities and Teachers Colleges in the four project provinces aimed to apply the project experience to the pre-service teacher education (SBEP NPMO, 2011b). A series of textbooks for pre-service teacher education programme have been developed by adapting the SBEP teacher training modules and adopting the learner-centred methodology. Four books named Pedagogy; Modern Educational Technology; Instruction of Chinese Language at Primary School and Instruction of Mathematic in Primary School have been published and are used in the pre-service teacher training programmes in nine normal universities or teachers colleges in the Southwest China area. In Guangxi Teachers College, a course named 'Participatory Instruction' was developed based on modules from the SBEP and has been offered to their student teachers since 2010. It was marked as one of the provincial-level excellent courses in Guangxi Autonomous Region.

Summary

In the SBEP, the teacher support system through county and township TLRCs has been used as a strategy to share resources and best teaching practices among teachers in remote areas; improve access to a wide range of professional development activities; foster cooperation between in-service teacher training providers and schools; improve the management of education. The success of it is not to create a new system but to work within the government system, the TSS in project counties corresponded with the local education administrative system, which avoided confusion or conflict in responsibility and authority over schools. The interventions implemented through the TSS were realistic since they supported and extended the development of the government's own initiatives on poverty reduction through enhancement of education opportunities. This increased the chance to sustain and promote the project initiatives. Another key element for success is the considerable commitment from local education authority, school leaders and teachers. In the context of China, it becomes a crucial factor to function the support system, especially after the end of the project. With financial support assured by the rising national and provincial education budgets, the professed political will to continue the reforms and the human capital in place, it is believed that the best practice of SBEP TSS will be expanded and sustained.

As Villegas-Reimers (2003) pointed out, 'continued teachers' professional development must be systematically planned, supported, funded and researched to guarantee the effectiveness of this process'. Schools, teacher-preparation institutions, local education authorities and other related institutions must work collaboratively to ensure a logical and consistent sequence of experiences can be followed. In the Chinese context, what needs further study and reflection, so as to develop an effective support system for rural teachers' CPD, is to explore approaches to merge a variety of county teacher training institutions into an integrated entity providing continuing support to teachers in remote areas; the capacity building of county trainers or teacher educators; and the quality assurance of CPD activities through local teacher support system.

Annexure

The framework of SBEP county teacher support system

Aims/goals

- To support the professional development of teachers in remote and rural areas
- To improve their teaching skills
- To expand their professional knowledge
- To improve students' learning and enjoyment in the classroom for the most disadvantaged girls and boys
- To contribute to the development of PRESET and INSET in rural areas
- To support the professional development of county and provincial trainers
- To support teachers and trainers in managing change improve ways of working
- To improve links and relationships between teacher education institutes
- To improve links with the parents and the wider community

Overall shared objectives

- Teaching and learning outcomes will be improved
- Teachers' capacity will be strengthened
- Teacher development support systems will be developed at school base
- Trainers' capacity will be strengthened
- Trainer support system will be developed at county level

(Annexure Continued)

(Annexure Continued)

Activities	Who Will Be Responsible?	How Much Time? How Long? How Often Meet/Do?	Output
Developmental observation and constructive feedback systems at county teacher training level	Provincial Output 2 teams and county Output 2 teams	Provincial trainers observe county trainers at least 3 times a project year	Observation and feedback systems developed so that county trainers can improve and develop together through using a system that is 'safe' and supportive
		County trainers do peer observation twice a project year using the forms and ongoing informally	Observation and feedback system developed for developmental purposes
			County Trainer Observation and Feedback Manuals developed at provincial level as part of the provincial support system to county trainers
			Completed observation forms for county trainers (evidence of how trainers are developing)
Developmental observation and constructive feedback systems at school base level	County Output 2 teams	County trainers to observe teachers at school base at least twice per project year	Observation and feedback systems developed so that peers at school base can improve and develop together through using a system that is 'safe' and supportive
	Key teachers and support from head teachers	Teachers to do peer observation at least once a year formally and ongoing informally	Observation and feedback system developed for developmental purposes.

Activity	Who	Timing	Outputs/Indicators
Provincial/county trainer training to ensure: Quality training skills to support school base INSET; Give basic ICT skills to ensure data collected and lessons/sessions/materials developed	NST and provincial trainers	Ongoing when system set up—integrate TOT as part of the INSET for trainers	County trainer support system for observation and feedback to remote and rural schools; Teacher observation and feedback manuals developed as part of the county support system for teachers; Completed observation forms for teachers (evidence of how teachers are developing); Trainer training materials; CPD handbook to include unit on ICT (basic skills for data collection, lesson and session planning, materials development)
INSET at school base level Run by key teachers	Head teachers at school level	Short term: Start to pilot INSET in one township per province	INSET plan which is integrated into the SDP; INSET key teachers identified to run short training sessions at school base
Run by county trainers	County trainers at county level	Long term: INSET programme to be established linking provincial, county and school levels	

(Annexure Continued)

(Annexure Continued)

Activities	Who Will Be Responsible?	How Much Time? How Long? How Often Meet/Do?	Output
Run by provincial trainers	Provincial trainers at provincial level		INSET schools identified to be used as 'centres' for INSET provided by county or provincial trainers
			INSET modules (SBEP modules not covered by the 15 days TT) delivered at school base by county trainers
			New INSET topics identified by provincial or county trainers for INSET at school base (this could include classroom research topics)
			INSET programme to be established linking provincial, county and school levels
Pilot systems	Head teachers, key teachers and identified members of the community	Ongoing when county TLRC and township TLRC set up—integrate these activities as part of the TSS	Members of the community identified to train as possible classroom language 'buddies' to support bilingual teaching strategies
'Buddy' systems using the community			
Classroom action research	Provincial and county trainers and classroom teachers		Provincial and county trainers to work with classroom teachers on classroom research topics
Mentor schemes using school HR	teachers		Teachers/school personnel identified as mentors for less experienced teachers 'Mentors' identified for students who have learning difficulties

Activity	Who	Notes	Outcome
Exchange programmes for teachers to have more exposure to wider range of experiences	Head teachers, key teachers and CEB		Links between different schools/institutions strengthened through exchange visits
Pairing pupils/schools	Head teachers and CEB		Strengthened links with communities specifically with parents
Parent training	Communities inc parents		
Other: Establishing support systems through establishing:	Head teachers, key teachers, classroom teachers	These activities would be ongoing	Professional development
Journal keeping for PD		Possibly pilot these as above	Journals (which could provide data to inform school policies on teacher development e.g., the type of further support for teachers)
Teacher SIG			Teacher forums (to discuss professional issues)
Teacher magazine			Teacher magazine published
Where feasible teacher networks			Teacher networks established through ICT

Abbreviations

CEB	County Education Bureau
CPD	Continuing Professional Development
HR	Human Resources
ICT	Information and Communication Technology
INSET	In-service training
NST	National Support Team
PD	Professional Development
SDP	School Development Plan
SIG	Special Interest Group

References

Beemer, Jr., and Halsey, L. (2011). China-UK Southwest Basic Education Project Completion Report, Independent Consultant's Report, DFID.

Department for International Development (DFID). (2006). Project Memorandum: Support to Government of China for Southwest Basic Education Project (2006–2011).

Drinan, Helen, and Liu, Jing. (2008). SBEP Document 107: Report on the Teacher Support Systems at County Level, SBEP NPMO, Beijing.

———. (2010). SBEP Document No.163: Report on the Field Visits to Duan County, Guangxi Province and Lan Cang County, Yunnan Province to Observe the Impact of the SBEP OP2 TSS, SBEP NPMO, Beijing.

Matachi, Atsushi. (2006). *Capacity Building Framework, UNESCO–IICBA*. Addis Ababa, Ethiopia: United Nations Economic Commission for Africa.

Ministry of Education, China (MoE). (1999). Regulation on the Continuing Education of Primary and Secondary School Teachers. MoE Order (1997) No.7, September 1999, Beijing.

———. (2002). Guidelines on Capacity Building of County Level Teacher Training Schools. MoE (TE) Circular No. (2002) 3, Beijing.

———. (2005). National Report on Education for All in China, with Focus on Education for Rural People. The 5th high level group meeting on EFA, Beijing.

———. (2009). *Educational Statistics Yearbook of China*. Beijing, People's Education Press.

———. (2011). Guidelines on Strengthening the Training for Primary and Secondary Teachers. MoE (TE) Circular No. (2011) 1, Beijing.

SBEP National Project Management Office (NPMO). (2007). China–UK Southwest Basic Education Project: A Survey Report on Teacher Training Needs, SBEP National Project Management Office, Beijing.

———. (2008). The Logic Framework of China–UK Southwest Basic Education Project, SBEP NPMO, Beijing.

———. (2010). A Handbook for Teacher Support System in Rural Areas, Beijing.

———. (2011a). China–UK Southwest Basic Education Project: End-of-Project Review, Qualitative Survey Report, SBEP NPMO, Beijing.

———. (2011b). Equitable and Quality Education: China–UK Southwest Basic Education Project (SBEP) End-of-Project Report, Beijing.

State Council of China. (2010). National Outline of Medium and Long-term Education Reform and Development (2010–2020), Beijing.

Villegas-Reimers, E. (2003). Teacher Professional Development: An International Review of the Literature. Paris: UNESCO–IIEP.

Yanqing, Ding, and Davison, A.J. (2011). China–UK Southwest Basic Education Project: End-of-Project Review, Quantitative Survey Report, SBEP National Project Management Office, Beijing.

Zheng, Xinrong, and Huang, Li. (2007). County Teacher Training School: A New Orientation of its Function (in Chinese), People's Education, Beijing.

4

School Cluster System as Support Mechanism for Teachers: A Case Study from Cambodia

F. Helen Drinan

Contents

List of Abbreviations

Introduction

Section 1: The Cambodian Ministry of Education, Youth and Sport (MoEYS): Policy in Relationship to Teacher Education and CPD

Section 2: Understanding the Context: A Brief Background to the History and Politics of Cambodia

Section 3: A Background to School Cluster Systems in Cambodia
3.1   Piloting of the System: 1993–1994
3.1.1   Scaling Up: 1995–1997
3.1.2   Post 1998
3.2   Organisation and Functions of School Clusters in Cambodia
3.2.1   Organisation

3.2.2   Functions
3.2.3   Teacher Training, Support, Methodology and Content

Section 4: Effectiveness and Outcomes
4.1   School Clusters and Sustainability
4.2   School Clusters and Equity
4.2.1   Focusing on Institutional and Individual Capacity Building rather than Construction
4.2.2   Setting up Working Groups
4.3   School Clusters and Cost Effectiveness
4.4   School Clusters and School Improvement Planning
4.5   School Clusters and Decentralisation
4.5.1   Heightened Local Management of Resources
4.5.2   Local Decision-making and Empowerment
4.5.3   Localised Capacity-building
4.5.4   Streamlined Absorption of Development Aid
4.6   School Clusters and Education Reform Processes

Section 5: Lessons Learnt
5.1   Mismatch of Education Providers' Expectations
5.2   Perceptions around Education
5.3   Shortage of Teachers: Double Shift Systems, Contract Teachers and Ethnic Minority Areas
5.4   Teacher Educators/Trainers

Section 6: The Future of School Clustering in Cambodia

References

List of Abbreviations

ACEID	Asia-Pacific Centre of Educational Innovation for Development
CAPE	The Cambodia Assistance to Primary Education Project
CFS	Child Friendly Schools
CPD	Continuing Professional Development
EFA	Education for All
EQIP	Education Quality Improvement Project
ESP	Education Strategic Plan

ESSP   Education Sector Support Programme
IBEC   Improved Basic Education in Cambodia
INSET   In-service Training
IOs   International Organisations
IPM   Integrated Pest Management
IRC   International Rescue Committee
KAPE   Kampuchean Action for Primary Education
LCSCs   Local Cluster School Committees
MoEYS   Ministry of Education, Youth and Sport
NGOs   Non-government Organisations
PAP   Priority Action Programme
PASEC   Programme on the Analysis of Education Systems
PRESET   Pre-service Training
SIP(s)   School Improvement Plans
TGL   Technical Group Leaders
TTCs   Teacher Training Colleges
UN   United Nations
UNESCO   United Nations Educational, Scientific and Cultural Organisation
UNICEF   United Nations Children's Fund
UNTAC   United Nations Transitional Authority in Cambodia
USAID   United States Aid
VSO   Voluntary Services Overseas

Introduction

This chapter seeks to link with Chapter 1 by integrating the common attributes found to contribute to quality CPD. It does this through looking at a case study from Cambodia. This case study will focus on a specific form of support system for rural teachers, that is, School Clustering. Therefore, the attributes from Chapter 1, such as, decentralisation and devolvement, sustainability and cost effectiveness will be considered in terms of this system.

As the School Cluster system in Cambodia is largely in the primary sector, support systems will be referring to teachers from this sector. However, the chapter provides a description of the overall country's strategy for CPD and the policies that are in the process of being implemented for both primary and secondary sectors.

The chapter is divided into six sections for ease of reading. Section 1 begins by providing a brief description and analysis of the Cambodian education policy in relation to teacher education and development, in particular to CPD. Section 2 looks at the historical and political contexts with which the School Cluster systems in Cambodia are embedded and which have had considerable impact on the development of the system.

Section 3 is the core section in that it considers both the evolution of the School Cluster system in Cambodia; the piloting phase and scaling up and also the organisation and functions of School Clustering in Cambodia; the implications for teacher development and support.

The effectiveness of the School Cluster system and its outcomes are analysed in Section 4. The penultimate section, Section 5, considers the challenges and puts forward caveats for setting up School Cluster systems. Finally, in Section 6 the future of School Clustering in Cambodia is discussed in light of the issues looked at in this chapter.

Section 1: The Cambodian Ministry of Education, Youth and Sport (MoEYS): Policy in Relationship to Teacher Education and CPD

The Cambodian Government, through the MoEYS, has long been committed to the quality of education and this is evident from the background and development of the School Cluster system in Cambodia. In addition the Education Strategic Plans (ESPs) make this clear, for example in the ESP 2006–2010 it is stated that, '[i]mproving the quality and efficiency of education services is one of the main policies … The MoEYS has made efforts to improve education quality by using all forms of capacity development for teachers in learning and teaching methodologies at all education levels' (MoEYS, 2006b).

More recently the ESP framework (2009–2013) states that, '[t]he Royal Government will pay attention to improve the quality of education by, … training teachers and upgrading teaching methodologies', as well, 'the government will continue to train qualified teachers in adequate numbers and effectively implement its teacher deployment policy' (MoEYS, 2010).

However the ESPs also give some insight into the challenges still facing the Cambodian government and specifically the MoEYS. Although there is a strong focus on the quality of education, the government is still grappling with a shortage of qualified teachers and with upgrading or certifying those that are already practising and in the system. For these reasons there is a lack of real attention given to CPD or teacher professional development as a lifelong and ongoing pursuit in the policy and planning rhetoric.

Further analysis of ministry documents reaffirms this and CPD can be seen in terms of what was referred to in Chapter one as the 'deficit model' to teacher professional development, that is a focus on 'plugging in the gaps' in teachers' knowledge through recertification and upgrading. Policy 2 for 'Improving the Quality and Efficiency of Education Services', includes the following in relation to teacher professional development:

- Improve pre-service and in-service teacher development. Increase service remuneration and incentives linked to teacher performance and standards.

A further interrogation of the policy reveals that teacher development, also referred to as 'continuous teacher development (in-service)', is seen in terms of upgrading and certification, for example:

- Upgrading staff competencies in various forms of training for all TTCs, including staff development programmes for teacher trainers to be conducted at the TTC level.
- Upgrading the capacity of primary-school teachers by training them to become basic education teachers so as to meet the projected growing enrolment of lower-secondary pupils in the years to come.
- Providing training on the use of new curricula and curriculum standards and on inclusive education for school teachers of all education levels.

While all the above policies for teacher development are commendable and necessary, three key elements for CPD seem to be missing:

1. Linking teacher professional development from pre-service through in-service and CPD. Therefore it does not appear to be considered as a lifelong learning process.
2. Integrating teacher development plans and policies with the School Cluster systems.
3. Recognising teacher development as not only an institutional capacity building initiative but also as an independent and personal development.

The policies serve to reinforce the idea of a 'deficit' and a 'standards-based' model to CPD in that teacher professional development is referred to more often in terms of pre and in-service rather than CPD. Both pre and in-service are linked to performance and standards rather than to a more reflective, individual and personal approach. The standards-based model also, 'relies heavily on a behaviourist perspective of learning, focusing on the competence of individual teachers and resultant rewards at the expense of collaborative and collegiate learning', according to Kennedy (2005: 241), which would concur with the type of teaching training often associated with upgrading and re-certifying.

Another factor to consider when looking at MoEYS policy towards teachers' professional development and one discussed in Chapter one is the stage of the national education system in Cambodia. Cambodia could be considered to be at, what is referred to by Verspoor and Wu (1990), the second stage, 'The second stage is the mechanical stage, where most teachers have received limited training and education and as a result they complete their work in a mechanical manner, following the textbooks and the national curriculum without giving any personal input' (cited in Villegas-Reimers, 2003: 124). As the chapter analyses the development of School Clustering in Cambodia and how it relates to teacher development many of these 'second stage' factors emerge.

These policies and their underlying concepts are pertinent to the evolution of the School Cluster system in Cambodia. However to understand more deeply how and why the Cambodian MoEYS are at the stage they are, it is necessary to understand the basics of Cambodia's historical and political background. As shall be seen in the next section this background has had a devastating impact on the education system and although progress has been made, many challenges still lie ahead.

Section 2: Understanding the Context: A Brief Background to the History and Politics of Cambodia

While looking at education and teacher support systems in Cambodia it is necessary to understand something of the turbulent past history and politics. The impact of the Khmer Rouge regime under the leadership of the infamous Pol Pot, which controlled the country from 1975–1979, had a devastating effect on the education sector. During this time many of Cambodia's intellectuals and academics were murdered or fled the country in exile. It was said that if you wore glasses or spoke a foreign language you were labelled 'teacher', 'an academic' or 'intellectual' and then executed.[1] More than thirty years on the affect of this brutal regime still lingers in the deep rooted psyche of those that lived through it.

During the 1980s and 1990s successive regimes and governments did not have the stability required to build a solid foundation to the education system. According to Ou Eng (2003), Deputy Director of the Planning Department in MoEYS and project director of EQIP, in the 1980s six-week teacher training courses were provided to train primary school leavers to be teachers. Indeed from the writer's own experience many of the teachers trained from 1995–1998 had only a fundamental level of education because the country was starting from 'Year Zero', an apt term that was used to describe Cambodia's position after the elimination of the Khmer Rouge.

Although the middle of 1990s saw many education reforms it also saw political instability and fragmentation so it was not really until 1998 when elections were held that international aid was fully restored and perhaps a sense of stability began to prevail. However history and politics have left a deep scar and education reform will be a long and slow progress as this World Bank Report on Cambodia from 2002 indicates,

> The education system (is) still ranked among the weakest in the world in 2000, more than 20 years after the end of the worst years of the conflict. The net enrolment rate was 84 percent in primary school, 17 percent in lower secondary school and 8 percent in upper secondary school. By one

---

[1] From personal discussions with teachers, trainers and lecturers in Cambodia during the period 1993–1999.

estimate the repetition and dropout rates were so high that it took 19 student years to produce a primary school graduate. (World Bank, 2002)

So by the end of 1990s and entering into the new millennium, Cambodia's education system was still seen to be having considerable challenges which related to the complex contexts mentioned earlier. Moreover, in a recent UNESCO report on the fragility of states it mentions,

> additionally, a discussion of education in Cambodia must also consider one of the fundamental factors limiting progress in education quality: teaching capacity, both at the individual and systems levels. While limitations in capacity appear to be less direct drivers of fragility, they in fact significantly amplify the effects of educational irrelevance, disparate access, community fragmentation, and the conditions that foster corruption within schools. (UNESCO, 2011: 39)

This would seem to indicate that poor quality of education could lead to further disaffection and frustration within the country.

However, as seen in the analysis of MoEYS educational strategy, there is a strong drive to focus on the quality of education and there have been considerable improvements, specifically in the primary education sector. One of the more successful education reforms is the School Cluster system which is now a nationwide system in Cambodia covering nearly all primary schools. The next sections describe and analyse the successes and challenges of this system.

Section 3: A Background to School Cluster[2] Systems in Cambodia

School Clusters commonly have at least two of the following purposes: economic, pedagogic, administrative and political. They can be briefly summarised as: economic in terms of cost effectiveness through sharing material, physical and human resources; pedagogic in terms of providing

---

[2] School Clusters have originally developed from micro-planning initiatives, treating each locality as an entity in itself but within a national framework (adapted from Bray, 1987). This implies a degree of decentralisation but equally of national standards. Once again this highlights the paradoxes of educational reforms as discussed in Chapter 1, that is, autonomy versus accountability to governments.

in-service training and teacher professional development support; administrative in terms of being responsible for educational management functions, specifically financial; and political as they can serve to increase community participation in decision-making, raise awareness of and reduce social, cultural, gender and regional inequities.

In Cambodia all four purposes come into play. The composition of School Clusters can be all primary, all secondary or a mix of both. In Cambodia the composition is largely in the primary sector. In addition Cluster School systems have shown to be effective in rural areas where there are small schools, with teachers having limited education and training and where resources are few, so well suited to the Cambodian context.

The concept of cluster schooling in Cambodia pre-dates 1998 and some believe evolved from Buddhist teachings. The roots of the Cluster School system can be found in the MoEYS plan, 'Perspectives for Quality Improvement in Teacher Education', (1990), which noted that such a system had, 'a potential strategy for development'.

Thus School Clustering has been supported by the MoEYS since 1990 in Cambodia. As Geeves (1999) writes in his review of cluster school development and recommendations for strengthening them in Cambodia,

> Clustering was originally undertaken as a strategy to encourage schools to identify local solutions for local problems and to enable strong schools to assist weaker schools in their vicinity through resource sharing. It was also a way through which the Ministry could provide resources to local primary schools from a severely stressed national budget. (Geeves, 1999: 5)

Conceptually the system is meant to be a 'bottom up' and 'grass roots' approach to school support and development. The phrase, 'local solutions to local problems', as seen in chapter one, was a one of the key characteristics for successful and effective CPD. However integrating concept and practice can often be difficult as is seen in the evolution of School Clustering in Cambodia.

3.1 Piloting of the System: 1993–1994

The year 1993 saw both political and educational changes. This was the period of UNTAC, the UN peace keeping force in Cambodia. It was also when UNICEF became majorly involved in supporting the MoEYS in establishing Cluster Systems in target areas which represented rural,

F. Helen Drinan   149

urban, frontier and minority populations. Under UNICEF, pilot school cluster programmes were implemented through the 'NGOs Consortium' and International Rescue Committee (IRC) working with Provincial Offices of Education in four provinces representing the four target areas: rural, urban, frontier and minority.

In 1993 the aim of the cluster school was, 'to redress the imbalance between schools by bringing them into an administrative group or cluster, mixing strong schools and disadvantaged schools in such a way that the latter benefit from the advantage of the former' (MoEYS, 1995: 1). Indeed the system appeared to be doing well in the pilot provinces under the support of International Organisations (IOs) and NGOs so a scaling up process began.

3.1.1 Scaling Up: 1995–1997

During this time big reforms in education were seen in Cambodia including new national curricula and textbooks for primary and secondary levels. The goal of the first Socio-economic Plan 1996–2000 was the 'revitalisation of (the) quality and effectiveness', of the primary and lower secondary education, (Royal Cambodian Government, 1996: Chap. 15). Amongst the quality improvement measures was the cluster schools enhancement:

> Strategies will include support for expansion of school clusters, with one being a core school and resource centre, wherever this model is feasible and cost effective. A variety of options will be studied and tested to reach those schools and pupils who live in more remote and minority areas. (Royal Cambodian Government, 1996)

At this stage there appears to be a recognition that 'one size does not fit all' and that variations of the cluster system model would have to be tried if all children were to be reached, specifically those in more remote areas which also tend to be the areas where minority groups live.

By 1995 the Cluster School system became a national approach and Provincial Offices of Education were required to 'cluster' all the primary schools in their province. They had to cluster according to a set of criteria and there were four main aims which were:

- To improve access, quality and administration of primary education
- To allow strong schools to assist weak schools through resource sharing

- To allow teacher meetings or exchanges
- To enhance the community contribution to the local school

Originally, the objectives of the School Clusters were both economic and pedagogic, the former because all resources (people, materials and facilities) in theory could be shared and the latter was meant to improve the quality of teaching and learning through teacher development, curriculum development and competition between pupils. Teacher development was seen as sharing ideas and tackling problems. MoEYS/UNICEF saw the teacher meetings at the core school as a type of in-service training where more experienced teachers helped less experienced and where enthusiastic teachers could, 'inject new life into the tired ones' (Royal Cambodian Government, 1996: 5).

Running parallel to the MoEYS/UNICEF clusters during this time was the USAID funded CAPE project. Although it was short lived and ceased to exist after July 1997, it is of significance because many of the managerial and organisational systems from the Kompong Cham Province Cluster were used as models for others. This included bringing capacity building and teacher training to the forefront of the School Cluster system. The cluster functions as described in CAPE documents were:

- Technical capacity building which included all activities in a cluster which improves the ability of staff to do their work, for example, teacher training.
- Accountability which meant holding staff in a cluster accountable for their performance, for example, if a school has a high rate of repetition, the director must be able to explain why this is the case.
- Resource sharing which meant sharing scarce educational resources, both human and materials, throughout the cluster, for example, sharing library books among all children in a cluster. (adapted from Bredenberg, 1997: 1)

By the beginning of 1997 there were 145 School Clusters in Cambodia supported by five organisations (CAPE [USAID], UNICEF-Sida, Redd Barna, CARERE and TOPS) (Geeves, 1999: 5). This was a high point for School Clustering and they represented 'model practice' which other clusters were meant to follow, 'as best they could until they too became

F. Helen Drinan   151

"supported" or until the program became sustainable and general within the national education system' (Geeves, 1999: 5).

However factional fighting during this period in Cambodia and culminating in July 1997 with the overthrow of the coalition government which had been brokered by UNTAC, saw the suspension and end of many education programmes. This saw the demise of the major Cluster School project, CAPE, funded by USAID. By the end of this period UNICEF became the most prominent and influential international agency supporting Cluster School education in Cambodia.

3.1.2 Post 1998

In the middle of 1998 a comprehensive external evaluation of this programme was made and revealed major problems. As Geeves (1999: 19) reports, the evaluation found that after five years of activity the achievements in UNICEF clusters were very narrowly focused, 'on construction and administrative infrastructure' and, 'only limited evidence of achievements outside the construction sector'. Indeed even UNICEF's own midterm review in December 1998 stated the same, 'problems related to quality and effectiveness of the programme (and) proposed solutions ... (were) not very realistic ... Goals have been achieved in few cases ... management style has not yet been decentralized' (UNICEF, 1998: Section 3.5 (UNICEF report) cited in Geeves, 1999: 19–20).

As a result, in the latter half of 1998 UNICEF began,

> To promote decentralization ... planning, budgeting and monitoring activities was shifted from national to provincial and individual School Clusters ... A shift away from construction to technical development, with an emphasis on quality of outcomes was also signalled as was a decision not to extend UNICEF support to more School Clusters. (Geeves, 1999: 21)

Therefore in 2001 and 2002, cluster boundaries were redrawn to create more reasonable entities in terms of distances between schools and to facilitate decentralisation. In doing this, it not only increased the number of clusters nationwide from 757 to 925 (Geeves, 2003) but also significantly changed the focus of the School Clustering with more of an emphasis on capacity building at local level and specifically focussing more on teacher development and support.

To this end new NGOs evolved. Significantly, the Kampuchean Action for Primary Education (KAPE) developed from a dedicated group of staff from the 1997 CAPE project and later, as a KAPE partner, the Improved Basic Education in Cambodia (IBEC) project funded by USAID. This project focuses on remote and rural areas and takes, 'an approach that emphasizes holistic programming, stakeholder-driven development, and improved educational relevance and management' (IBEC Project, 2009).

Through the evolution of the School Cluster system in Cambodia from its early, small beginnings in the 1990s to the national system it is now (by 2007 there were 1,044 School Clusters in Cambodia), there are familiar paradigm shifts emerging which form part of the lesson learning process, for example, the movement from centralisation to decentralisation; from a focus on administration and construction to a focus on capacity building; quality and access to teaching and learning.

On the other hand what also emerges is that the system operates on two-tiers with some schools heavily supported by IOs/NGOs and others that are not. Therefore serious challenges to sustainability are clear and need to be resolved. In the next section on the organisation and functions of the cluster systems these challenges are discussed further.

3.2 Organisation and Functions of School Clusters in Cambodia

3.2.1 Organisation

Internationally there is wide diversity in the organisation of clusters and the Cambodian School Cluster system is no exception. On the surface level the structure of the clusters in Cambodia is made up of the 'core' or 'central' school which often houses the Resource Centre. The Core School is usually located in the geographical centre so that all other schools are meant to be less than 7 km away. Directors and teachers meet at the Core School for professional development once or twice in a month on Thursdays.

Other member schools are called Satellite Schools where teachers usually meet for Thursday meetings or a nearby school on days when they do not travel to the Core School. The number of schools within a cluster varies from five to eight in a neighbourhood or district.

According to Geeves (1999) there are four main types of Cluster Schools in Cambodia: (1) Regular Clusters: where all the schools are within 7 km and travel between them is easy. (2) Populous Clusters:

F. Helen Drinan   153

where schools are close together and very large, usually only in towns. (3) Remote Clusters: where the distance between most of the schools is vast and Cluster meetings cannot be held. (4) Irregular Clusters: where most schools are close together but one or two or three are very distant.

Figure 4.1 shows a typical, surface definition of a School Cluster which focuses primarily on the geographical arrangement of the schools.

Initially the organisation and management of the cluster system in Cambodia was heavily 'top-down' and centralised with a hierarchy of committees. These were: the National Cluster School Committee, Provincial Cluster School Committee and District Cluster School Committee and finally and most innovatively the Local Cluster School Committee (LCSC).

The members of the LCSC are all the Directors of Primary Schools in the Cluster, Technical Group Leaders (TGLs), community representatives,

Figure 4.1
A typical, surface definition of a School Cluster

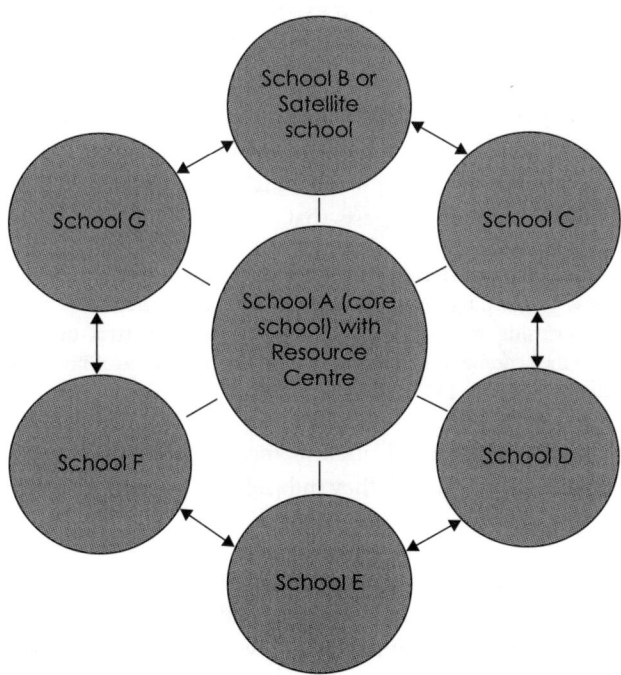

the local Lower Secondary School Director (if there is one in the Cluster) and representatives from the Commune Council. When School Clusters receive support from IO/NGOs, the LCSC is an important body for deciding how to use the funds.

The Cluster Director is one of the School Directors and is responsible for chairing meetings of the Local Cluster School Committee, helping School Directors in their management tasks and helping TGLs organise Thursday technical sessions. The TGLs are chosen from the teachers at each grade level from schools in the Cluster. The TGLs are responsible for carrying out the Thursday technical sessions and assisting teachers at their grade level to improve their teaching.

By the new millennium the School Cluster organisation was realigned according to Bredenberg, 'to give greater focus to internal functions that (did) not entail material resource sharing. Capacity building and accountability (or monitoring) functions should be the focus of this realignment' (Bredenberg, 2002: 23). Bredenberg recognised that, '[w]here LCSCs and teacher supervision networks have been well organized, they offer a tremendous means to expedite interventions of quality that seek to promote innovation' (Bredenberg, 2002). Therefore Bredenberg begins to look at School Cluster organisation at a deeper level.

Bredenberg who has worked for decades on School Cluster systems in Cambodia rightly suggests that the former description of the School Cluster organisation is too simplistic as it fails to focus on the functions of the School Cluster. He suggests that

> [t]hinking of the clustering process in terms of function can provide a practical way of grasping the activities that must be set in motion in clusters ... models focusing on function can be described as 'deep' structure frameworks because they can be quite explicit in guiding the process of implementation. (Bredenberg, 2000: 17)

Therefore, further we will look at the functions within the School Cluster organisation and how they interrelate.

3.2.2 Functions

The four cluster functions described by Bray in 1987 have already been discussed. Broadly, these are, pedagogic, administrative, economic and political. In Cambodia when the LCSCs were initially set up their functions were to: share resources, stronger schools help weaker schools, build capacity, mobilise the communities, respond to local problems with local solutions. Lately these functions have been streamlined to include:

- Resource Sharing
- Capacity Building
- Accountability

These three functions have been referred to as the core functions of the School Clusters because they cover the technical input the clusters can provide. Thus, as Bredenberg puts it, 'the emphasis of the scheme is on the inputs more directly related to improving quality of educational services to the largest number of children possible' (Bredenberg, 2000: 19). These are now considered in terms of how they relate to improving the quality and support of teachers in the School Cluster system.

Resource Sharing: Sharing resources means both human and material resource sharing and has always been one of the key functions of School Clustering. For the purpose of this chapter the most important sharing of resources is the sharing of personnel between member schools specifically for teachers' professional development. In Cambodia this has been most pertinent and has meant that those schools that have lacked strong human resource bases have had access to more experienced personnel. One of the key ways this is done is through:

Cluster-based Teacher Supervision System[3]: Technical support is provided to teachers through this system. It has been developed by using the Thursday 'technical meetings' and through the development of a network of TGLs within the clusters. These TGLs provide teachers with teacher training and supervision systems. These systems are considered to be the most important by teachers as Bredenberg points out, 'it should not be forgotten that teacher training/supervision represented an important area which many cluster school practitioners identified as among the most successful achievements of cluster-based interventions' (Bredenberg, 2002).

---

[3] The Supervision System for teachers can equally be part of the section on Capacity Building and Accountability. Indeed all three functions are clearly seen in this system.

Another important aspect of this system in the cluster context is that it promotes locally based modes of teacher supervision and teacher training. This has been developed through intensive training of the TGLs who are cluster based. Bredenberg describes the TGLs as

> master teachers who plan teacher training activities on Thursdays and do follow-up supervisory visits during the month. This system is intended to increase the overall frequency of teacher supervision and to give it more of a supportive focus in contrast to 'check and control' inspections that sometimes characterise district and province based supervision. Because TGLs are teacher peers, their classroom visits are less likely to be threatening and thus can more easily focus on providing help to fellow teachers. (Bredenberg, 2002)

This teacher supervision system holds teachers accountable for their teaching and performance.

Indeed this system is a good example as shown in Figure 4.2 of how the functions of sharing resources, capacity building and accountability are integrated and synergised. This is discussed further under the functions.

Figure 4.2
Integration of functions

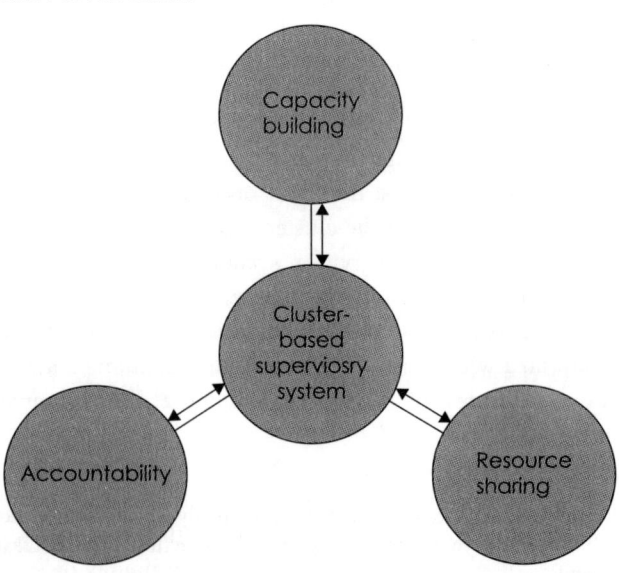

A more traditional way of resource sharing is through:

Using Resource Centres: Within the Cambodian School Clusters and the hub for sharing resources is the Resource Centre.

Initially the Resource Centres were used more for developing and generating material resources and traditional in-service training rather than building capacity or developing school–community relationships. These are relevant activities and Cambodian Resource Centres are still used in such a way: producing teaching and learning materials, borrowing materials, training teachers on new strategies and techniques as well as methods of organising and managing the classroom activities, the gathering venue for the teachers' Thursday sessions.

However, the Resource Centres have become more of a conduit or link between teachers from the different schools; between external experienced trainers/TGLs; between education management staff and between school and community. Therefore a more needs and local-based type of resource sharing is being developed. The Thursday teacher development meetings provide a good forum for assessing these needs for teachers.

In addition the Resource Centres are used as venues for training supervisors and school managers on how to support teachers and students within the clusters both technically and academically. Schools and communities use the centres to organise joint planning activities too.

Other resource sharing mechanisms which have been developed in Cambodian School Clusters are mobile libraries and the Cluster School Library which support study and research for both teachers and students. These have been used effectively by teachers in their personal development and in classroom action research. However from lessons learnt it is imperative that the School Cluster staff understand the purpose of sharing the resources from school to school and how to use them, as in the past some of these activities have been carried out simply because it has been mandated from an authority above. This is why the next function 'capacity building' is so important at all levels.

Capacity Building: In addition to the Cluster-based Supervision System described above under Resource Sharing, there have been several other interventions that have allowed staff in the School Cluster systems to build up their skills and knowledge to be able to do their job. The following relate to teacher professional development and community development.

Teacher Professional Development: In terms of continuing professional development for teachers in Cambodia the 'deficit' model has been applied. Thus the emphasis in terms of capacity building has been to upgrade and recertify teachers. Indeed this is an ongoing process and one that is seen as a necessity. However, teacher professional development in Cambodia is evolving and there are innovative initiatives to further develop and build capacity of teachers. These initiatives are largely undertaken by projects supported by the donor community and NGOs.

One particularly successful project in Cambodia which helped target the needs of the teachers was the World Bank funded EQIP. EQIP managed the clusters' resources and gave the responsibility for writing grant proposals to the schools and communities. It had considerable impact on the School Cluster system and specifically on teacher development. Some of the activities and systems put in place through these proposals for teacher professional development are:

- Training in child-centred methodology (see more under Section 3.2.3)
- Revitalising Thursday training days
- Using experienced trainers from across the sector; Teacher Training Colleges, the Inspectorate and from district level (master trainers)
- Creating a relaxed and happy environment
- Using demo lessons based on students' needs
- Encouraging teachers to understand their pupils holistically
- Training includes materials development and use of materials

So in terms of systems to support teachers it is seen that by providing grants at local cluster school level and allowing local people (school staff, parents and community) to make decisions on what is needed most, teacher professional development needs are regarded as a priority. It would appear that releasing grants and giving schools their own budgets to propose and develop their own activities not only ensures that they meet the needs of the context but also ensures a level of commitment to monitor and evaluate the process too. This would concur with the key concepts for quality CPD discussed in Chapter one.

Mobilising Communities: According to Giordano there are four main facets to the relationship between School Clusters and the community:

'The first concerns community participation in decision-making concerning the School Cluster; the second is the financial or material support given to a School Cluster or resource centre by the community it serves; the third is the role of the School Cluster or resource centre vis-a-vis the community it serves; and the fourth involves parental involvement with their children's education.'

These four facets are not easy to achieve in any context and the Cambodian context is no exception. Thus building the relationship between the School Clusters and communities has had its trials and tribulations. Some of them being, according to Geeves (1999),

> [a] lack of vision for the school-community relationship so that the relationship was limited to issues of construction and nothing else; [t]he need for real tasks to stimulate community involvement and to encourage a mutual responsibility; [o]vercoming pre-conceptions about working with community members; [o]pening up the curriculum process.

However, through time many of these issues have been overcome and there are many examples of successful school-community initiatives which involve capacity development and resource sharing:

- Implementing projects between the old and the young, for example, gathering and telling stories which are also used in the classroom.
- Parenting and nutrition classes with inputs from local NGOs which impacts teaching and learning as children are healthier and parents more aware of the link between good nutrition and learning.
- Involving of students, teachers, farmers and parents in the Integrated Pest Management (IPM) Student Field Schools which also involved the rural development department.
- Authorising decentralisation of school funds and school planning particularly through NGO initiatives has meant that decision-making has become much more devolved and schools and communities have more say in how, where and what funds are spent on so they reflect local needs and concerns.
- Giving communities the responsibility for their own improvements and development gives a sense of ownership and commitment.
- Providing budgets to clusters means they can implement, monitor and evaluate their own plans and activities.

- Using the Resource Centres in the School Clusters for community activities including capacity building and awareness raising.

Accountability: As Bredenberg points out, '[t]he other major benefit that clusters can provide to efforts to improve the quality of education in schools relates to its accountability function' (Bredenberg 2000: 21), and this is clearly seen in terms of teacher professional development and support.

As has been seen under the Resource Sharing and Capacity Building functions, the Teacher Supervision System being used in Cambodian School Clusters can provide valuable feedback on many teacher development and cluster activities, for example, on the

- quality of teaching and learning;
- quality of support to teachers;
- quality of the relationship between school and community;
- use of resources (people, financial, material);
- use of libraries;
- use of systems in place, for example, rotation systems for resources;
- use of records and data.

The effectiveness of this function in an education system will depend on historical and political contexts. However, School Cluster systems, as in Cambodia, can be developed to allow the implementation of activities which are accountable and which complement the other two functions: resource sharing and capacity development.

What is seen from the Cambodian experience of the organisation and functioning of School Clusters is the necessity for flexibility and ability to change. Over the years there has been a shift from a centralised, 'top-down' approach to the organisation and management of the clusters to a more decentralised and localised approach.

The addition of the EQIP in the late nineties highlights how necessary it is to give responsibility and ownership to those who are directly affected by the reforms. It also highlighted the correlation of effective planning and successful School Clustering. Indeed Giordanno equates effective School Clustering to the use of development plans, such as those developed under the EQIP in Cambodia through direct transfer of funds to school level. This, she believes, also enabled school to monitor the impact of their improvement projects, 'In Cambodia, where previously there were no effective mechanisms in place to monitor and evaluate cluster performance, EQIP helped to, "create a culture of evaluation in Cambodia", (World Bank, 2004a: 12 in Giordano, 2008: 125) and built capacity at the district level to do so' (Giordano, 2008: 125).

Finally, it can be seen that if these three functions are cross-referenced with institutional sectors, School-Clustering development can enhance institutional building. This is Bredenberg's point, that the organisation and functions of School Clusters should be analysed more deeply than purely by geographical arrangement. Table 4.1 shows how both organisation and functions intersect to provide a clear framework for indentifying activities that need to be done and can also help evaluate the functions of each institutional sector (adapted from Bredenberg 2000: 20).

Table 4.1
A multi-sectoral classification scheme for cluster functions

Sector / Function	Resource Sharing	Capacity Building	Accountability
Resource centre			
Cluster School Committee			
Teacher Supervision Systems	A	B	C
Parent Boards			
Testing Committees			
Other			
Possible activities			
A	Organise a cluster-based mentoring scheme		
B	Identify and train mentors		
C	Track mentor scheme through observation and mentor/mentee portfolios		

Source: Adapted from Bredenberg (2000: 19).

3.2.3 Teacher Training, Support, Methodology and Content

Current teacher training, methodology and content are driven by Cambodia's policy and commitment to establishing 'Child Friendly Schools' (CFS). Since 2002 and in cooperation with IOs and NGOs, the MoEYS have been pursuing UNICEF's Child Friendly Approach to teaching and learning.

CFS programmes have been introduced into Cambodian clusters and expanded to Lower Secondary schools too. According to Bunlay et al. (2010: 9),

> One MoEYS official described CFS as fitting easily within the cluster school system. He explained that one or more classrooms at the core school would be targeted to become 'child friendly', and then once successfully implemented, the child-friendly model could be expanded to other classrooms at the core school and eventually in the satellite schools within the cluster.

Bunlay et al. (2010) go on to describe:

> The technical approach by the Child Friendly Schools program at the primary level, applied most often in the context of NGO-supported programs, employs the use of a school grant (usually about $4,500 per school), and an activity menu to facilitate objective-based planning that is locally driven, for a 'holistic approach to educational development'.

However, the methods and content of the teacher training in the School Clusters in Cambodia follow the CFS approach to teaching and learning. This means that methodology focuses on child-centred learning and includes:

- Teaching and learning through creative ideas
- Participation and cooperative learning
- Research, analysis and critical thinking
- Problem solving
- Innovation and encouragement of creative and divergent thinking

Accordingly these methodologies apparently focus attention on generating the four Khmer compassions: Metha (empathy), Karuna (loving, kindness), Muktetha (feeling arising from seeing the reduction in suffering of others) and Obeka (equanimity). They are aimed at the holistic development of schools, including inclusive education, child-centred teaching and learning and conducive and gender-responsive learning.

The MoEYS plan for INSET also calls for providing in-service training on the concept and practices of child-friendly schooling to all current teachers as one of the main activities for their 'continuous teacher development'. The MoEYS officials described the technical meetings, held monthly at the cluster level, as the key vehicle for providing this in-service training. Thus MoEYS is placing a high priority on the development of what are known as 'child friendly experimental classrooms'. In the Cambodian case, technical support activities include

- intensive training of teachers;
- refurbishing classrooms to create learning corners;
- group work stations;
- increased access to learning materials.

Teachers are trained in methods that promote

- cooperative learning techniques;
- critical and creative thinking;
- more child-friendly modes of student assessment (e.g., the use of student portfolios).

Specifically, professional developmental activities at the School Cluster level include the following:

- Stand-alone teacher trainings
- On-the-job support
- Periodic refresher trainings (twice a year)
- Embedding active-learning methodology into curriculum and learning materials
- Ongoing support for trained staff at any time throughout the year
- Holding teacher meetings and other group discussions on the success and challenges of implementing these pedagogies
- Annual evaluations of teacher classroom instruction to assess their success and effectiveness of the use of these pedagogies
- Feedback and follow-up with teachers and school officials

Section 4: Effectiveness and Outcomes

4.1 School Clusters and Sustainability

As can be seen the Cambodian School Cluster system is heavily dependent on donor funded projects, NGOs and IOs to the degree that there is a two-tiered system of school clustering nationwide. Even when measures for sustainability have been included in the design of the project, to maintain the level of effectiveness and momentum is very difficult. The World Bank in its completion report for the Cambodian EQIP stated that, 'one of the challenges of the sustainability of the EQIP model is to maintain the necessary injection of new ideas that came with the technical assistance provided by Volunteer Services Overseas and the province-level Lead Technical Advisers' (World Bank, 2004: 11).

There are other issues to the challenges of sustainability in Cambodia too namely that School Clustering was never actually institutionalised. This alone does not necessarily mean that the system will not be sustained but it would certainly help. Another area the writer feels was neglected from the start was capacity building of all staff in School Clusters. It was seen that from the inception of the clusters, the emphasis had been on constructions. This was rectified after 1998 and with the support of donor funded projects and NGOs and IOs with projects focussing more on quality outputs and capacity building. However, in terms of CPD, there still appears to be a lack of overall vision and therefore a lack of sustainability.

However with the functions of School Clustering focussing more on accountability including monitoring and evaluation, it is more likely that issues of sustainability will be addressed and integrated into future initiatives in School Cluster systems. Indeed looking at School Clusters and equity it can be seen how sustainability issues are also being addressed.

4.2 School Clusters and Equity

Equity has always been a key reason for clustering schools in Cambodia, that is, to lessen disparity between schools through the sharing of all resources. There have been challenges for the Cambodian MoEYS in achieving this, not least the fact that there is a two-tiered system of School Clustering with some clusters supported and others not. This is not to imply that the unsupported clusters are less equitable in their approach but it is fair to assume that in terms of resources the former will be more adequately served.

Another challenge presented itself in the early years of School Clustering in Cambodia when there was a focus on construction and buildings especially at the core school which often housed the resource centres and/ or libraries. What transpired was that core schools got the lion's share of facilities, equipment and resources to the detriment of the satellite schools. Indeed as the KAPE reports, 'due to the inoperative nature of the resource sharing systems in a large number of clusters, many of the resources placed in core schools did not benefit satellite schools' (KAPE, 2001: 12).

These dichotomies indicate the challenges to equity, access and quality of education when setting up School Cluster systems and the fact that contexts and needs differ from one area to the next.

Since 1998, however, many initiatives have been implemented which begin to overcome these challenges and to minimise the inequities within and between School Clusters. These remedies include:

4.2.1 Focusing on Institutional and Individual Capacity Building rather than Construction

As has been seen through the evolution of the School Clusters in Cambodia it has been necessary to move away from quantitative to qualitative measures to improve the School Clusters. This has been done by reducing construction and focusing on resource sharing, capacity building and accountability as described in the last section.

4.2.2 Setting up Working Groups

In terms of teacher support the most important working groups set up in the Cluster Systems are the LCSC the TGLs and master teachers. The LCSCs have provided the forum for planning and decision-making at local level which have included heads and teachers. This has ensured that funding has been spent on needs-based, relevant training and support for teachers.

The TGLs as part of the Teacher Supervisory system have provided teachers with experience and support especially in the rural and remote areas. In turn the TGLs have also been trained and supported at district levels. Another cluster body are the cluster-based master teachers who facilitate a wide range of quality improvement inputs such as; testing programmes, teacher training and student support.

The fact that these working groups are made up of people from the institutional framework ensures there is sustained support within the schools.

Devolved Planning and Management through Grants: The direct disbursal of funds at local level has meant that capacity in education management is being built at school, district and provincial levels. It was also seen that MoEYS staff, within three years, according to Geeves (2003), was able to run the grants fund independently from donors and NGOs in an accountable and transparent manner.

As Giordano points out, '[p]roviding grants for education improvement projects has shown to be one of the most effective methods of supporting local initiatives for education improvement though clusters' (Giordano, 2008: 123) but also because what transpired was that the majority of cluster projects funded by EQIP in Cambodia targeted teacher development, 'with teacher development expenditure correlating with improved pupil performance' (Giordano, 2008: 124).

The Development of Manuals to Make the Sharing of Resources More Explicit: Materials development is all too often overlooked in teacher development systems but is core to sustainability and key to building confidence and capacity in educators.

In Cambodia there have been a number of diverse initiatives in the development of manuals and materials to improve the organisation and functions of the School Clusters. These include management manuals for the LCSCs; training manuals for TGLs; resource sharing manuals to ensure that resources are used equitably; checklists and menus for training and activities; newsletters; module design for teacher training and so on.

Income Generation Schemes to Provide Funds to Enable Directors and Teachers to Travel to Core Schools to Share Resources: In some clusters sustainability has been addressed through income generation schemes, for example, credit schemes which are administered by the cluster from a central fund. As Bredenberg (2000: 15) points out, 'these funds are usually enough to assure the continuation of cluster school activities albeit at a lower level of intensity than was true during the period of donor support'.

4.3 School Clusters and Cost Effectiveness

As already has been mentioned one of the reasons for School Clustering is economic, specifically in contexts where financial resources are scarce. School Clustering enables sharing of all resources which is particularly pertinent to poor areas (usually rural and remote) where resources are generally lacking. However, there is relatively little information on how cost effective School Clustering really is and as Mac Neil says in his paper on school and cluster based teacher professional development, '[i]n many cases, the "project effect" has masked government intentions and ability to devote resources to teacher in-service programs as long as outside funding is in place' (MacNeil, 2004).

In other words, and this is very much the case in Cambodia, it is difficult to gauge how cost effective the School Cluster system is because of the two-tier system. As has been seen through initiatives, like the grant system through EQIP, School Clusters are now responsible for their own planning and managing of resources and as was seen most of the grants went on teacher development and subsequently these expenditures on teachers' development, 'correlated with improved pupil performances' (Giordano, 2008: 124). However, whether this is true for whole country is unclear and as noted in Mark Bray's 1999 book on household and community financing in Cambodia, some clusters reduced disparity between schools but it was not found uniformly.

What does appear to be reiterated in evaluations of projects is the cost effectiveness of effective professional development, as the World Bank found in the end of Implementation Report, there is evidence that, 'small amounts of money devoted to teacher training can have large impacts on learning' (World Bank, 2005). So, although the evidence for the cost effectiveness of School Clustering is inconclusive and more information is needed in this area, it would appear that given the experience of EQIP that when School Clusters use grant money on teacher development there is an impact on pupils' learning and the school development as a whole.

The World Bank in its report on EQIP which worked with the School Clusters stated that

[t]eacher development captured as much as 57 per cent (in the second year) of the total spending, and this category was consistently the largest budget item. Teacher development involved hiring trainers to provide classes, providing materials for these training sessions, and providing teachers with cash 'incentives' to attend. (World Bank, 2005)

In addition, it acknowledged that one of the most important inputs to ensure changes in the quality of education is in teacher training,

> money invested in teacher development had the highest payoff in terms of student retention, promotion, and especially in student learning. A one dollar per pupil increase in EQIP money devoted to teacher training generally led to between 0.70 and 1.05 points higher on the EQIP exams. (World Bank, 2005)

4.4 School Clusters and School Improvement Planning

In 1995 the Asia-Pacific Centre of Educational Innovation for Development (UNESCO–ACEID) stated, '[i]deally clusters do not simply serve as channels for orders from the top of the bureaucracy down to the school level, but must have the autonomy to develop self-reliance and their own plans and programmes for quality improvement and local capacity building' (UNESCO–ACEID, 1996).

According to the evaluations conducted as part of donor projects in School Clusters in Cambodia (Bredenberg, 2002; Geeves, 2000; Wheeler, 1998) this seems to have happened to some extent. The cluster school model has been most successful in facilitating school improvement planning. Although there is considerable variation between the plans and different clusters at least now there is a rational relationship between objectives, activities set and the real needs of the cluster.

In the Cambodian School Cluster systems, there has been an attempt to delegate some responsibility for the planning, management and financing of education to the local level through the EQIP grants and LCSCs so that the clusters, 'become a formal unit in the administrative hierarchy between the districts and the schools' (Giordano, 2008: 39). Furthermore Geeves states that '[t]he Ministry now relies on the local School Cluster committee for technical assistance on school planning and management of operational funds' (Geeves, 2003).

In addition the SIPS play an important role in teachers' professional development in the School Clusters as teachers are involved at each stage of the main common features of developing SIPS, which according to Geeves et al. (2005) are:

- Stressing the importance of consultation between the School Director, teachers and community members in developing SIPs (in line with the government's policy of decentralisation) and requiring the signatures of community representatives, along with educational officials, on completed plans.
- Training stakeholders to conduct a process of planning which identified local needs, set related objectives, agree on activities to achieve these objectives and to set indicators and benchmarks which would enable measurement (see next point).
- Stressing the importance of relating activities in the SIP to addressing the major education issues of enrolment, drop out, repetition, promotion and participation by girls which are the targets of the Ministry's Education Strategic Plan (ESP), Education Sector Support Programme (ESSP) and the government's commitment to Education for All (EFA).
- Recognising that the best way to strengthen the relationship between school and community to enable decision making at local level and that this would only be meaningful if real and significant resources were available, real decisions about their use were made locally and stakeholder involvement was genuine (adapted from Geeves et al., 2005: 3).

4.5 School Clusters and Decentralisation

It has been seen that School Cluster systems can provide a vehicle to promote decentralisation: an opportunity to manage both the administrative and the technical systems at local level through local committees. Indeed one of the primary rationales in starting the cluster school initiative was to promote decentralisation. In terms of CPD decentralisation is necessary if teachers in rural and remote areas are going to be reached and supported effectively.

During the early period of cluster school development, efforts to promote decentralisation were greatly hampered by what Geeves (1999) refers to as, 'the anomaly of a unidimensional framework,' that was implemented directly from the MoEYS. During this period not only was the curriculum highly centralised but also there was intense rivalry between two large bi-lateral projects[4] with very differing ideologies on how education systems should run. Similarly there have been different approaches to disbursing grants at local levels,[5] whilst both influencing the decentralisation process, both are working through different systems.

However, things have improved and the record of School Clusters to promote decentralisation, particularly in the period after 1998, appears to be increasingly positive. A version of cluster school guidelines issued by MoEYS in 2002 have helped to ensure a much more flexible approach to cluster school development than past versions. There are numerous provisions to ensure that cluster design can be fitted to local circumstances such as recognition of possible variations in the structure of the LCSC depending on the locality in which a cluster is located (e.g., urban, remote, etc.) (Bredenberg, 2002: 13). According to Bredenberg in his analysis of the processes and outcomes of School Cluster systems, there appear to be four areas where clusters have succeeded in promoting decentralisation:

4.5.1 Heightened Local Management of Resources

Decentralisation in the local use of resources has been achieved through the decision of the MoEYS in collaboration with donors to route funds more directly to schools via cluster school networks. At the cluster level, the utilisation of funds has been greatly facilitated by the introduction of objective-based planning, mostly through Logical Framework Approaches. This reform of the planning process allows each LCSC to analyse its own problems and to determine its own objectives, activities

---

[4] CAPE, which has already been referred to and which had a profound impact on the evolution of School Clustering in Cambodia and PASEC an EU funded Franco-phone programme which was the antithesis of CAPE in that it promoted a more centralised approach to teacher education in particular (author's experience and opinion of the programme).

[5] EQIP which focused on disbursement of grants to clusters and Priority Action programme (PAP) which focused on individual schools (author's understanding of the grant systems).

and budgetary requirements based on this analysis. Planning together as a group of schools helps to ensure that more competent school directors can work with the less competent ones to produce a rationalised plan that benefits everyone (Bredenberg, 2002: 13–14).

4.5.2 Local Decision-making and Empowerment

This facility relates to the one above. With their strong focus on planning, cluster school projects have provided a structured context for schools to collectively make decisions based on rationalised assessments of local need. Because schools are often limited in their exposure to activities to solve problems, cluster school projects have begun to move in the direction of using activity menus to facilitate local decisions by providing choice among a wide variety of possible options. These activity menus outline all the technical support which is available to them. Activity Menus may differ among provincial sites within each province depending on the technical expertise (Bredenberg, 2002: 13).

4.5.3 Localised Capacity-building

Another important potential in the cluster context has been its ability to promote locally based modes of teacher supervision and teacher training. This has been approached primarily through intensive training of TGLs who are cluster based. TGLs are master teachers who plan teacher training activities on Thursdays and do follow-up supervisory visits during the month (Bredenberg, 2002: 13).

4.5.4 Streamlined Absorption of Development Aid

Dealing with schools collectively rather than individually has enabled development projects to greatly increase both the amount of aid that can be disbursed and the number of beneficiaries of that aid. Working through an established network of school directors, cluster based master teachers and community members enables project staff to achieve tremendous savings in their use of time, particularly with respect to training activities and development (Bredenberg, 2002: 14).

This in turn has meant that teachers work collectively and in networks which can help communication between schools and with central provincial education offices. In this way important teacher development activities can be streamlined through the cluster system.

School Clusters in Cambodia have achieved a great deal in promoting 'upward accountability' to District and Provincial Offices of Education. Upward accountability refers to requiring clusters to develop performance standards with respect to student learning, classroom practice, etc., and to monitor their own progress towards these explicit standards for reporting upwards. There is still more work to be done with 'downward' accountability of schools to parents, however, with more community involvement in planning and decision-making at cluster level and more awareness raising of the importance of teaching and learning, these issues can be overcome.

There are encouraging signs that the MoEYS is committed to a more decentralised approach as is evident from the ESP (2006–2010) it states,

> [a]t the same time, the MOEYS has decentralized some functions to the sub-national level. MOEYS has provided school operation budgets to all schools and all education levels across the country. Communities, parents, local authorities and local and international organizations have also taken an active part in education activities to contribute to improving education quality. (MoEYS, 2006a, 2010)

4.6 School Clusters and Education Reform Processes

The shift from a more centralised approach to decentralisation in Cambodia started around the new millennium and was part of comprehensive education reform processes. More recently there have been paradigm shifts within School Clustering which directly relate to these reform processes, most noticeably in the area of active learning and child-friendly schools which encompass child rights and welfare. As mentioned earlier, School Clusters have been key in using and promoting CFS approaches. This is evident in teacher training and development from PRESET onwards.

The CFS approach was expanded in 2002 to other provinces which established a steering committee comprising of representatives from NGOs and key MoEYS departments, notably, the Teacher Training Department and Pedagogical Research Department. This was to oversee the programme and also to provide consistency.

In 2004, reports Bredenberg, the Ministry initiated a pilot programme to expand the Child Friendly Schools approach into the lower secondary (i.e., junior high) school sector so that children who studied in child-friendly primary schools could continue such experiences (Bredenberg, 2004). Thus providing consistency and stability to the child throughout their school experience.

In addition the Ministry's 2006–2010 plan included the introduction of the principles of child-friendly schooling into the pre-service teacher preparation curriculum in all teacher training colleges. The plan also calls for providing in-service training on the concept and practices of child-friendly schooling to all current teachers as one of the main activities for their 'continuous teacher development'. The MoEYS officials described the technical meetings, held monthly at the cluster level, as the key vehicle for providing this in-service training (Bredenberg, 2004).

Section 5: Lessons Learnt

5.1 Mismatch of Education Providers' Expectations

As has been noted many times in this chapter the School Cluster system in Cambodia is heavily supported by donors, NGOs and IOs. This is not uncommon in countries that are recovering from conflict and trauma such as Cambodia experienced. However what has been seen in the Cambodia case study is that only too often there has been a lack of shared vision amongst those meant to be supporting and strengthening the education system.

In Cambodia there is strong evidence of rivalry between bilateral projects in the earlier days with CAPE striving for a more decentralised and capacity building approach and the centralised approach of the PASEC project. Lately there have been similar spates between the EQIP working with the cluster system and PAP working more at single school level. Not only is there a need for mutual understanding and cooperation across the sector but also the MoEYS, which naturally is keen to receive the support, needs to be able to coordinate parallel, or rather multiple, national programmes which have very different expectations and approaches to education reform.

5.2 Perceptions around Education

Another challenge centres around the perception Cambodians have of education, as reported by one tertiary professor: the 'embedded model of hierarchical relationships between teacher and pupil, where the focus is on teaching rather than learning, means that there has been no historical aim towards developing a facility for lifelong learning' (VSO, 2008: 33 cited in UNESCO, 2011: 40). Then the suggestion that '[q]uality training efforts might be beneficial in reorienting teachers to a more student-centred teaching approach' (UNESCO, 2011).

In addition, parents and the wider community need to understand more about teaching and learning. There need to be awareness raising programmes so that parents can understand why CPD is important and necessary not only for the teacher's development but also for the benefit of their child's learning. Teachers need to have enough time to know and understand where families come from and who they are.

In this respect the World Bank's Implementation Completion Report on EQIP talks of lessons learnt and this one is relevant here,

> To change attitudes and pedagogical practices at the classroom level requires sustained effort over time and support at all management and policymaking levels. Champions of change at the central, provincial and district levels are particularly important in a context where hierarchal relations dominate. Furthermore, technical assistance is important for the injection of new ideas and continuous reinforcement of those new ideas. Capacity building is a necessary condition to effect lasting institutional change. This is especially important and useful at decentralized levels. (World Bank, 2004: 13)

Indeed this has been an ongoing issue, not only in Cambodia but other countries too, the issue of, as Ayres (1997) puts it, '[t]he tendency to appreciate form rather than substance'. In the writer's own experience there has always been too much emphasis and focus on developing and displaying teaching aids and not enough on using these teaching aids in the classroom and how they link with lesson plans and the curriculum. If resource centres are to be the hub of developing and sharing resources they should not only be material resource sharing but human too. The resource centres are natural venues for the in-service type of training, such as, upgrading and recertifying teachers. In addition and very importantly it should also be a place where teachers can continue to develop through CPD activities.

5.3 Shortage of Teachers: Double Shift Systems, Contract Teachers and Ethnic Minority Areas

Teacher shortages continue to hamper Cambodia's education system and for this reason the MoEYS relies on the double shift system and contract teachers, specifically in rural areas.

In theory a double shift system should mean teachers teach two four-hour blocks each day. As a UNESCO report points out, 'this may involve teaching two different classes—one in the morning and one in the afternoon—further complicating established problems of insufficient time for planning and administration. There are reports of teachers combining two classes into one larger one as the double-shift option is clearly not preferred' (UNESCO and INEE, 2011: 41). This clearly has implications for any cluster system and in these areas they are often unsupported clusters.

Most teachers in Cambodia need to supplement their income because they are underpaid and doing a double shift would prohibit this, as Geeves and Bredenberg believe, '[combining classes] may be because it prevents the teacher from holding a second job and most payments for the second shift are delayed, reduced, or paid at the end of the year' (Geeves and Bredenberg, 2004). The World Bank gives credence to these reports, as it states that 'while two thirds of rural primary teachers claim to work double shifts, three quarters also claim to have a second job' (Benveniste et al., 2008), 'usually in farming' (VSO, 2008 cited in UNESCO and INEE, 2011: 41).

A common feature in countries with acute teacher shortages and large rural and remote areas, is the recruitment of what are called 'contract teachers', locally recruited and often unqualified. In Cambodia these teachers pose both challenges but also possible solutions to providing quality education in schools.

In Cambodia there are a lot fewer than once was, for example, from 2001 to 2002. Recently contract teachers have been reduced to fewer than 3 per cent from 9 per cent of total teachers in primary schools. However over 13 per cent of teachers in remote areas are still 'contract teachers' (adapted from UNESCO and INEE, 2011: 40). Some see this as an issue: 'There does not appear to be a consistent method to deal with this problem and school directors continue to hire them as needed' (VSO, 2008 cited in UNESCO and INEE, 2011: 40). However, as Bredenberg points out, '[c]ontinuing to appoint Contract Teachers also enabled the

MOEYS to address chronic teacher shortages in many rural and remote areas characterized by a widening "gap" between the number of primary teachers and classes'.

In their monograph, 'Contract Teachers in Cambodia', Geeves and Bredenberg are able to clarify the MoEYS policy on how to use and develop contract teachers especially those in ethnic minority areas:

> The Contract Teachers who remained after the cuts of 2001–02 and 2002–03 are concentrated in former conflict and remote areas, primarily because these are the places in which the MoEYS has had most difficulty implementing its polices of re-deploying experienced teachers, or deploying newly qualified teachers, to remote schools, despite offering a variety of incentives. (Geeves and Bredenberg, 2004)

'The MoEYS currently aims to provide fully certified teachers to all primary schools in the country. Focusing on developing local teachers (including teachers on contracts—especially in ethnic minority schools) may prove a pragmatic complimentary strategy' (Geeves and Bredenberg, 2004). In addition they point out that locally resourced teachers, such as contract teaches can

- provide their own socio-economic support;
- speak ethnic minority languages, the locally-hired teachers can bring vernacular instruction and culturally relevant content into the classroom.

They suggest that contract teachers can be developed in a number of ways:

- Offering on-the-job training to local people to retain them in schools as paraprofessionals.
- Assisting them to gain full teacher status through participation in teacher education. (Adapted from Geeves and Bredenberg, 2004)

5.4 Teacher Educators/Trainers

The role of teacher educators or trainers was raised in Chapter 1 also under 'challenges'. This is because they are too often forgotten and yet are pivotal in the facilitation and management of the capacity building at local levels. Therefore it is necessary to ensure that time and training is

F. Helen Drinan   177

given to them as well as ongoing support so that they can provide quality inputs at school level.

As Geeves and Bredenberg mention in their Planning document for an ADB project,

> [t]raining is seen as a core component of the project. It is clear that sustainable improvement in remote schools depends upon well informed education officials working at Provincial and District levels to provide support and responsive management. They in turn must have access to and support from specialist personnel at national level. The quality of training programs and the trainers will be critical in achieving such an enabling environment. (Geeves and Bredenberg, 2004: 11)

More recently a VSO reiterated similar sentiments:

> The lack of quality teacher trainers presents another major impediment to progress. Cambodia currently suffers a serious shortage of experienced and thoroughly qualified teacher trainers, in large part a result of the disassembling of the teaching service in the 1970s. Because pulling qualified trainers from current experienced teaching ranks would only exacerbate shortages, development partners may have an opportunity to focus on this area. (VSO, 2008 cited in UNESCO and INEE, 2011: 40)

Herein lies the weakness, too often training programmes and trainers do not deliver the necessary quality. This can be for a number of reasons but in the Cambodian case it is mainly to do with selection. The selection of trainers has come from the more senior ranks who have either not been in the classroom for a very long time or never been in one. They do not have the skills to train adults and worst of all they do not have the interest in improving the quality of education. Relevant and appropriate selection and selection criteria of trainers is therefore crucial. In addition to the selection of suitable trainers is the content and design of the training materials which should be relevant, appropriate, participatory and with a focus on child-centred or child friendly teaching and learning.

Section 6: The Future of School Clustering in Cambodia

In conclusion it is pertinent to consider views from key 'institutions' with a long history in Cambodia and the development of the School Clusters there. What do they think is the future for School Clusters in Cambodia?

In the World Bank's Implementation Completion Report for EQIP in 2004 the tone was sombre,

> The future of the school cluster system in Cambodia is uncertain. Whether on a formal or an informal basis, provinces which have had a positive experience with clusters are likely to continue to rely on them as a decentralized support network, fostering the exchange of experiences and offering a framework for regular in-service training. The effectiveness of clusters, however, will ultimately depend on the availability of district level facilitators to motivate and facilitate professional dialogue and pedagogical reflection. (World Bank, 2004: 11)

In a slightly more optimistic light, the long term advocate and veteran Cambodian educator, Kurt Bredenberg, feels,

> it is clear that school clusters as a development strategy appear to be deeply entrenched in the minds of many local educators, particularly at provincial level. Perceptions of its waning popularity aside, its abrogation would surely be deeply disruptive to the education system. What is needed, however, is a modification in the design of school clusters to accommodate changes in the educational landscape. (Bredenberg, 2002: 10)

It is interesting to note that both believe clusters will continue to operate in some shape or form: whether in those provinces where they have been successful or whether because they are so firmly entrenched in the system. However both views recognise that there needs to be change within the Cluster System. The World Bank statement suggests that changes need to come more from grass roots, at least at district level and possibly the need for more capacity building to build up that 'critical mass' of trainers/teacher educators/leaders to steer teaching and learning at cluster level in a more professional and reflective manner.

Bredenberg's suggestion could be interpreted in a similar way in that he implies that the clusters need to be more flexible and 'organic', able to change not only to national educational reforms, which one would hope emanates from the clusters, but also be aware and amenable to wider, more regional and global changes. The 'educational landscape' should also include inter-sectoral or cross-sectoral approaches, informal and non-formal education, so that clusters embrace and expand their concept of 'education'.

What also needs to be considered in terms of support to teachers and their CPD is a more holistic way of looking at it and as Bredenberg says to consider the 'educational landscape'. As the writer implied earlier when discussing teacher training at cluster level, the focus has been more on the traditional in-service style of training. This is also necessary especially where a system has many unqualified or under-qualified teachers.

However, by now the clusters should be embracing CPD in all its forms and encourage teachers to pursue their professional development formally, informally and non-formally and creating opportunities for them to do this. In this way teachers can realise their own professional strengths and build confidence in their field and at the same time improve learning in the classroom and enhance the teaching profession so that we can banish the notion that 'teachers have a low status and are not respected by society' (Cambodian Independent Teachers Association, cited in UNESCO and INEE, 2011: 41), which further contributes to the undesirable appeal of the profession.

Capacity building, and equitable distribution of this capacity to provide quality education would seem to be key priorities for the cluster systems now, to avoid this very sombre and worrying statement on Cambodia's education system from UNESCO's report on 'Fragile States', coming true,

> [l]imited teaching capacity, and thus poor quality of education, has driven and may continue to drive fragility in a number of ways. Poor quality education can serve to amplify society's lack of confidence in state-provided services that have again failed to deliver promised indications of modernisation. Furthermore, the distribution of existing capacity is such that it contributes to further inequity within society, particularly among the rural and poor populations. Finally, there is an inherent danger in an unhappy educated class: some of Cambodia's most troublesome times were in part fuelled by disenchanted intellectuals and their frustrated pupils. (UNESCO and INEE, 2011: 41)

References

Asia-Pacific Centre of Educational Innovation for Development (UNESCO–ACEID). (1996). *Partnerships in Teacher Development for a New Asia*. Bangkok, Thailand: UNESCO Principal Regional Office for Asia and the Pacific.

Ayres, David M. (1997). From Tradition to Modernity: Education, Development and the State in Cambodia, 1953–1997. PhD thesis, University of Sydney.

Benveniste, L., Marshall, J., and Araujo, M.C. (2008). *Teaching in Cambodia*. Phnom Penh, Cambodia: World Bank.

Bray, M. (1987). *School Clusters in the Third World: Making Them Work*. Paris: UNESCO–UNICEF.
Bray, M. (1999). *The Private Costs of Public Schooling: Household and Community Financing of Primary Education in Cambodia*. Paris: International Institute for Educational Planning (IIEP)/UNESCO.
Bredenberg, K. (1997). *A Training Manual for Preparing LCSCs*. Phnom Penh, Cambodia: CAPE/USAID.
———. (2000). *Can School Clustering Enhance Education Effectiveness? Promises and Pitfalls*. Phnom Penh, Cambodia: KAPE.
———. (2002). *Cluster School Development in Cambodia: Analysis of Process and Outcomes*. Phnom Penh: UNICEF/Sida.
———. (2004). *The Child Friendly Schools Movement and Impacts on Children's Learning: Practical Applications in Cambodia*. Phnom Penh: UNICEF/Sida.
Bunlay, N., Bredenberg, K., Sophea, H., Singh, M., and Wayne E. Wright. (2010). *Active-Learning Pedagogies as a Reform Initiative: The Case of Cambodia*. Phnom Penh: American Institutes for Research under the EQUIP1 LWA, USAID.
Eng, Ou. (2003). Cambodia's Experience with EQIP–The Education Quality Improvement Project: Ministry of Education Youth and Sports, Phnom Penh, Cambodia.
Geeves, R. (1999). *Project Preparatory Study No. 2: Review the Various Models of Cluster School Development and Make Recommendations to Strengthen the Cluster System of Cambodia*. Phnom Penh: MoEYS, Planning Department.
———. (2000). *Similarities, Differences, and Viability of Various Models of Support to Cluster Schools in Cambodia*. Phnom Penh: UNICEF/Sida.
———. (2003). *Operational Planning for School Cluster Development: Inception Report*. Phnom Penh: Ministry of Education, Youth and Sports, UNICEF/Sida.
Geeves, R., and Bredenberg, K. (2004). *Contract Teachers in Cambodia: An Abstract*. Phnom Penh: Kampuchean Action for Primary Education (KAPE)/World Education.
Geeves, R. (Lead Consultant), Bredenberg, K., Nhoeurn N.S., Huon, H.S., Sina, and Saran, C. (2005). School Improvement Planning. Inception Report: Consultancy Team KAPE, Consultancy team World Education/Cambodia.
Giordano, A., Elizabeth. (2008). *School Clusters and Teacher Resource Centres*. Paris: UNESCO, International Institutes for Education and Planning.
Improved Basic Education in Cambodia (IBEC) Project. (2009). Phnom Penh, Cambodia: World Education Inc./KAPE: USAID.
Kampuchean Action for Primary Education (KAPE). (2001). *Developing School Clusters in Cambodia: Suggestions for Future Practice and Increased Coordination among Program Components*. Phnom Penh, Cambodia: The Ministry of Education, Youth and Sports Publishing House.
Kennedy, A. (2005). Models of Continuing Professional Development: A Framework for Analysis. *Journal of In-service Education*, 31(2): 235–250.
MacNeil, D. James. (2004). School- and Cluster-based Teacher Professional Teacher In-service Programs and Clustering of Schools Development: Bringing

Teacher Learning to the Schools. Working Paper #1 under EQUIP1's Study of School-based: World Education/USAID.

Ministry of Education, Youth and Sport (MoEYS). (1990). *Perspectives for Quality Improvement in Teacher Education.* Phnom Penh, Cambodia: Author.

———. (1995). *Cluster School Education in Cambodia.* Phnom Penh, Cambodia: Ministry of Education, Youth and Sports Publishing House.

———. (2002). Education Sector Support Review 2002. Education Sector Performance Report, Phnom Penh.

———. (2006a). *Education Strategic Plan 2006–2010.* Phnom Penh, Cambodia: MoEYS.

———. (2006b). *Education Sector Support Program 2006–2010.* Phnom Penh, Cambodia: MoEYS.

———. (2010). *Education Strategic Plan 2009–2013.* Phnom Penh, Cambodia: MoEYS.

Royal Cambodian Government. (1996). *First Socioeconomic Development Plan 1996–2000.* Phnom Penh, Cambodia: Royal Cambodian Government.

UNESCO and Inter-Agency Network for Education in Emergencies (INEE). (2011). *Education and Fragility in Cambodia.* Paris: International Institute for Educational Planning (IIEP) and UNESCO.

Verspoor, A.M., and Wu, K.B. (1990). Textbooks and Educational Development. Education and Employment Division, Population and Human Resources, Department Paper No. PHREE/90/31, World Bank, Washington DC.

Villegas-Reimers, E. (2003). *Teacher Professional Development: An International Review of the Literature.* Paris: UNESCO–IIEP.

Wheeler, C. (1998). *Rebuilding Technical Capacity in Cambodia.* Phnom Penh: UNICEF/Sida.

World Bank. (2002). Achieving Education for All in Post-Conflict Cambodia, Washington DC.

———. (2004). Document of the World Bank. Report No: 29679, Washington DC.

———. (2005). Cambodia: Quality Basic Education for All, Washington DC.

5
Pedagogical Workshops as a Rural Teacher Support System in Mozambique

Ajuda de Desenvolvimento de Povo para Povo (Development Aid from People to People)

Contents

List of Abbreviations

Section 1: Purpose of the Document

Section 2: Mozambique at a Glance
2.1   Mozambique—Current Demographics
2.2   Education in Mozambique: Problems, Constraints and Challenges
2.3   ADPP in Mozambique and How It Contributes to Improve Education Quality

Section 3: Pedagogical Workshops: Purposes and Functioning

Section 4: Impact of Pedagogical Workshops at the School and Community Level

Section 5: The Scale up of Pedagogical Workshops

Section 6: Lessons Learnt

References

List of Abbreviations

ADPP	Ajuda de Desenvolvimento de Povo para Povo (Development Aid from People to People)
CPD	Continuing Professional Development
DFID	Department for International Development (United Kingdom)
DAF	Direção de Administração e Finanças Administration and Finance Directorate
DMM	Determination of Modern Methods pedagogy
DPEC	Direcção Provincial de Educação e Cultura (Provincial Education Directorate)
EP1	Escola Primária de Primeiro Grau (Primary School of First Grade)
EP2	Escola Primária de Segundo Grau (Primary School of Second Grade)
EPF	Escola de Professores do Futuro (School of Future's Teachers; ADPP Teacher Training College)
GoM	Government of Mozambique
INSIDA	HIV/AIDS national survey
MFA	Ministry for Foreign Affairs of Finland
MINED	Ministério da Educação (Ministry of Education)
NGO	Non-governmental Organization
OWU/ISET	One World University/Instituto Superior de Educação e Tecnologia (Higher Institute of Education and Technology)
PEE	Plano Estratégico da Educação (Strategic Plan for Education)
PW	Pedagogical Workshop
SADC	Southern Africa Development Community
SDEJT	Serviço Distrital de Educação, Juventude e Tecnologia (District Education, Youth and Technology Service)
ZIP	Zona de Influencia Pedagógica (Zone of Pedagogic Influence; Education Cluster)

Section 1: Purpose of the Document

The objective of this chapter is to picture the basic structure or mechanism of a rural teacher support system in Mozambique. It will help to identify the fundamental similarities and features of successful rural teacher support systems in different countries or contexts based on case studies for the reference of governments of UNESCO Member States and other stakeholders. It illustrates the case of the Pedagogical Workshops (PW) developed by Ajuda de Desenvolvimento de Povo para Povo (ADPP; Development Aid from People to People) in Mozambique.

The chapter seeks to present the lessons learnt from the mechanism of a rural teacher support system developed by ADPP Mozambique since 1998, the PWs, which are part of a process that enables teachers, students and communities to gain life skills that contribute to improve teaching skills and community development.

It presents a participatory tool which involves an in-service teacher training process for use by education practitioners who are tasked with supporting and capacity building of rural teachers and the communities around rural schools. The participatory in-service teacher training process provides practitioners with an overview, understanding and guide which integrate training into local development and life skills activities.

ADPP has developed and expanded PWs in most provinces of Mozambique, through an in-service teacher training programme implemented through a network of PWs. These are located in each district which serve as resource and training centres for teachers to ensure that they use the most updated teaching methods, lesson planning and school management techniques. This has been contributing to reduce dropout and repetition rates of pupils. To support these interventions, ADPP's efforts aim to ensure that the community participates in school councils and activities designed to reduce health and social risks that prevent children from participating effectively in school.

This chapter introduces the country and the educational situation in Mozambique and a framework to describe PWs, the problems addressed by this tool, the participatory community based process, its purpose, role and components, the results and lessons learnt.

Ajuda de Desenvolvimento de Povo para Povo 185

Section 2: Mozambique at a Glance

Mozambique is a country by the Indian Ocean in south eastern Africa, with a 2,470 km coastline. About half of the country is made up of flat coastal plain. Heading inland, the land rises, and high plateau and mountains run along the western and northern borders, ranging from 200 m to the highlands over 1,000 m.

The capital, Maputo, is in the extreme south with a population of around 1.5 million. The two most populous provinces are the coastal provinces of Zambézia in the centre and Nampula in the north.

2.1 Mozambique—Current Demographics

Mozambique's population is currently about 24 million, growing at 2.6 per cent annually. In southern Africa, Mozambique ranks third in population size, after South Africa and Tanzania. Population density was calculated in 2002 to be 23 per km^2. Over 50 per cent of the population are under 18 years, and are officially children. For every 100 women there are 93 men.

Urban dwellers account for 31 per cent of the population, increasing at only 1 per cent per year according to the 2007 census. These figures are significant for education planning in Mozambique for two reasons. First, it is less costly, everywhere, to provide education services for clustered populations in towns. However, in Mozambique, due to the colonial legacy of education provision noted above, education facilities beyond lower primary classes are still mainly located in the towns, thus failing to reach almost 70 per cent of the population who lives in the rural areas, and who are likely to remain in rural areas in the future. Recent focus of sector expansion has targeted rural areas, but provision of full primary schools and post-primary facilities remain an urgent need.

The 2007 census reported that one third of households (31 per cent) were headed by women. In a significant number of child-headed households (6,149), the head of the household was 12 to 14 years. This has implications not only for schooling the siblings, but the head of the household, too. A study published this year updates information on family education status and occupations: 23 per cent of household heads had never attended school, 44 per cent have lower primary education;

15 per cent have upper primary; and 11 per cent have either junior or senior secondary education. Nearly two thirds (65 per cent) of household heads are working in the agricultural sector, mainly in the informal sector. This implies very low family incomes.

2.2 Education in Mozambique: Problems, Constraints and Challenges

Despite Mozambique's impressive post-war economic growth and advances made in ensuring access to primary education, massive disparities in wealth remain. Poverty levels show clear geographic and gender-based trends: a girl in Zambézia is much less likely to lead a long productive life than a boy in Maputo city. The Government of Mozambique (GoM) adopted the Free Primary Education policy in 2003, which has helped to substantially increase school enrolment and achieve the Millennium Development Goal of universal primary education. Mozambique has also made progress in getting boys and girls into schools in almost equal proportions—47 per cent for girls and 53 per cent for boys (SADC Gender Protocol Barometer, 2011). However, girls are dropping out of school at much higher rates than boys. Girls account for the majority of the students who drop out of primary and secondary school in the centre and north of the country. In 2010, 32.6 per cent of girls failed the first level of secondary school and 33.3 per cent failed the second level. It is thus not surprising that Mozambique has the lowest literacy level for women among SADC region countries (33 per cent for women and 57 per cent for men). Despite positive trends—raising overall literacy from 39 per cent in 1997 to 50 per cent ten years later—almost two-thirds of Mozambican women are still illiterate. Mozambique is mindful of the broader Education for All goals which encompass equity and quality in education, lifelong learning and effective education outcomes, but has focused efforts on formal schooling for children rather than giving simultaneous attention to non-formal programmes for adults, adolescents and youth.

The nexus of high teacher–pupil ratios (national average of 1:66) and a high prevalence of teachers without formal teacher training (approx 26 per cent of teachers throughout the country) result in pupil dropout levels of 21.2 per cent (1st level primary) and 45.5 per cent (2nd level primary). The context is compounded by the difficulty of recruiting and retaining motivated trained teachers to work in rural areas.

Ajuda de Desenvolvimento de Povo para Povo   187

In Mozambique, the Ministry of Education (MINED) recognises that the quality of education and teacher training provided in institutions is often poor. MINED has defined expanding access to education, improving educational quality and sustaining expansion and improvement as priority activities, particularly where teacher training is part of the programme. Teachers at all levels are often under qualified for the posts they hold, many are entirely untrained and the majority have received only six years of schooling and one year of professional training. In 2011, a new curriculum was approved to expand teacher training for three years, with the view of establishing a viable system of teacher training that will place more emphasis on pedagogical skills, and will be robust enough to provide a continuing basis of common experience for the next generation of new teachers and providing more systematic opportunities for in-service training—for both established and contract teachers and for those without any formal training—to enhance their professional competence and allow them to gain additional qualifications.

Since national independence in 1975, Mozambique has used 21 different teacher training 'models' to train future teachers. This has resulted in several different types and levels of teacher training institutions and also different 'models of training' (programmes of study) of different lengths. The 'nationally defined minimum standard' for the training of teachers has changed repeatedly over the years, in accordance with the changing conditions and needs of the country. The different teacher training models tend to be referred to in shorthand in a way that is conveniently descriptive: the number of years of schooling that the prospective teacher has received plus number of years of training, that is, 4+4, 6+1, 7+3, 10+2, etc.

The Mozambican Strategic Plan of Education 2012–2016 recognises that the nature of teacher training in Mozambique, with its many models constantly changed over the years and its poor quality has resulted in a dearth of competent teachers, particularly in reading and mathematics, and that this dearth has had negative consequences on the quality of education. Despite efforts by the Government of Mozambique (GoM) to improve the quality of education, some gaps still exist, such as poorly trained teachers, the limited availability of materials, and a weak budget framework that does not comprehensively cover the needs of education in the country. The high incidence of repetition and dropout indicates the low achievement in primary schools, as identified by the MINED statistics (2009).

Teacher recruitment and deployment is centrally planned but organised at provincial level: each province trains, recruits and deploys its own teachers. In general, graduates from provincial teacher training colleges are required to teach in that province. The numbers of teachers trained do not necessarily correspond to the needs of the province, and there is considerable variation between provinces in terms of both pupil–teacher ratio (PTR) and the ratio of pupils to qualified teachers (PQTR). Rural provinces, such as Niassa, have a higher PTR and a higher PQTR, reflecting both a higher number of unfilled posts and a greater proportion of untrained teachers than is the case in other less rural provinces (Mulkeen, 2005: 7).

The schools in rural areas are suffering from poor educational outcomes, which can be observed from the high drop-out and repetition rates, as well as poor academic achievements. Low access and completion rates may be an indication that parents give low priority to education for their children. These problems are especially notable among girls and are caused by a number of factors such as weak management, poorly trained teachers and lack of proper teaching aids and study material. The high cost of education, poor quality of teaching processes, distance to school, and the opportunity costs of attending school—which are higher for girls than boys, as girls are typically expected to do more domestic work than boys—are the main socio-economic factors affecting girls' education. Additionally, pregnancy, early marriage, gender-based violence, communities' negative attitude toward girls' schooling, and child labour are also of concern.

Research has shown that many adolescent girls particularly in rural areas spend up to four days away from school per month due to difficulties associated with menstrual hygiene. Lack of protective sanitary materials, poor sanitation, lack of water, lack of separate toilets, etc., create fear and discomfort in these girls, resulting in poor learning and performance in class. In Mozambique, gender disparities are evident at all levels with girls' schooling lagging behind that of boys. This is evidenced by the low youth female literacy rates (63.68 per cent) compared with 78.09 per cent of male youths.

Another reason for the low academic achievements mentioned earlier is that teachers lack experience in, and do not understand the importance of, developing and using supplementary pedagogical material to support the students' learning process. In addition, rural Mozambican teachers often do not have the skills to manage the large, overcrowded classes that they have to face. As a result, a very large part of a student's time is spent simply waiting for instruction or listening passively to others instead of actively participating.

2.3 ADPP in Mozambique and How It Contributes to Improve Education Quality

ADPP is a Mozambican registered NGO and member of the International Federation of Humana People to People (HPP). According to the HPP Charter, the role of development is to create a world in which we can all live in harmony. To equip future generations with a solid education, strong will and determination to achieve development. In order to achieve this, people will have to draw from concepts, strategies and methods which have been successful and can be adapted in other contexts where poverty hampers people's growth and development.

ADPP has been working with the sector of education in Mozambique since its establishment in 1982, and currently runs five schools for children, three vocational schools, eleven teacher training colleges and one university (focusing on trainers for teachers and fighting poverty). One of ADPP's main strengths is that it has strong linkages with the Government of Mozambique, which gives the organisation and its programmes long-term sustainability. Such linkages also exist with a number of international organisations (NGOs, foreign embassies and intra-governmental agencies) with whom ADPP has a working policy.

ADPP Mozambique has been working in partnership with the MINED for many years and training primary teachers since 1993. ADPP has made a strategic choice to focus on teacher training in order to increase access to primary education and improve education quality, with the objectives of

1. educating qualified teachers, creating continuity in supply;
2. raising the quantity and quality of teachers in primary schools to better meet the needs of rural areas; and
3. promoting education and development in a wide range of aspects in the community.

ADPP Mozambique has trained 13,800 primary teachers by 2014. ADPP graduates accounted for 16 per cent of the teachers trained in Mozambique between 2005 and 2011 and the vast majority of ADPP graduate teachers—100 per cent of them until 2009—begin their careers working in rural primary schools.

ADPP works in strong collaboration with local communities in order to develop health and education projects that address community concerns. The collaborations require a paradigm shift from traditional practices to an approach that involves: acknowledging community contributions, recruiting and training local people to participate in training, improving communication, sharing power, and valuing local practices. ADPP's management systems support local participants by emphasising the importance of peer leadership, supervisory support, and community liaison in the implementation of community-based services, which use culturally appropriate strategies.

Section 3: Pedagogical Workshops: Purposes and Functioning

Access to education and improvement of education quality has been orienting ADPP interventions in the education sector in Mozambique. Parallel to teachers training in the 10 Teacher Training Centres, ADPP has introduced and expanded the PWs, as a tool to develop continuous in-service teacher training activities. The PWs are aimed at the improvement of the learning environment in primary schools and increasing educational opportunities while strengthening community members' effective participation and support of education through capacity building activities.

Well-qualified and trained teachers are a prerequisite for achieving educational quality. Teachers' employment conditions and working environment are also central to educational quality, as they have an impact on teachers' motivation, which in turn affects the way they are able to perform in the classroom and interact with their pupils. Most of the 21 different teacher training programmes are no longer offered within teacher training institutions, but are still valid in the sense that a large proportion of currently serving teachers have been trained through one or other of these earlier models of teacher training. Currently, the minimum school-leaving qualification for someone wanting to enter the teaching profession as a primary teacher is tenth grade.

The MINED is striving to meet the demand for trained teachers across the system. MINED has embarked on a massive recruitment of teachers who have no teaching qualification to teach in primary schools as a stop-gap measure. This measure is a necessary step in addressing the problem of teacher shortage in primary schools. In other words, to achieve universal access and completion of EP1 as well as ensure an unfettered transition to EP2, there is a dire need for a vigorous recruitment policy and an effective in-service training for teachers, as well as expansion of the existing pre-service teacher training institutions in the country. This perhaps is one of the surest ways of meeting the demand for an adequate number of qualified teachers in the primary school sub-sector of the national system of education in Mozambique.

According to Ministry of Education Statistics 2010, the percentage of teachers with no in-service pedagogical training is 26 per cent in the country. This naturally, affects the quality of education taking place, which in turn negatively effects pass and drop-out rates. The following challenges have been highlighted as obstacles to the delivery of quality education in Mozambique: many teachers lack the abilities in planning, designing and making teaching aids; many teachers lack basic academic and professional skills for effective classroom interaction and many teachers fail to prepare and use schemes of work, lesson plans and lesson notes.

Furthermore the teachers with the lack of teaching qualification are unable to manage the increasingly large class sizes. Due to lack of appropriate training in teaching methodology, many children are unable to progress without qualified support and the dropout and repetition rates increase on a yearly basis. Serious interventions are therefore needed to secure the quality of teaching taking place in the rural schools. The only solution is to train the teachers while they are in-service.

Through its programme of decentralisation, the Government of Mozambique has placed a great deal of emphasis on the development of local centres on a provincial level which can lead MINED's new strategic interventions. The decentralisation plan, which is due to finish in 2014, emphasises the importance of developing provincial institutions and networks which support in-service training and assist to adapt the national in-service training programme (in development at present) to the local context. In all provinces, ADPP is involved in this process and the interventions in this project support the national in-service training curriculum.

The PWs seek to address specific aspects of education quality based on the following assumptions: (1) Constraints in the state budget reduce the number of teachers trained and therefore contribute to high pupil-teacher ratios, therefore the training of more teachers with external support is key. (2) In-service teacher training must ensure that teachers have the capacity to effectively meet the requirements of the national and local curriculum, including lesson preparation, and the capacity to deal with social and cognitive challenges in learning. (3) The quality of primary education can be improved through the introduction of additional reading and writing tuition for the first grades, as this ability is critical for the success of the whole process of education. (4) The existing disparities in the completion rates of girls and boys must be addressed as a matter of priority. Evidence shows that in the first grades of EP1 there are no significant differences in the enrolment of boys and girls. However, in the final grades and in the transition to EP2, the percentage of girls tends to drop. In the aggregate first level (Grade 5) primary school completion rate there is still a gap between boys (79.7 per cent) and girls (74.4 per cent).

ADPP has been implementing community development, health and education programmes in Manica Province, in the central region of Mozambique. Manica suffers from a high HIV rate at 15.3 per cent (INSIDA, 2009), which greatly effects the quality and quantity of basic education taking place in the province, as children are affected by the death of their parents (thus changing living situations, leaving school to earn an income to support younger siblings) and the absence of infected teachers, etc. The primary school network is better than most provinces in terms of infrastructures, but the classrooms are overcrowded (1:66 is the Teacher–Pupil ratio) and 52.5 per cent of teachers don't have any pedagogical education as opposed to 26 per cent on the national level (Ministry of Education Statistics, 2009).

In 2009, in addition to this, 43 per cent of households in Manica suffered food insecurity, of which 19 per cent experienced chronic food

Ajuda de Desenvolvimento de Povo para Povo   193

insecurity. This was due to a series of climatic shocks (drought and intermittent flooding) which resulted in an 82 per cent crop failure. This has further jeopardised the ability of families to send children to school due to lack of cash for school uniforms, books and increased emphasis on crop production to make up for the food losses incurred in 2009.

Furthermore, Manica was highlighted as a priority province for Institutional Development in the ESSP 2006–2010/11. Problems in the communities related to health, low income, gender issues and weak local organisation have a negative effect on the outcome of the education the children and youth receive and in many cases even hinders many children from attending school. Many of the rural communities suffer from lack of basic health infrastructures and lack of social services.

The first PWs were established in Manica province where there are 676 primary schools and many are located in isolated areas. Considering that many teachers didn't have a proper education and their academic results were among the lowest in the country, ADPP has developed a programme in coordination with the provincial department of education (DPEC Manica), in which a considerable number of primary school teachers in the province have the opportunity to be involved in a three-year in-service training. The programme aims to increase the knowledge and skills of 559 primary school teachers and develop 26 model schools with improved educational conditions connected to 13 PWs in 10 different districts in the province. The PWs are now part of the pedagogical structures in the districts in close cooperation with the District Education, Youth and Technology Service (SDEJT).

An in-service teacher training programme has been implemented through a network of PWs located in each district which serve as resource and training centres for teachers to ensure that they use the most updated teaching methods, lesson planning and school management techniques. This has contributed in reducing dropout and repetition rates of pupils. To support these interventions, the PW project ensures that the community participates in school councils and activities designed to reduce health and social risks that prevent children from participating effectively in school.

The objectives for setting up and scaling up PWs in rural districts of Mozambique are three-fold: (1) To support teachers in their pedagogical work by providing means and tools that help them to improve the quality of teaching; (2) to strengthen leadership skills of the ADPP teacher graduates to be able to implement development projects that bring the community closer to the education process; and (3) to empower children and youth and mainly girls and women so that they engage in the social and economic development of their communities by strengthening their capabilities.

PW is a way that brings modern information, communication and education technologies to the doorsteps of rural communities. It maximises the investment in the training of the 'Teachers of the Future' and creates centres for outreach work. The main outcomes of PWs in rural areas are translated in better learning opportunities for children and adults and their empowerment with skills to participate more effectively in the social and economic development of their districts.

PWs are resource centres to be used by teachers to plan their lessons, share experiences and produce didactic materials; teachers have the opportunity to learn and use computers and the internet where it is possible, and interact with the community. It is the meeting point for the Zone of Pedagogic Influence (ZIPs).

An important component of the PWs are the resources which are allocated in the form of equipment and materials, which enable the creation of a learning environment where different stakeholders can interact: computers, printers, scanners, television and DVD, photocopy machines, books, magazines, laminating and binding machines, are some of the resources that are allocated to each PW.

The issue of trained and untrained teachers delivering low quality primary teaching is being tackled by the PWs. This model of in-service teacher training aims at increasing the delivery of good quality primary education. It helps to produce a group of well-trained teachers who can help to provide models of good classroom practice, motivating their students and contributing for children's retention and progression. This model provides opportunities for continuing professional development of teachers in rural areas, where communication and access to resources are limited and constrained.

In order to ensure the sustainability of the PWs, a management body is normally elected to work together with the PW manager and coordinator. This committee includes a school's headmaster, a representative of the school administration, a representative of the district educational services, two community members, and one person from IRDP (local committee of development). This group meets regularly to monitor the functioning of the PW, solving problems, approving norms or regulations and programmes, suggesting more activities and supervising the financial management of the PW.

The PW coordinators structure their work in two main ways: Some (most) coordinators of the PWs are teaching or are pedagogical directors or even directors in the primary schools near or connected to the PW where they are working. In this case there are two coordinators at the PW. One is in the PW while the other is working in the primary school and then they switch according to the timetable of the school.

The second way of organising is where some graduates are working full-time with ADPP to only work with the PWs. In this case there is only one coordinator at the PW. Each coordinator has a work programme aligned with the elements of the PW that he/she is developing all the time and the planning exercise is made together with the PW managers and approved by PW Management Committee.

The PW Management Committee members include a teacher, one or two community members, an officer from the SDEJT and the coordinators. The PW Management Committee ensures that more people get involved and become responsible for the PW resources available for the community. This structure has allowed ownership by the community and support by the district local authorities.

The PW coordinators and managers are selected from some of the most active and best qualified teachers around the PW in coordination with the SDEJTs. Their task is to implement the programme of in-service training of teachers. Every quarter they will participate in a training programme which will enable them to fulfill their mission. They hold the in-service training sessions, train the teachers in how to use computer educational equipment and be instructors on how to produce didactical materials, how to make good plans for lessons and how to acquire information. The PW staff interact closely with the traditional leaders and seek out possible solutions to local problems and seek support from the people around them. They link with all sectors, women, youth, elderly, HIV/AIDS positive, etc. and make them part of the programmes.

Community development activities are managed by the PW manager; at the PWs, those activities bring together community members, students and teachers. The PW offers an equipped and comfortable venue for seminars and meetings in the district and village which is used for public meetings and local authorities.

The activities implemented in PWs are broadening the execution and sustainability of the day-to-day operation of the PWs to concretely and systematically reach out the essential needs of the community, and in this process mobilise more children and youth to get involved while building up their lives.

The main party involved in the implementation of the PWs are the Provincial Department for Education (DPEC) and SDEJT. As the DPEC sets the targets for in-service training, monitors the pass and repetition rates, manages the teacher placement process and oversees the quality of teaching taking place in the province, it plays a fundamental role in the design, implementation and evaluation of the PW projects.

A partnership is established between ADPP and the local authorities of education. ADPP, SDEJT and DPEC sign a three year agreement for project period and the intention is to extend it to guarantee the PWs sustainability. As the DPEC sets the targets the roles of each party are clearly specified. DPEC's roles include the identification of the placement of new PWs; approval of the teachers' deployment to new PWs as coordinators and managers, enabling the teachers to work half of their day at the PW and keep the position for time span of the project; paying salaries for the teachers who are managing the PWs; supporting the in-service training by ensuring local schools adhere to the schedule; and providing technical support for monitoring and evaluation.

Equally, SDEJT and its most local mechanism—the ZIP are involved in all activities taking place in the PWs. SDEJT representatives participate (when possible) in training sessions for in-service teachers; they ensure that the material and methodology supports the objectives of MINED and contribute with technical skills in the areas of school management and monitoring; they support the DPEC's role in monitoring and evaluating the PW project and support new initiatives for the ZIP which are promoted by the PW managers. SDEJT representatives also benefit through the utilisation of the workshop resources to learn management skills such as work-processing and Excel, etc. And they are part of the PW management committee.

The in-service training component involves primary and secondary teachers working in rural schools around the PW. The manager together with a ZIP coordinator or a school headmaster organises the training which includes teaching methodologies, lesson planning, time management, team work, bilingual education, active learning, pedagogical skills to address social and cognitive challenges in learning, gender equality, parents' involvement, school management, etc. Teachers with or without training have access to training, production of didactic materials using local resources and development of local curricula. A successful model of extra-curricular reading and writing tuition for the first grades, combined with competitions aimed at stimulating the pupils' motivation has been developed and implemented in PWs. Reading and writing skills are essential to enable children's progress throughout primary education.

Section 4: Impact of Pedagogical Workshops at the School and Community Level

The PW's goals are to create better learning opportunities for children and adults, to empower them with the skills to participate more effectively in the social and economic development of their district.

The main focus of the PWs is on capacity building, empowerment and community ownership. These three elements are key to the achievement of the project's outcomes. Quality of education depends on capacity building of teachers, school councils and local authorities. The teachers are trained in-service in order to improve their skills and be able to implement a more child-centred approach, and to develop extra-curricular activities so that the school environment improves. The teachers are trained in pedagogical methodologies which enable them to be more proactive in their work. The pre-service training of significant number of women empower them to play a more active role in raising the quality of education, and serve as role models for girls. Empowerment is also a key element for school council members (Parent–Teacher Associations). The community leaders and parents who gain awareness of their rights and responsibilities are able to actively participate in the school management and in the district council sessions in planning and monitoring of local policies, mainly education-related ones. Figure 5.1 illustrates the functions of PWs.

Figure 5.1
The functions of PWs

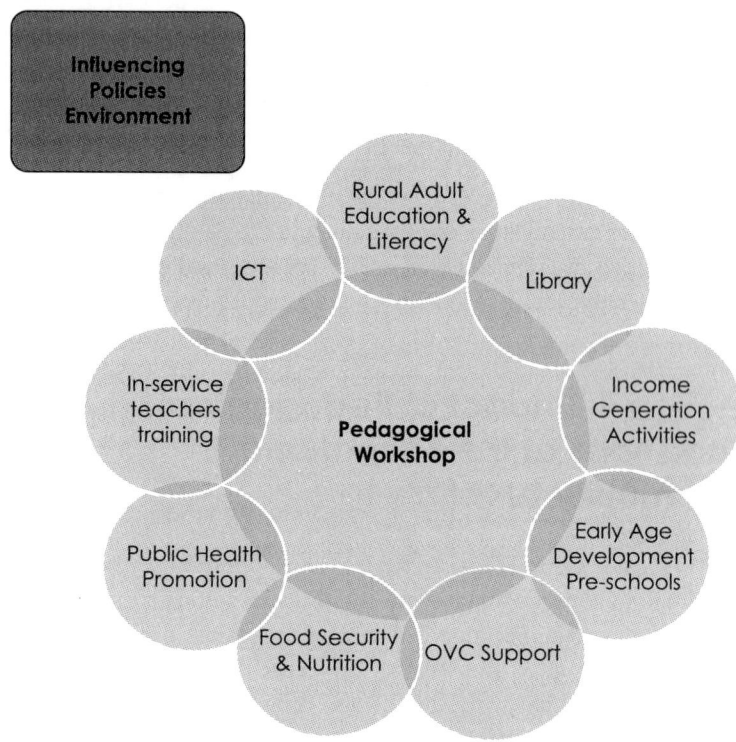

Source: ADPP.

PWs have promoted and supported the use of ICT tools: training of teachers to manage computers and use modern digital tools. This means access to studies, comments from other peer teachers, working groups for planning, debating and sharing of experiences. The digital libraries set up in the PWs have made the training more effective, and the use of DMM (Definition of Modern Methods), a system of teaching and learning implemented by ADPP, has been helping teachers to develop a more child-centred methodology.

Rural teachers who work in difficult conditions have raised their motivation and become multi-faceted professionals who see education as part of community development, and mainly see themselves as agents of change. The retention and completion rates in schools around PWs have improved.

There is a general public recognition, especially at district and local level, of the importance of the PW, as a catalytic resource for community mobilisation, and teachers' and students' engagement in community development. The improved capacity and personal progress of most staff and people involved in implementing and managing PWs is quite visible and measurable.

There is also cooperation among different stakeholders at the community level who understand and share the same vision regarding their problems and how PWs help to address them.

Section 5: The Scale up of Pedagogical Workshops

ADPP-Mozambique has started the implementation of PWs in the Teacher Training College in Chimoio, in Manica province in 2000, with the support of W.K. Kellog Foundation, in partnership with local government structures and surrounding rural communities. Table 5.1 illustrates the scaling up efforts by ADPP that has reached more than 20 districts in rural areas of Mozambique.

ADPP has been able to raise funds in order to establish and implement PWs. This has been done over the years in partnership with international NGOs and donors. PWs are a three year project, implemented by ADPP trained staff, usually a former graduate of the teacher training centre; the management of the PW is done in close collaboration with local district authorities at the provincial and district levels. As per agreement with education authorities, PWs are handed over to the SDEJT which ensures the sustainable continuation of the project.

With support from MINED and encouraged by pilot projects in Manica and Cabo Delgado, ADPP Mozambique has been developing its full-scale PW Programme in Mozambique. At present there are 42 PWs in most of the provinces which serve as a vital source of support for teachers in rural settings where no other teaching materials could be accessed. Over the past 10 years, the model for the PW has evolved into a locally-driven centre, run by local teachers (ADPP graduates where

Table 5.1
Pedagogical workshop by province in Mozambique

PW/year	Total no. of PW/Province	Provinces	Districts
2002(6); 2007(1); 2012(1)	9	Cabo Delgado	Chiure, Ancuabe, Pemba Metuge, Macomia, Meluco, Mueda, Mocimba da Praia and Quissanga
2001(2); 2006(10)	10	Manica	Guro, Macossa, Bárue, Gondola, Manica, Sussundenga and Mossurize
2006(1)	1	Inhambane	Inhambane City
2002(2), 2006(2)	4	Zambézia	Namacurra
1999(3); 2008(2)	5	Maputo Província	Matola, Moamba, Boane and Marracuene
2010(2)	2	Nampula	Nacala Velha and Nacala Porto
1999(2); 2008(2); 2010(1)	5	Sofala	Nhamatanda, Caia and Dondo
2010(1)	1	Tete	Chiuta
1999(1); 2009(3)	4	Gaza	Chibuto, Chokwé and Guijá

possible) and partly financed by income from courses held at the centre. This model has proved to be effective in improving access to quality education in rural areas as well as stimulating general development within the communities around the PWs.

In order to ensure the sustainability of this approach, the programme is designed in such a way that most of the initiatives and the basic materials take place at the primary school level and PW level which are managed by school teachers as coordinators and managers. If after the three years of the project, MINED advices that the PW structure and its asset should be managed by the DPEC as part of the decentralisation process, ADPP prepares an exit strategy. If this is not suggested by the DPEC, the PW remains under ADPP Management for the foreseeable future. ADPP looks after the resources purchased as part of the project and ensures that the assets continue to be utilised for the progress of teacher training in the future. Out of 43 PWs established since 2000, 28 have been handed over to district authorities of education; ADPP still manages 3 PWs in Cabo Delgado Province and 12 in Manica Province, with the financial support of Agencia Española de Cooperación Internacional para el Desarollo (AECID; Spanish Agency for International Development Cooperation) and Ministry of Foreign Affairs of Finland (MFA Finland), respectively. Given the constraints in the allocation of the education budget, the sustainable character that defines the concept of a PW has allowed their continuation, as community owned centres of local development. The PWs raise their own funds through income generating activities started by ADPP and these cover running costs and maintenance of facilities.

There are factors that should be taken into account by education authorities which might impede programme sustainability in the long run, and these include:

- Heavy reliance on technical assistance with little training of local staff, including education technical staff in district services, to effectively take over implementation.
- Initial considerable level of investment may result in resource unavailability (e.g., no way to find replacement parts or afford maintenance) when project disbursements end, and the importance to monitor and ensure maintenance.
- Low level of community involvement and lack of sense of ownership.

Section 6: Lessons Learnt

Community development through education and health promotion using the PWs has meant developing organisational and leadership capacity, building on strengths, respecting community values and learning from experiences. The main lessons after more than a decade of implementing PWs are around creating and adjusting plans to address concerns, make decisions about resources, share responsibilities and develop communities in action. There are important lessons that have been learnt over time:

- Each community is different. It is different in its needs, financial capacities, and the physical organisation of the village, the people who are involved and the gender relations. In this respect, it is important to fit the activities and norms specifically to each community, and be sensitive to these differences. Sometimes, small changes need to be made in order to fit the same activity to two different communities.
- It is important to involve the community in the management of the PWs so that it develops the ownership of the development process. This can help create a greater understanding and collective decision that show that all stakeholders share the same interest.
- It is important to think from the beginning about financial sustainability of the PWs, and the early start of income generating activities will ensure benefits for all.

'Ownership' of the PW objectives is vital, and an enabling environment should exist for local governmental institutions and community organisations to establish a collaborative partnership in undertaking the responsibility for developing a local 'vision' and strategy and for designing/planning, allocating resources, implementing and monitoring/evaluating of development activities that better cater to local needs. It is important that the various local players, teachers, students, school headmasters, PW managers, local authorities, local leaders and formal and informal local entrepreneurs become the driving force towards development and develop a 'sense of shared ownership', and jointly manage their development initiatives.

Community development based on a learning community approach fosters the acquisition of information, knowledge, skills, attitudes and values that together build a community's capacity to successfully respond to, and direct economic and social change. Allied to the improved quality of education that PWs contribute to, ADPP's experience should be regarded as an important tool that should be replicated and adopted by education authorities in many other sub-Saharan countries.

As an innovative approach built-in partnership with communities, schools, local institutions and community organisations, PWs promote outreach and extension opportunities for people in remote and rural communities. PWs develop skills and qualifications to enhance employment and self-employment, provide community services and skills development initiatives that promote collaborative community efforts to reduce disadvantage and exclusion of people with few assets and opportunities.

References

INSIDA. (2009). The 2009 National Survey on Prevalence, Behavioral Risks and Information about HIV and AIDS. Instituto Nacional de Saúde (INS), Mozambique.
MDG Mozambique Report. (2010). Ministry of Planning and Development, Government of Mozambique, National Statistics. Printing Laranja. LDA.
Ministry of Education Statistics. (2009). Statistics of the Ministry of Education, Annual School Survey 2009, Ministry of Education and Culture, Directorate of Planning and Cooperation. Maputo, December 2009.
Mulkeen, Aidan. (2005). *Teachers for Rural Schools: A Challenge for Africa*. Association for the Development of Education in Africa (ADEA), International Institute for Educational Planning, Paris.
SADC Gender Protocol Barometer. (2011). Eds Colleen Lowe Morna and Loveness Jambaya Nyakurajah. Johannesburg: Gender Links.
Statistics of the Ministry of Education, Annual School Survey. (2009). Ministry of Education and Culture, Directorate of Planning and Cooperation. Maputo, December 2009.
Statistics of MINEC. (2009). Ministry of Education and Culture, Directorate of Planning and Cooperation. Maputo, December 2009.

6

Rural Teachers' Continuing Professional Development Support System: The Case of Ethiopia

Theodros Shewarget Belew

Contents

List of Abbreviations

Section 1: Background
1.1 The Education Policy
1.2 The CPD Design
1.3 Challenges and Problems of CPD

Section 2: The Initiation of the New CPD Framework
2.1 School-based CPD
2.2 Cluster-based CPD
2.3 Administrative and Training Structures of the Pilot Programme

Section 3: The Concept and the Rationale Establishing CRCs in Ethiopia

Section 4: The Organisational Model of CRCs

Section 5: Monitor and Support of CRCs: The Supervision in CRCs

Section 6: Effectiveness of the CRCs

Section 7: Lessons Learnt

Section 8: Future Plan

References

List of Abbreviations

AREB	Amhara Region Education Bureau
BESO	Basic Education System Overhaul
CPD	Continuous Professional Development
CRC	Cluster Resource Centre
EFA	Education for All
ETP	Education and Training Policy
JICA	Japan International Cooperation Agency
KT	Key Teacher
LS	Lesson Study
MoE	Ministry of Education
M&S	Mathematics and Science
NCU	National Coordinating Unit
NGO	Non-governmental organisation
NSC	National Steering Committee
NT	National Trainer
RSC	Regional Steering Committee
SMASEE	Strengthening Mathematics and Science Education in Ethiopia
TEI	Teacher Education Institute
TVET	Technical, Vocational Education and Training
T&L	Teaching and Learning

Section 1: Background

1.1 The Education Policy

Education is believed to be basic for political, social and economic development of a society. Educated citizens can have the potential to improve both the volume and quality of their products or services. Education is a basic human right that should be met by each government (UNESCO, 2005). To initiate action to implement this basic human right, all countries are expected to achieve Education for All (EFA) goals by 2015.

In Ethiopia, since the 1994 Education and Training Policy (ETP), much effort was made in expanding education throughout the country. Considerable achievements were made that led to the successful achievement of the EFA goals. According to this ETP, the education structure is divided in to three main levels. These are primary, secondary and tertiary. Parallel to general education, diversified Technical Vocational Education and Training (TVET) is being provided for those who leave school from any level of education. Primary education is further divided into two cycles. The first cycle, grades 1–4 (7–10 age group), mainly deals with basic education. The second cycle, grades 5–8 (11–14 age group), focuses on general knowledge. The gross enrolment of primary education reached 96.4 per cent in 2011/12. In addition, there were 13,963 pre-school, 308,286 primary and 52,731 secondary (total 374,980) teachers in the same year (Ministry of Education [MoE], 2010/2011).

ETP has also set high standards for teachers and described a new approach to education. At the heart of this new approach was the promotion of more active learning, problem solving, and student centred teaching methods. The policy clearly indicated that emphasis should be given to upgrading and updating both in pre-service and in-service teachers. It was recognised that teachers were the key to school improvement and therefore a programme of In-service Continuous Professional Development (CPD) was developed in 2005. CPD Guidelines were produced outlining the new strategies and courses developed for the induction of newly deployed teachers and for CPD priority programmes.

1.2 The CPD Design

CPD is a part of life-long learning used to update teachers with new methodologies and teaching practices that improves the quality of classroom instruction. In Ethiopia, teachers following pre-service programmes are required to do two years induction professional training. After completing the induction training, each teacher must take part in planned CPD for a minimum of sixty hours each year.

Newly deployed teachers are expected to work through a two year induction programme, produced at national level and supported by mentors. There are four components to the induction programme:

- Professional Development—this component contains activities that the new teacher will carry out to develop their expertise in the classroom.
- Action Research—this is recognised as a valuable method of enabling teachers to improve their practice by evaluating their teaching and what is happening in their classrooms. The projects planned in this induction programme will develop the new teacher's action research skills.
- Professional Appraisal—these are formal meetings and discussions between a new teacher and a mentor, in which evidence of the new teacher's performance is reviewed. These meetings will form the basis upon which it will be decided whether the teacher gains their full license.
- Classroom observations (part of Professional Development)— these will be carried out by the mentor. Feedback from these observations will guide the teacher's professional development.

All other teachers were expected to carry out the CPD programme produced at national level. This programme consists of three course books which teachers worked through in small groups within clusters of schools. Each course consisted of three units covering aspects of teaching and learning and school ethos. The groups were designed to be led by facilitators, usually selected from experienced members of the school staff. The expectation was that these groups would meet at least two hours every week.

1.3 Challenges and Problems of CPD

In 2008, a study, conducted by MoE in collaboration with Haromya University, examined the structure of the CPD system and the progresses that had been made. The study came up with important findings that illuminated the then status of CPD. The major findings showed that in most of the visited schools, maximum of which were rural schools, CPD had not been structured adequately.

The major findings were as follows:

- The study generally revealed that in nearly four out of five schools the structure of CPD was either absent or inadequate.
- Nearly all (29 of 31) CRCs (Cluster Resource Centres) sampled were not adequately prepared to run well-organised, inspiring and transforming CPD activities.
- In schools where CPD had begun, teachers were however able to demonstrate a reasonable mastery of the contents (of the CPD courses) they had covered before and up to the time of the study.

The study also identified the following six major challenges:

- Failure to synchronise the career structure and the CPD values and activities.
- CPD facilitators' high turnover.
- Time constraints on teachers as well as their school leaders.
- CPD programme's lagging behind its time and the tendency of rushing to cover the course.
- Total absence or inadequacy of the minimum resources required to run CPD.
- Lack of systematic collaboration and coordination between Education Bureaus, TEIs and NGOs.

Among the challenges mentioned above facilitators' turnover, time constraints and inadequacy of minimum resources are the most pertinent problems that rural teachers faced in implementing the CPD programme.

Section 2: The Initiation of the New CPD Framework

The 2008 study that examined the structure and implementation of the then CPD programme came up with the following recommendations.

- The MoE, together with the regional, zonal and woreda (district) education offices should develop a clear, transparent and self-controlling CPD structure which clearly stipulates terms of references

for responsibilities on how CPD should be run, evaluated and improved.
- The goals and objectives of the CPD programme should be clearly defined and delineated so that stakeholders build shared visions and understanding among themselves and there is no room for ambiguities, uncertainties or excuses for not implementing it.
- CPD structure and outcomes should be regularly monitored and evaluated. The existing collaboration between TEIs (Teacher Education Institutes) and schools through practicum could be used to develop monitoring and assessment systems for CPD.
- A Guideline must be produced to synchronise CPD with the career structure.
- Raising awareness of CPD at schools and teacher level is important.

Furthermore, different studies, such as the national learning assessments study, conducted in two yearly intervals have shown that students' achievements were far from the national standard. According to the national standard, students are expected to score at least 50 per cent in the achievement tests. The situation was more serious in mathematics and science subjects. Realising this, in 2009 the MoE in collaboration with the Japan International Cooperation Agency (JICA) conducted a study to examine the then situation of teaching and learning of mathematics and science in grade 7 and 8. The study also investigated the skill gaps in teaching science and mathematics among teachers. This study has come up with the following findings.

- In most cases, the teaching methods employed in schools are still teacher-centred, despite the fact that training was offered to many Maths and Science teachers on 'active learning' or 'student-centred approach' in PRESET and INSET programmes.
- Student participation in the teaching and learning process is very limited due to the fact that inadequate practical activities arose from lack of chemicals, laboratory equipment, teaching learning aids etc.
- Teachers lack the necessary facilitation skills such as properly structuring and leading group discussion, question and answer activities, demonstration, etc.
- Teachers use very limited assessment techniques (Question and Answer methods or assignment or written test), which may not be

enough to measure the progress of students' knowledge, attitude and skills.
- The instructional medium (English) is acting as a barrier to effective learning. That is, due to a communication gap, sometimes learning contents could not be understood by the students. Consequently their performance is usually low.
- Teachers do not use teaching and learning aids adequately, because of shortage of resources, lack of skills and lack of improvisation skills.
- Although teachers have got used to preparing annual plans and weekly/daily lesson plans, more efforts have to be paid to the quality of them. Teachers do not exercise good lesson planning that enables them to make their lessons effective.
- Teachers sometimes face problems in understanding their subject content.
- There is recognition from the teachers' and the students' sides that co-curricular activities would help to develop a positive attitude in learning Maths and Science subjects. However, the implementation is seen only in some schools.

The study has also come up with the following recommendations:

- Teachers should receive more practical training continuously in order for them to be able to understand and to use 'active learning' in Maths and Science lessons. In this way, they can also take advantage of the existing system, such as the CPD programme.
- Teachers should be capable of employing practical work/experiments and problem solving methods which could help to promote the development of the scientific inquiry skills and mathematical skills.
- Teachers need to have adequate facilitation skills to carry out lively explorative group discussion among the students. Their questioning techniques should also promote higher order thinking, such as applying, analysing, evaluating and creating.
- In order to develop positive attitudes and interests in students towards Maths and Science (M&S) subjects, formative assessment should be encouraged. In addition, particularly for M&S subjects,

assessment techniques such as, practical work and project work should be practiced. This could help to develop the psychomotor (skill) domain of students.

The recommendations of the two studies were used as a basis for developing a new framework for CPD. The new CPD framework was developed in 2009 with the objective of providing teachers throughout Ethiopia with a clear structure and rationale for CPD. It was developed based on the best national and international practice and designed to function in the Ethiopian context. The framework links teachers' career ladder with their professional competencies and appraisal. In this framework, CPD is considered to be delivered through two modalities. These are school-based CPD and Cluster-based CPD.

2.1 School-based CPD

Schools are responsible for the organisation and management of school-based CPD. Even though, teachers participate in cluster training programme, they should exchange experience and support each other based on the context of their own schools. At CRC level, the training and support is general but each school has its own need and problems to be solved. The framework states that:

> CPD needs to be conducted in school settings and linked to school wide efforts. Teachers work with each other, observing each other, planning lessons together, team teaching and undertaking action research together. The importance of teachers talking together about their practice cannot be exaggerated. These processes need to be frequent and regular within the school. (MoE, 2009)

As mentioned in the above principle, schools are required to identify key issues that challenge the school's teaching and learning process. They are required to prioritise problems according to their impact on the quality of the class room instruction and prepare appropriate trainings. Teachers are expected to identify their needs based on the school priorities and plan their own CPD plan. Each department should do the same thing with members of the department.

In addition to the school activities, each school, has to share the national and regional priorities with all teachers and integrate them into the work of the institutions with their own priorities. It is the responsibility of school leaders to implement school based CPD by creating a conducive environment in their schools. In this regard, the framework clearly states that:

> The role of the institution's leadership is crucial. Institution leaders have to recognize themselves as educational leaders and must be involved in the identification of the institutional CPD needs and the planning of activities. Leaders must also be involved in the CPD activities, and conduct formal professional discussions with staff. (MoE, 2009)

In school based CPD, the induction programme for newly deployed teachers provides action research, experience sharing among teachers within the same school and classroom observation. In Cluster-based CPD updating trainings designed at a national level are covered. School improvement programmes, English language improvement programme, trainings designed to improve M&S classroom instruction are some of the main programmes included in this modality. The framework has explicitly indicated the roles and responsibilities of CPD stakeholders as follows:

Teachers are responsible for
- engaging in their own CPD throughout their careers;
- in consultation with others (for example, mentor, supervisor), identifying personal CPD needs in the light of the institution's Annual CPD Plan and individual Professional Competencies;
- working collaboratively with colleagues to improve teaching and learning;
- carrying out sixty hours CPD each year;
- putting CPD into practice in the classroom;
- being committed to supporting the wider CPD needs of their institution;
- maintaining a Professional Portfolio to record all their CPD and other professional activities.

School leaders are responsible for
- ensuring that learning and student achievement is inclusive, and at the centre of strategic planning and resource management;
- creating a CPD management strategy within the institution;
- ensuring that an effective CPD needs analysis is carried out each year;

- together with colleagues, identifying issues for consideration as CPD priorities;
- ensuring that the institution/department/faculty produces an Annual CPD Plan and manages the budget;
- regularly monitoring the effectiveness of the changes to teaching and learning;
- ensuring the quality of engagement of teachers in CPD activities, monitoring and assessing the content of individual Professional Portfolios and giving constructive feedback;
- collaborating with other local institutional leaders to facilitate effective responses to shared CPD issues;
- collaborating with woreda, zone and REB professionals to ensure that national and regional CPD priorities are addressed in institutional CPD planning;
- taking part in regional and national CPD activities which ensure that their own knowledge and experience is up-to-date;
- ensuring that all teachers in schools take part in sixty hours of CPD activities each year.

Clusters are responsible for
- establishing and supporting the Cluster CPD Committee;
- managing and coordinating CPD activities within the cluster;
- collating and sharing individual school CPD plans;
- supporting, as appropriate, the Annual School CPD plans;
- supporting Teachers' Professional Portfolio development;
- providing opportunities for collaboration and the sharing of good practice within the cluster, for example, samples of good lessons, effective teaching strategies, innovative use of readily available materials for practical lessons, etc.;
- making resources available for cluster schools to use in the classroom;
- providing training opportunities as required;
- supporting the delivery of the Induction Programme for Newly Deployed Teachers;
- supporting inclusive education;
- reporting annually to the woreda on cluster CPD activities;
- maintaining an effective communication system between all the schools.

Woreda and Sub-City Education Offices are responsible for
- annually producing local CPD plans;
- ensuring that all schools have annual CPD plans;
- monitoring and evaluating the CPD activities of schools;
- collecting data about CPD activities in the woreda/sub-city;
- collecting data of individuals' and schools' participation in CPD;
- providing support and training to clusters and schools via the supervisors;
- raising awareness of and promoting inclusive education in all schools;
- collaborating with school directors to administer the 'Induction' CPD process and to moderate the judgments on passing/failing;
- providing support and advice on the maintenance of professional portfolios;
- overseeing and facilitating the work of clusters and kebeles (lowest administrative part of the government next to woreda) in their support of the CPD effort.

Regional Education Bureaus/Zones are responsible for
- analysing and identifying regional priorities, production of materials and delivering training to implement them;
- sharing information with all stakeholders;
- annually producing and circulating regional CPD plans;
- appointing a responsible person for CPD;
- allocating the resources needed to implement the regional CPD programme including the development of Teachers' Professional Portfolios;
- ensuring that resources are written in the language that teachers will understand best, with high quality translation, produced in sufficient quantities (minimum ratio of 1 booklet to 20 teachers) and distributed throughout the region;
- monitoring and evaluating the CPD programme regionally and producing an annual report which should be submitted to the Process for Teachers and Leaders Development, MoE;
- raising awareness of and promoting inclusive education throughout the region through CPD;
- overseeing and facilitating the work of CTEs in their support of the CPD effort;

- giving support to woredas, zones and sub-cities within the region;
- compiling Educational Management Information System (EMIS) CPD statistics for the region and submitting them annually to the MoE.

The MoE is responsible for
- analysing and identifying national priorities, production of materials and organising training to implement them;
- annually producing and circulating national CPD plans;
- raising awareness of the need for CPD;
- designing, implementing and reviewing the National Framework for CPD;
- monitoring and evaluating the CPD programme nationally and producing an annual report;
- producing support materials to be used throughout the Federal Republic;
- helping to increase capacity by training trainers;
- raising awareness of and promoting inclusive education through CPD;
- collating and reporting EMIS CPD statistics;
- producing an Annual CPD Plan for employees of the MoE;
- giving support to regions;
- conducting consultation meetings on achievements and challenges (MoE, 2009).

Since the development of the new framework many activities have been accomplished both from school- and cluster-based CPD programmes. The activities of school-based programmes are by and large a preparation for implementation which include the development of needs-based CPD materials.

The CPD materials so far developed includes:
- Primary school science module
- Primary school mathematics module
- Training tips for science module
- Training tips for mathematics module
- Classroom management

- Training tips for classroom management module
- Continuous assessment module
- Training tips for Continuous assessment module
- Mentoring
- Practical skills in mentoring
- Portfolio with toolkits

2.2 Cluster-based CPD

Teaching skill gaps, instructional problems, and other issues related to the quality of classroom instruction common to all teachers in the country which are commonly known to the system as national priorities are considered in Cluster-based CPD. One good example is the CPD programme designed to improve the quality of primary school M&S classroom instruction. It is a pilot project named 'Strengthening Mathematics and Science Education in Ethiopia' (SMASEE) that was designed in collaboration with JICA. This project was designed in response to the problems identified by the national learning assessment and other studies. According to these studies, students' performance of primary M&S was poor and less than the national standard, teaching method was chalk & talk, teacher centred and insufficient introduction on activities, and students were passive participants in the classroom (MoE, 2010). The aim of the project was to establish a model of the CPD system for grade 7 and 8 primary school M&S teachers.

2.3 Administrative and Training Structures of the Pilot Programme

Similar administrative structures were in use which extends from the federal to woreda levels. The federal level administrative structure is as shown in Table 6.1.

The Regional administrative structure is as indicated in the Table 6.2 and has a similar outline with that of the federal level.

At Wereda level, administrative structure indicated in the Table 6.3 is in use.

In a similar manner the training structure was formed at different levels. In general the training structure follows a cascade model which emanated from federal to cluster level.

Table 6.1
The federal level administrative structure

Name of Bodies/Units	Responsibilities	Actors
National Steering Committee (NSC)	• To be responsible for overall project decisions. • To work towards implementation and institutionalization of regular INSET.	The State Minister of General Education, other high level officials, Head of REBs & JICA.
National Coordinating Unit (NCU)	• To coordinate overall project. • To conduct National INSET. • To develop work plan. • To carry out regular communication with stakeholders of the project.	Process Owner of TELDCP, Process Owner of CDICP and 8 MoE Officials & JICA.
National Trainers (NTs)	• To develop training materials. • To conduct National INSET session. • To develop M&E tools. • To support Regional trainers.	8 MoE officers as full time National Trainers and 8 part-time National Trainers.

Source: MoE, 2010.

Table 6.2
The regional level administrative structure

Name of Bodies/Units	Responsibilities	Actors
Regional Steering Committee (RSC)	• To be responsible for the implementation of the project activities in each region. • To approve disbursement of funds. • To work towards implementing & institutionalising regular Regional INSET.	Bureau Head, Rep. Bureau of Finance, Other Process Owners, Deans of CTEs and Rep. of NCU, JICA Experts, Regional Coordinator (Secretary).

(Table 6.2 Continued)

(Table 6.2 Continued)

Name of Bodies/Units	Responsibilities	Actors
Regional Coordinating Unit (RCU)	• To coordinate Regional INSET activities. • To prepare the work plan. • To conduct M&E of INSET. • To develop bi-annual report. • To prepare the framework for implementing & institutionalizing regular INSET.	Process Owner of TELDCP (Regional Coordinator), Process Owner of CDICP, 4 Subject specialists from TELDCP and CDICP, Rep. of CTEs, Rep. of NCU, Experts of TDP (Secretary).
Regional Trainers (RTs)	• To participate in National INSET. • To conduct Regional INSET session. • To conduct M&E and prepare reports. • To support KTs' activities at CRCs.	Lecturers from CTEs, REB officers, Secondary School Teachers and Upper Teachers.

Source: MoE, 2010.

Table 6.3
The Wereda level administrative structure

Name of Bodies/Units	Responsibilities	Actors
Woreda Coordinating Unit (WCU)	• To select Key Teachers from CRCs. • To sensitise stakeholders of schools to the importance of M&S. • To give necessary support to CRC schools and satellite schools for the effective implementation of training of M&S teachers. • To promote activities related to M&S.	1. Experts of Teacher Development Process 2. Curriculum Expert 3. Woreda Supervisor * At first, WCU will be established in SMASEE pilot zone.

(Table 6.3 Continued)

(Table 6.3 Continued)

Name of Bodies/Units	Responsibilities	Actors
Key Teachers (KTs)	• To participate in regional INSET. • To conduct trainings at CRC and school levels. • To provide technical support to school teachers in M&S. • To facilitate the M&S related activities at CRC and school levels.	Proposed criteria for selection of KTs are: 1. Minimum qualification of Diploma 2. Must be a professional in M&S 3. Must have minimum 5 years teaching experience * 4 KTs (Math., Phy., Chem., Bio.) will be selected from CRC in pilot zone

Source: MoE, 2010.

Figures 6.1 and 6.2 show the detailed training structures at different levels.

So far, the project has developed a three-year training curriculum as given in Table 6.4 based on the needs assessment conducted at the beginning of the project.

Figure 6.1
Detailed training structure at federal level

16 National Trainers
(8 full time NTs and 8 part-time NTs)

272 Regional Trainers
(Amhara: 96 [8 x 9 SMASEE zone + 24 x 1 SMASEE pilot zone])
(Oromia: 160 [8 x 17 SMASEE zone + 24 x 1 SMASEE pilot zone])
(Addis Ababa)

Source: MoE, 2010.

Figure 6.2
Detailed training structure at region level

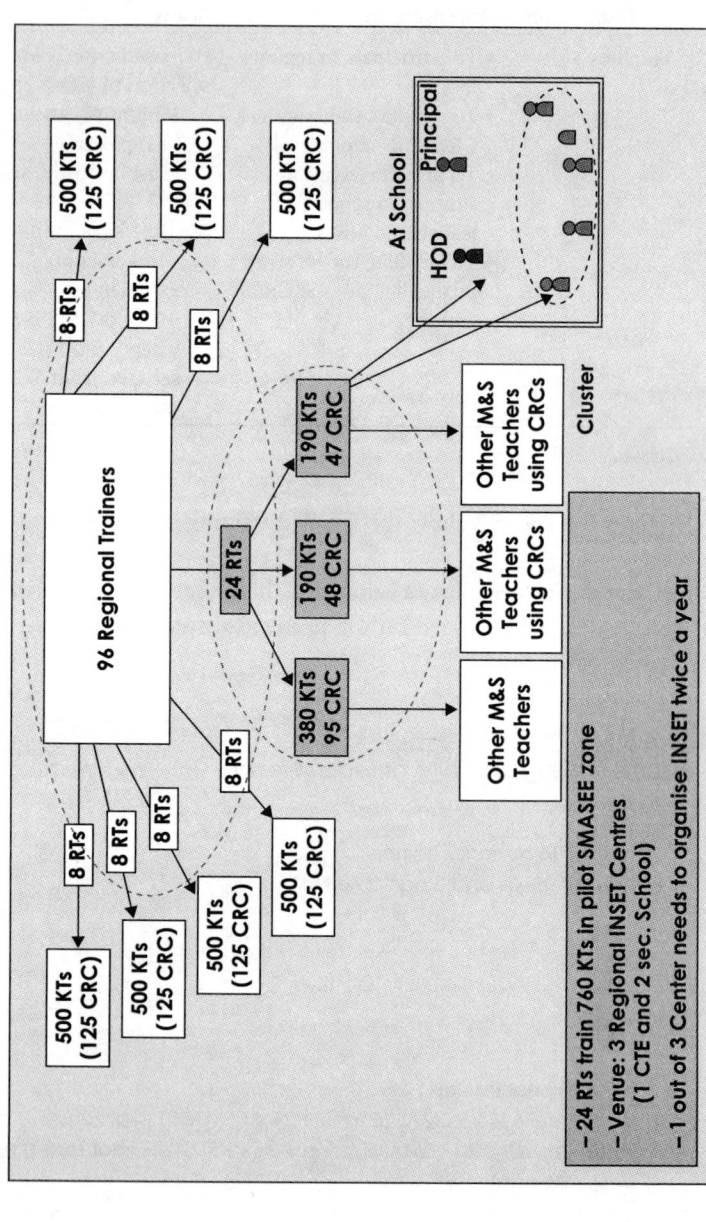

Source: MoE, 2010.

Table 6.4
Three-year training curriculum

	Year 1	Year 2	Year 3
Overall objective	To enable RTs to train and KTs to actualise 'active learning lesson' in G 7&8 M&S lessons through planning lessons effectively, using appropriate teaching methods, facilitation and assessment skills as well as effective use of Teaching and Learning (T&L) materials.		
Areas/issues to be covered	1. Lesson planning (**P**) 2. Teaching methods (e.g., practical work, experiment and problem solving) in order to cultivate students' scientific inquiry skills and mathematical skills (Activity-based and Student-centred methods: **AS**) 3. Facilitation skills for instructional activities (**F**) 4. Assessment techniques for student's learning (**A**) 5. Communication skills (**C**) 6. Use of T&L materials for better lesson delivery (**T**)		
Focus/emphasis	• Lesson planning (**P**) • Teaching methods (**AS**)	• Use of **T&L** materials (**T**) • Facilitation skills (**F**) • Communication skills (**C**)	• Assessment skills for student's learning (**A**)
Theme	**Lesson planning and teaching methodology** for 'active learning' in M&S lessons.	Enriching M&S lessons with effective use of T&L materials and facilitation skills.	Sustaining good M&S lessons with updating lesson study (LS) (Reflection and evaluation).

(Table 6.4 Continued)

(Table 6.4 Continued)

	Year 1	Year 2	Year 3
Objectives	The participants will be able to: • Describe 'active learning' in M&S lessons. • Define LS approach. • Prepare, implement and evaluate 'active learning' M&S lessons through LS approach.	The participants will be able to: • Identify appropriate T&L materials for M&S lessons. • Improvise necessary T&L materials to M&S lessons. • Utilise the T&L materials effectively. • Practice and update LS.	The participants will be able to: • Use assessment to improve T&L process. • Practice and update LS.
Contents/sessions	• Introduction to active learning and its methods for M&S lessons (e.g. group work, experiment, demonstration, project work, etc.). • Introduction to LS approach. • Implementation of LS by subject groups. • Lesson planning and evaluation.	• Type of T&L materials. • Improvisation of T&L materials. • Facilitation and communication skills. • Implementation of LS.	• Assessment techniques for T&L. • Implementation of assessment. • Self-evaluation/reflection. • Implementation of LS.

Source: MoE, 2010.

Table 6.4
Three-year training curriculum

	Year 1	Year 2	Year 3
Overall objective	To enable RTs to train and KTs to actualise 'active learning lesson' in G 7&8 M&S lessons through planning lessons effectively, using appropriate teaching methods, facilitation and assessment skills as well as effective use of Teaching and Learning (T&L) materials.		
Areas/issues to be covered	1. Lesson planning (**P**) 2. Teaching methods (e.g., practical work, experiment and problem solving) in order to cultivate students' scientific inquiry skills and mathematical skills (Activity-based and Student-centred methods: **AS**) 3. Facilitation skills for instructional activities (**F**) 4. Assessment techniques for student's learning (**A**) 5. Communication skills (**C**) 6. Use of T&L materials for better lesson delivery (**T**)		
Focus/emphasis	• Lesson planning (**P**) • Teaching methods (**AS**)	• Use of T&L materials (**T**) • Facilitation skills (**F**) • Communication skills (**C**)	• Assessment skills for student's learning (**A**)
Theme	**Lesson planning and teaching methodology** for 'active learning' in M&S lessons.	Enriching M&S lessons with effective use of T&L materials and facilitation skills.	Sustaining good M&S lessons with updating lesson study (LS) (Reflection and evaluation).

(Table 6.4 Continued)

(Table 6.4 Continued)

	Year 1	Year 2	Year 3
Objectives	The participants will be able to: • Describe 'active learning' in M&S lessons. • Define LS approach. • Prepare, implement and evaluate 'active learning' M&S lessons through LS approach.	The participants will be able to: • Identify appropriate T&L materials for M&S lessons. • Improvise necessary T&L materials to M&S lessons. • Utilise the T&L materials effectively. • Practice and update LS.	The participants will be able to: • Use assessment to improve T&L process. • Practice and update LS.
Contents/sessions	• Introduction to active learning and its methods for M&S lessons (e.g., group work, experiment, demonstration, project work, etc.). • Introduction to LS approach. • Implementation of LS by subject groups. • Lesson planning and evaluation.	• Type of T&L materials. • Improvisation of T&L materials. • Facilitation and communication skills. • Implementation of LS.	• Assessment techniques for T&L. • Implementation of assessment. • Self-evaluation/reflection. • Implementation of LS.

Source: MoE, 2010.

From the curriculum above the first and second year curriculum were implemented in 2011 and 2012 respectively. The formative evaluation made at the end of the first year implementation indicates that teachers were happy with the training and had started using the skills and knowledge they gained from the training. In some schools students achieved better results than the year before.

This promising and positive result encouraged the government to scale up and implement it at a national level. A permanent new administrative structure which is responsible to the nationwide implementation has been established at a federal and directorate level. Establishments of similar administrative units at regional level have already started and plan to be completed by August 2013.

Section 3: The Concept and the Rationale: Establishing CRCs in Ethiopia

The main objective of the school is to promote quality education by creating an effective school. Scheerens (1992) stated that '[i]n educational discussion, the term "effective" is often associated with the quality of education' (3). Similarly Elliott (2001) suggested that, the major elements of effective schools are strong student achievement, instructional leadership, well-defined goals, training decisions, sense of order, monitoring student achievement, academic progress, and other effective school activities. Coleman (1994) also stated that 'Leadership is consistently recognized as being a vital factor in school effectiveness' (67). Therefore, where resources are scarce governments often establish cluster systems in order to create effective schools.

The concept of Clustering Schools was introduced in the 1950s (Khaniya, 1997). Different countries use different terms for CRCs. These are CRC, school CRC, zones, complexes, school learning cells, clusters or satellite schools, etc., (Khaniya, 1997). In Ethiopia, the CRCs' system started in collaboration with the BESO (Basic Education System Overhaul, a project supported by USAID working on primary school education) and UNICEF in 1995 and 1998 respectively as a pilot project in different regions in the country (MoE, 2001). After four years of this pilot project, the importance of establishing CRCs became clear and well received by stakeholders. The MoE accepted it as an approach and used them to implement a CPD programme and expanded it all over the country.

The main objective of CRCs is also to improve the quality of education. It has four other purposes: pedagogical, economical, administrative and political (Bredenberg and Dahal, 2000).

Pedagogical Purpose: The pedagogical purpose mainly focuses on teachers' professional development. According to Villegas-Reimers (2003: 29),

> Successful professional development opportunities for teachers have a significant positive effect on students' performance and learning. Thus, when the goal is to increase students' learning and to improve their performance, the professional development of teachers should be considered a key factor, and this at the same time must feature as an element in a larger reform.

These include enriching curriculum materials, improving measurement skills, supporting teachers through supervision, sharing school experience, conducting monitoring and evaluation, promoting active learning, practicing action research, producing educational media, improving teachers' motivation, improving special needs education and preventing HIV/AIDS (Villegas-Reimers, 2003; EQUIP1, 2004).

Economic Purpose: The economic purpose focuses on sharing materials or resources, utilising allocated budget, and raising funds for different activities. Sharing of experts and resources between schools enhances the in-service training of teachers (Grauwe, 2001). Bredenberg and Dahal (2000: 2) also suggested:

> The sharing of resources, both material and human, is usually one of the most central functions in a cluster. This function has a strong bearing on a number of other goals variously adopted by school clusters in many different settings. For example, sharing personnel between member schools for the purpose of teacher education, test development, and other capacity building activities enables those schools that lack a strong human resource base to access more experienced personnel.

Political purpose: The political purpose has two dimensions: achieving EFA goals and involving communities in education. As mentioned above, all countries are committed to achieve EFA goals by 2015. This needs a political commitment. The other dimensions of community involvement are sending children to schools, reducing drop-out rates, enhancing girls' education, enriching the curriculum, supporting financially, solving school and teacher's problems, and strengthening school and community linkage.

Administrative purpose: This focuses on establishing a well-organised information system, solving different problems, improving the management system of a school, motivating and apprising teachers' performance, and distributing educational materials (AREB, 2005; Khaniya, 1997). It is difficult for students and teachers to facilitate learning without textbooks and educational materials. In most cases, textbook and educational materials will not reach schools quickly. Therefore, Resource Centres play an important role in distributing the necessary materials to schools. According to Khaniya (1997: 61),

> the use of the resource centres to distribute textbooks to children and educational materials to cluster schools would be very useful. Since the RCs [CRCs] are centrally located, schools would find it easier to ask their students to get books in time if they were distributed through the RCs [CRCs]. In addition to textbooks, other educational materials can also be supplied to cluster schools through the same channel.

Based on the international experience, we developed a chart as given in Figure 6.3.

As indicated in the chart, pedagogical objectives include capacity building, curriculum development, continuous assessment, supervision, experience sharing, monitoring and evaluation, CPD, action research, teacher motivation, special needs, and HIV/AIDS. The economic objectives comprise of resource sharing and utilisation, monitoring of school finance, income generating, and utilisation of professional linkage.

Administrative objectives include: gathering and organising information, solving problems, performance evaluation, and facilitating administrative benefits. To achieve EFA goals and to create community linkage are some of the political objectives of CRCs.

To make these objectives effective, the CRCs' supervisors are assigned these tasks in each of the CRCs. The supervisors have roles and responsibilities of executing CRCs' objectives.

Figure 6.3
Four objectives of CRCs

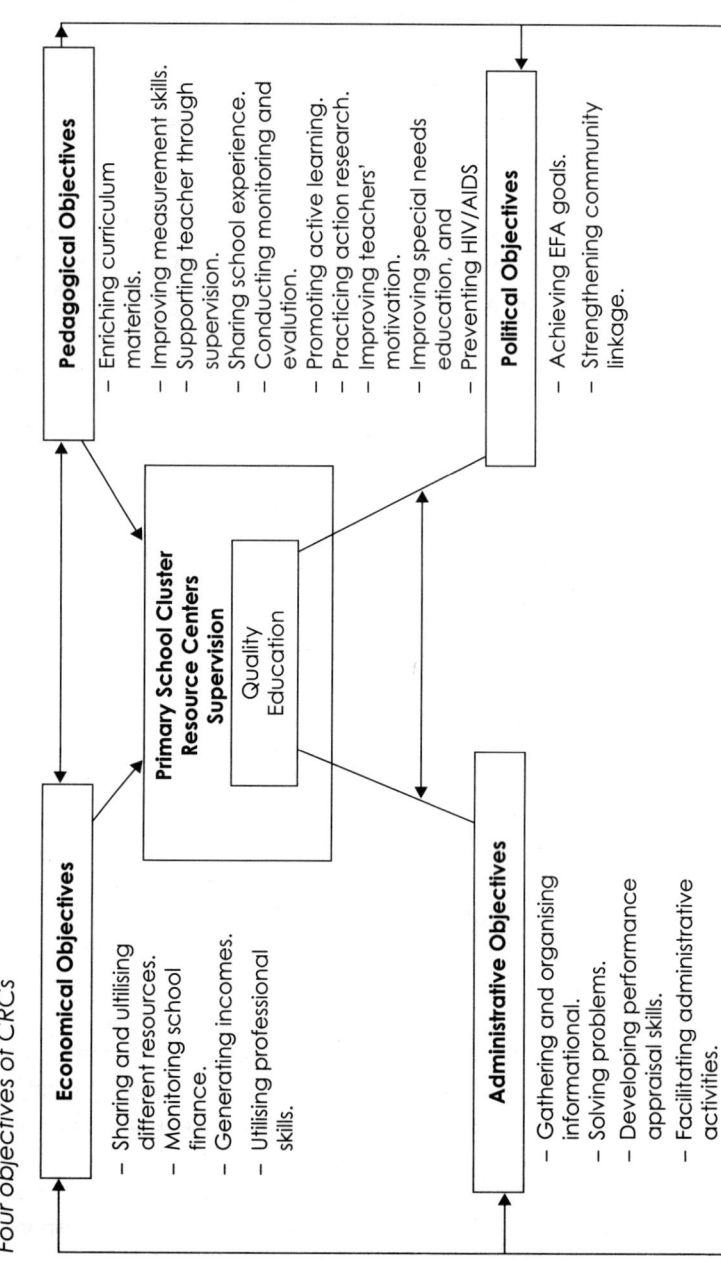

Source: Adapted from AREB CRCs' objective model (AREB, 2005).

The research findings stated that School Clusters will be established by one of the following two initiatives:

> In some countries, school clusters are born of the professional needs of individual head teachers and emerge through grass-roots initiatives (Bell, 1988). In others, they are mainly imposed by the central level. In either case, they are advocated particularly for dealing with the question of school-based management with respect to relatively small schools. (Perera, 2000: 78)

These two modalities took the initiative because there were growing demands of teachers as well as educational institutes to improve quality. However, there were scarce resources to improve the quality of education. To maintain this quality education, it is very important to establish a system to enhance professional development and other activities which bring quality education.

According to MoE (2001: 4–5), the rationale to establish CRCs is

> once teachers were trained and placed in the teaching profession, there was no in-built, systematic arrangement by which their professional upgrading/ updating could be facilitated. This is one of the main reasons why teachers have not adopted more widely the 'new' learning approaches. There is an urgent need to introduce this more up-to-date, learner-centered methodology in the classroom in order to: make the curriculum more flexible; make curriculum content more relevant to the local environment, and to the present and future needs of the learners; produce materials that are learner-centered and match the demands of the curriculum.

Section 4: The Organisational Model of CRCs

Different countries use different types of School Cluster organisational models. The most commonly used models are hierarchical, horizontal and hybrid.

Hierarchical model: It is highly centralised and employs a top-down way of communication. The centre school or CRC is responsible for all kinds of the School Cluster's functions, 'the RC [CRC] was, from the very beginning, expected to provide a broad range of services. It had to mobilise its human and physical resources to cater for the needs of the satellite schools and the non-formal classes (Khaniya, 1997: 22). It also serves as the training venue for CPD, administration and information dissemination (MoE, 2001). The model is useful for the centre to be equipped with different materials so as to monitor and support satellite schools. However, the model doesn't encourage satellite schools to act according to their needs and to solve their problems.

Horizontal model: It is a less centralised type of communication between the centre and the satellites. The centre is considered as a satellite and there is the opportunity to make contact with other schools, the centre as well as the satellites (MoE, 2001). All the schools, including the centre, share the resources equally and have equal responsibilities. It is difficult to manage this model because 'there is no central coordination and schools may limit their activities and resources to themselves' (AREB, 2005).

Hybrid model: This model is a combination of the hierarchical and horizontal models. The centre school will manage the administrative functions and the programme. It also serves as a centre of communication between schools. The challenge is that all member schools should share the resources and play an active role to perform the CRCs' functions. In the infant stage of CRCs, Ethiopia used the hierarchal model; currently it is practicing the hybrid model.

In Ethiopia, three to five schools are clustered in rural areas and two to three schools in urban areas (AREB, 2005; MoE, 2001). This depends on the numbers of teachers and proximity of schools to each other. It may also be difficult to cluster few schools because of their distance from the centre school. In this case, direct support will be given by Woreda Education Offices which work to strengthen the pedagogical centres of the schools.

In most cases, the training programme of CRCs follows a cascade model. Drawing regional trainers, they receive training at Federal level. Regional trainers will share their experience, knowledge and skills to key teachers at the regional level. About seven key teachers are selected based on their performance and training facilitation skills in each CRC. These key teachers will also train teachers in their respective CRCs. The M&S cascading training model is indicated in Figure 6.4 as an example.

Figure 6.4
The mathematics and science cascading training model

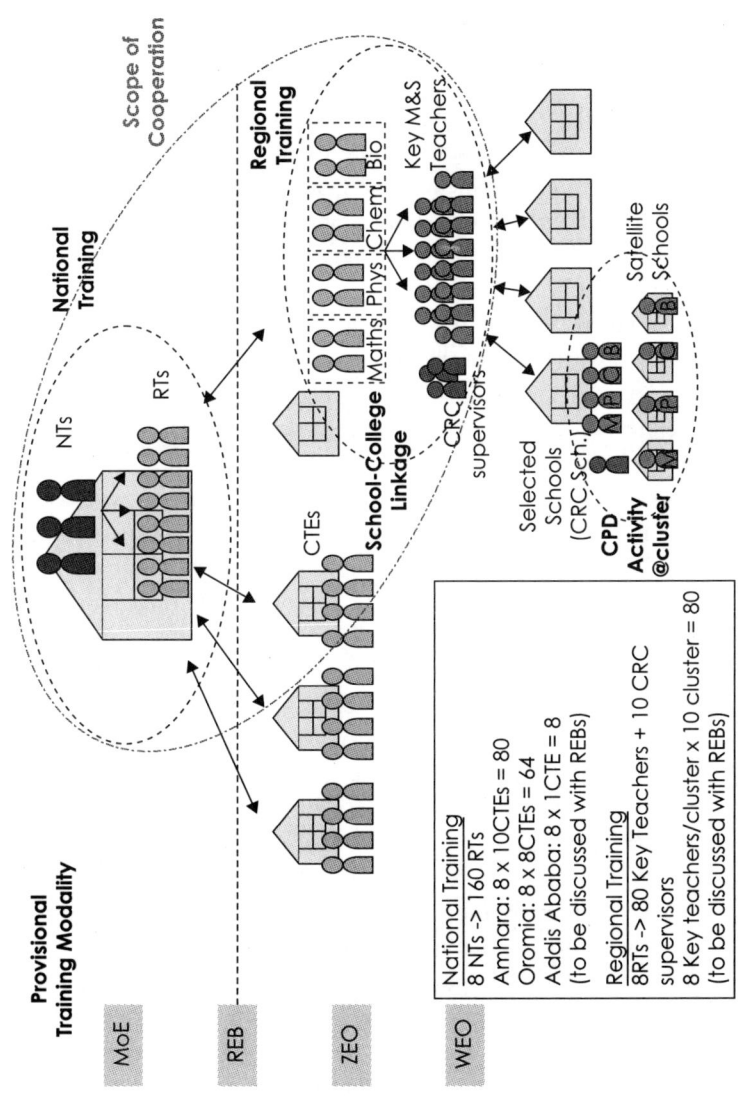

Source: MoE, 2010.

As explained in Section 2 of this chapter, the SMASEE project introduces training and administrative structures emanated from federal to school level. This structure is adapted to the national CPD programme. The administration at the national level is led by an administrative unit organised at a directorate level. The directorate has permanent staff who follow the day-to-day activities of the national programme.

At Regional level a similar unit to the federal is established with permanent staff responsible to the regional CPD programme. This unit will have regional permanent trainers and part timers selected from Teachers' Colleges and schools in the region and will receive their training at national level.

At woreda level, a focal person is assigned to follow and support the day to day activities of the CRCs in the woreda. CRCs are led by CRC's supervisor. Training at CRCs is provided by key teachers selected from satellite schools and trained at regional level. These key teachers are selected based on their experience and performance in the school. The school principal together with the cluster supervisor will do the selection. Each CRC has a limited annual budget that covers training.

CRCs are supposed to be used as the nearest training centre for the schools. Teachers of the satellite school receive their national training at the CRC. These CRCs are also used as a resource centre for teachers of satellite schools to share their experience with their colleagues, make their teaching aids using resources in the centre, and disseminate their success stories and best practices. Teachers from nearby schools use the centre at any time convenient to them. But, for trainings and workshops the centre will arrange times suitable to all teachers in the satellite schools. Most of the time the trainings and the workshops are arranged during weekends and semester breaks.

The other service the CRCs provide to the satellite school is the follow-up support. After each training and workshop, the cluster supervisor visits satellite schools to support teachers. One supervisor assigned at a cluster is supposed to support teachers in five schools. The supervisor is expected to visit a school at least once in a week. During the visit the supervisor has meetings with teachers, school management and students. The meetings, particularly with teachers, held after a series of classroom observations focus primarily on the classroom interactions among teacher and students.

These supervisors' support is very much appreciated by teachers. The reports of field visit done by the regional education bureaus and federal MoE reveal that teachers are positive to supervisors' visits and witnessed that they have improved their teaching skills as a result of the visits.

Section 5: Monitor and Support of CRCs: The Supervision in CRCs

In earlier times, the supervision system was based on district education offices. Each district education office had two or three supervisors. These supervisors had no capacity and time to support more than 30 schools in the districts. They gave supervision support one or two times in each school in the academic year. This was also more focused on inspection rather than support. To minimise, if not to alleviate, this situation, it was decided to bring supervision support closer to schools by assigning a supervisor in each CRC.

Cluster supervisors' role: The CRCs objectives can be fulfilled when there is a strong supervision and support system. Supervision plays a great role in making schools effective and improving the quality of education. Khaniya (1997: 23) suggested that 'it [supervision] was also supposed to provide teachers with the necessary professional support; supportive supervision of the schools in the cluster area was the most important activity of the RC [CRCs]'. The CRCs' support system has a great role to play in improving the quality of education. The supervisors have to perform their tasks, fulfilling the CRCs' objectives. To achieve these objectives, they are performing the following major tasks:

CPD: As mentioned earlier, professional development is a key factor for teachers' performance. To update teachers with new methodologies, supervisors are expected to train teachers continuously. Supervisors are coordinating CPD programmes in their assigned CRCs. This function also includes disseminating new ideas, providing in-service training, and promoting action research, active learning methods, curriculum enrichment, etc.

School visits: One of the major tasks of supervisors is school visits. Supervisors visit schools regularly for the continuous support of teachers. When they visit schools, they observe teaching as well as other aspects of classroom functioning. They sit with the teachers and discuss the problems that they face in carrying out classroom activities systematically. Some of the visits are full, short or a follow-up visit. In 'full supervision', the supervisor will focus on classroom observations, feedback meetings and discussions which take place each week. This is followed by a regular report.

Report: After every activity or school visit, supervisors prepare and submit reports to the Woreda Education Office.

Advice and guidance: Supervisors identify strengths and weaknesses in the performance of teachers and head teachers. Based on this, they give advice and guidance to teachers and head teachers.

Sharing of experience: Supervisors identify the best practice of individual teachers and institutions and coordinate experience sharing among teachers and schools.

Teachers' motivation: One of the supervisors' roles is to motivate teachers by creating a conducive environment for work and appreciating their work. This will enhance teachers' involvement in CRCs' activities and will promote their classroom teaching.

Section 6: Effectiveness of the CRCs

As mentioned earlier in this chapter, CPD as a programme was introduced to the system in 1995. Since then, much has been done to strengthen and expand it to all administrative regions of the country. But, due to different reasons primarily related to lack of awareness about the programme among teachers, school leaders and other educational personnel the programme was not as effective as it was designed. Through time, the CRC model created a learning environment for teachers. Nowadays, sharing experiences and supporting each other in schools and CRCs has increased among teachers.

In earlier times, the focus of CPD was limited to an induction programme for newly deployed teachers and proper CPD that covers three generic materials. Gradually, demand increased from different stakeholders particularly the government which stipulates the focus to specific areas like English language, Science and Mathematics improvement programmes. The first organised cluster based intervention was the SMASEE. It was a pilot project planned to be implemented in some school of one city and two national regional states. The training in these programmes was planned to be delivered to the classroom teachers at CRCs level. Therefore, it was necessary to establish strong CRCs at these pilot regions. The regional education bureaus under the pilot project have done a lot in this regard. The formative follow up reports, the field visits, and the pilot regions' education bureaus reports have revealed the 484 CRCs have been established and trained 1,936 teachers in the first year of the project implementation (MoE, 2012, SMASEE first year implementation report). The field visit reports further reveal that the practise of school-based CPD programme in the pilot schools has revived teachers' interest in school-based. CPD increases and teachers started using the skills and knowledge they gained in the first round of the training. These are promising results which have laid down a good foundation for establishing good and functioning CRCs. Establishing well-functioning CRCs is one area of support for rural teachers.

Section 7: Lessons Learnt

Strengthening CRCs: It was a challenge to establish CRCs in the early stage. The programme was started as a pilot and efforts were made to expand the best practices of these pilot schools to others. The result of these schools helped to convince stakeholders and to expand throughout the country in a short period of time.

Increased school-based support system: At the beginning, there was no systematic support system in schools and it was difficult to convince teachers to support each other. In order to change this situation, a series of workshops were organised at federal, regional, woreda and school levels to encourage school-based and CRC level support system. Now, schools and teachers are identifying and prioritising their needs. Based on this, teachers are preparing their plans, exchanging experiences, and helping each other, with focus on each subject's contents and methodologies. If there are strong head teachers and CRC supervisors, the support system will be very strong and will result in better student performance.

Capacity building in material development: Materials are prepared at federal and regional levels. Different workshops were organised on interactive material production for school-based and cluster-based training. It has become a common practice for schools to prepare modules for their CPD training, and sharing these materials at school as well as CRC levels.

Capacity development of CRC supervisors: It is important to facilitate the activities of CRCs by assigning responsible personnel. Initially, the CRC activities were run by CRC committees which were comprised of member schools. In this regard, the regions decided to assign competent supervisor in each CRCs. Now, the performance of CRCs has improved wherever there are strong supervisors.

In general, in order to support rural teachers in their endeavour to improve their professional competency and teaching skills it is vital to strengthen establishments such as CRCs by assigning resources and supervisors. SMASEE's experience has shown that CRCs can effectively work if there is follow up and support by a nearby education bureaus. Therefore, to deliver effective support for teachers in rural areas through CRCs it is very important to provide capacity development trainings for educational leaders working at different levels.

Section 8: Future Plan

As mentioned earlier in this chapter, different efforts have been tried to support all teachers in their activities to improve their teaching skills and improve the quality of education. The MoE has developed a document that guides future activities of pre- and in-service teacher trainings. This document is known as the 'Teachers, School Leaders, and Supervisors Development Guideline (Blue Print)'. The blue print contains general directions to be followed by all implementing entities including education bureaus regarding programmes of pre- and in-service teacher, school leaders and supervisor's development. This document is the basis for all existing and future plan related to teachers development.

To reach rural teachers and provide appropriate support that augment their professional development the government planned strengthening efforts have already started, for example, the Science and Mathematics Programme and other new programmes like the English Language Improvement Programme and through school-based and Cluster-based CPD programmes. Among others, the future plan includes the following activities:

- Developing the capacity of CRC supervisors and school leaders.
- Strengthening school based support system.
- Motivating teachers to be more active in the participation of school-based and cluster level support system.
- Carrying out assessment to identify training needs at national and regional levels.
- Organising capacity building programmes for regional trainers in identifying needs.
- Strengthening school–college linkages so as to support schools and cluster activities.
- Expanding English, Mathematics, and Science improvement programmes to all schools.
- Preparing supplementary materials and modules.
- Equipping CRCs with basic materials.

References

Amhara Region Education Bureau (AREB). (2005). *School Cluster and Supervision System*. (Unpublished Material).

Bredenberg, K., and Dahal, N. (2000). *Can School Clustering Enhance Educational Effectiveness? Promises and Pitfalls*. Phnom Penh, Cambodia: unpublished.

Coleman, M. (1994). *Leadership in Educational Management: The Principles of Educational Management*. London: Longman.

Elliott, D. (2001). *Change Agent Play Book: Coaching Teachers for Excellence*. Claremont: Learning-light Press.

EQUIP1. (2004). Cluster Schools and Teachers Professional Development. *EQ Review*, 2(2). Available at: http://www.equip123.net/EQ_Review/2_2.pdf (accessed on 15 February 2005).

Grauwe, A. (2001). *School Supervision in Four African Countries: Challenges and Reform* (Vol. I). Paris: IIEP/UNESCO.

Khaniya, T. (1997). *Teacher Support through Resource Centres: The Nepalese Case*. Paris: IIEP/UNESCO.

Ministry of Education of Ethiopia (MoE). (2001). *School Cluster Organization and Management Guideline*. (Unpublished Material).

———. (2009). *Teachers' Development Guideline (Blue Print)*. Addis Ababa, Ethiopia: EMPEDA.

———. (2010). *Project Documents on National Pilot Project for Strengthening Mathematics and Science Education in Ethiopia*. (Unpublished).

———. (2010/2011). *Annual Abstract*. Addis Ababa: Professional Printing Press.

———. (2012). SMASEE First Year Implementation Report. (Unpublished).

Perera, W.J. (2000). School Autonomy through School-based Management: The Case of Sri Lanka. *Improving School Efficiency: The Asian Experience*. An ANTRIEP Report. Paris: IIEP/UNESCO.

Scheerens, J. (1992). *Effective Schooling: Research, Theory and Practice*. New York: Cassell.

UNESCO. (2005). *Education for All*. Retrieved from http://www.education.nic.in/htmlweb/efa.htm Education: Right to Education. Retrieved from http://www.unesco.org/education/en.ev(2005). EFA Global Monitoring Report. Retrieved from http://www.unesco.org/education/gmr_download/chapter4.pdf

Villegas-Reimers, E. (2003). *Teacher Professional Development: An International Review of the Literature*. Paris: IIEP/UNESCO.

Summary and Policy Recommendations

F. Helen Drinan

It is evident from these chapters that there are a number of choices of systems, models and activities to support teachers' CPD in rural areas: from large scale School and Teacher Networks, to Mentoring Systems, Cluster Schools and Cluster Resource Centres, to Pedagogical Workshops involving the community and to school-based activities, such as observation and feedback. In many cases a combination of systems and activities are used in a given context.

However, equally and inevitably, there are paradoxes which challenge these teacher support systems, such as, political priorities, funding, time and commitment.

In this final part, it is pertinent to consider some of the paradoxes and tensions in the policy and practice of CPD as they are reflected in each of the chapters presented from Romania, China, Cambodia, Mozambique and Ethiopia. They are not seen as negative forces but as elements which can help inform Teacher Education and Development Policy. The challenges selected are generic and apply to the case studies in this book. They do not cover more specific challenges, such as teacher recruitment and deployment.

Teacher Support Systems as an International Priority for Quality Education

As has been noted several times throughout this book, the role that teachers play in relation to education quality is crucial and CPD for teachers is a vital element of this.

However, often other global realities in education take precedence, for example, teacher shortages, which mean that budgets put money into pre-service or initial teacher training rather than into in-service and CPD, which is often not considered a priority at all.

Alternatively, mass INSET programmes are implemented without thought to quality of training or follow up measures, such as, CPD systems. Consequently these, often costly programmes fail but are repeated a few years later without heeding lessons learnt.

Policy recommendation: CPD for teachers should be made a priority internationally so that it becomes a reality for all teachers not just the few. PRESET–INSET and CPD should be considered part of the same continuum and integrally linked. Therefore they should be given equal consideration so that when governments, supported by donors, prepare action plans based on the EFA mandate, CPD should be an integral part of their Teacher Education and Development policy.

Sustainability

Sustainability is a key element to any education initiative and has been highlighted on more than one occasion in these chapters. In setting up the Mentor System in Romania, Sandi recommends 'grassroots interventions need to be combined with nationwide policies and actions'. In the SBEP example from China, Liu Jing recommends that teacher support systems match government policies or work with them in order for them to be successful and sustainable. In the Cambodian example, Drinan, suggests that if the system is accountable and has a strong monitoring and evaluation framework in which it works, the support system will be sustainable. In the Mozambican case, the point of financial sustainability is made.

Policy recommendation: CPD and teacher support systems should be made sustainable in a number of ways; working with the government and within national policies, making them accountable, making them financially viable by providing sufficient funding for teacher support systems.

Capacity Building

Very much linked to the issue of sustainability and highlighted by Belew, in the Ethiopian Case Study on Cluster Resource Centres, is capacity building at all levels but in particular for those with a supervisory role or those who are in a management and leadership position to continue to develop the teacher support system. This can be done by giving them the skills to manage and lead systems and also to create new materials, curriculum and courses. By building capacity in this way, a critical mass of change agents is created who are able to provide, for example, continuation of donor-funded projects and the essential follow up support that teacher professional development systems need.

Policy recommendation: Capacity building to provide sustainability and follow up support should be core to teacher development programmes and be one of the key goals of a teacher support system.

Ownership and Community Development

It has been shown in nearly all the case studies that a teacher support system based on local needs is more successful and sustainable than a system or model that is transferred from another country as explained further also. As the Mozambican case study points out, 'an enabling environment should exist for local governmental institutions and community organisations to establish a collaborative partnership in undertaking the responsibility for developing a local vision and strategy'.

In addition to this, it has been shown that teacher support systems can and do involve a wider community than just a school's environment. Indeed as the Mozambican case study goes on to point out it can, '... build a community's capacity to successfully respond to and direct economic and social change'.

Policy recommendation: Teacher Support Systems should be based on local needs and contexts. They should involve those who they will directly affect as well as the wider community.

Transferring Wholesale Systems and Models

As is pointed out from Chapter one onwards, too often programmes and projects funded by international donor agencies rely on foreign experts or institutes to advise and suggest systems and models of teacher development.

In the Cambodian Case Study it was seen that it was sometimes conflict or mismatch of expectations of foreign donors that could slow down or cause duplication of activities in teacher professional development interventions.

So it is pertinent to be aware that sometimes teacher support systems come from a western perspective and context with assumptions being made on this basis. Wholesale transferral of systems is seldom effective. A good example of this is the transferral of various National Qualification Frameworks from one country to another, for example, South Africa importing frameworks from New Zealand/Australia/Scotland, and translating them onto a different context without considering lessons learnt from the original experience.

Policy recommendation: Therefore, if systems and models from another context are being introduced, the needs of the new context and also the lessons learnt from the original context should be the basis from which systems or models grow. In addition foreign experts should have a background in, not only the specific subject area, for example, teacher education, but also experience and a deep understanding of developing contexts.

Monitoring Impact and Evaluation

The case studies in this book provide excellent examples of how to monitor and evaluate teacher support systems. Belew in his case study from Ethiopia describes the importance of the Cluster Resource Centre's supervisors who not only report to the Woreda Education Office but also give advice and guidance, share experience and provide a conducive environment for teachers to work and appreciate their work, thereby improving teachers' motivation.

However, assessing the impact of teacher support systems on the individual and on the whole school, institutional development is often the weakest part of the chain of planning activities. Therefore it is important to execute it well. Recent research has found that impact evaluation is effective when there are clearly pre-defined outcomes and a suitable method for collecting evidence of its impact. Some examples of suitable methods for collecting evidence are: discussions with teachers; heads; support staff; parents; colleagues or focus group interviews; pupil interviews; focused classroom observation; using external expertise to gain a more objective opinion.

Policy recommendation: Leadership teams within schools and outside schools, who might include teachers, school directors, teacher trainers, teacher education managers from tertiary institutes, members of the community (parents) and students should be made responsible for monitoring impact and evaluation of CPD systems. These teams would have to be able to:

- understand how to evaluate quality and not just to monitor compliance;
- write guidelines on impact evaluation;
- analyse the data from an impact evaluation and;
- use the information from the evaluation to further improve CPD at all levels.

The Role of Teacher Educators

'Who trains the trainers?' and 'Who are the trainers?' are familiar refrains in setting up teacher support systems. It is still is an area for more research and development. All too often teacher educators are neglected but they too need training. This training will not be that different from teacher training in that it needs to provide both content and pedagogical skills training.

Sandi in the Romanian case study reminds us of the importance of selecting, training and recruitment of mentors and that it should be based on, 'their prior teaching and training experience and knowledge', and then lists specific criteria. Hernandez (1998) in Villegas-Reimers (2004: 138–139) lists a few principles that should guide the education of teacher-educators. These should be made part of any government's teacher education policy.

Policy recommendation:

- As the work of teacher-educators has a strong influence on the work of teachers, they should model and illustrate a variety of teaching methods, techniques, and processes; therefore, they need to be educated in pedagogy.
- Processes to prepare teacher-educators must be based on practical issues related to the day-to-day work in the classroom. The work of teacher-educators must include not only teaching, but also research directly related to their area of expertise.
- Teacher-educators must know and understand the institutions where they work and where their students will work.
- Teacher-educators must know the national education system in depth, and must understand the context in which it is implemented.
- Teacher-educators must know how to work in teams and collaborate in their work. Teacher-educators must enjoy teaching. This disposition will generate a positive attitude towards teaching in their students.

Teacher Incentives

Providing incentives are often used to alleviate the problems faced by teachers due to low salaries, and to improve the retention of teachers in the system. However, many of the incentive mechanisms described in teacher education and development literature would not be necessary if sufficient career and professional development opportunities were available to teachers. In a study of five African countries Webb (2010) found that, 'the creation of professional development opportunities linked to an appropriate career structure as one of the most important strategies to address poor salaries. It is also central to the improvement of education delivery in the countries concerned.'

Another caveat on incentives from Webb (2010), 'While it is easy to understand the rationale for such incentives, it is equally important to recognise that their impact on the quality of education might be negative ('double-class' and 'double shift' payments, extra duty allowance, etc.) as well as positive (easier access to study leave, scholarships, etc.). As such they should not be viewed as an alternative to the establishment of a model which allows teachers to seek promotion and its associated financial reward as part of a career-long process of development.'

Policy recommendation: Ministries in charge of education should ensure that CPD is linked to an appropriate career structure and that teacher support systems consider not only extrinsic motivation but also intrinsic motivation.

Institutional (systemic) and Individual (personal) Drivers

As has been seen in the chapters, looking at the importance of context on the support systems for rural teachers, governments can swing from institutional or systemic professional development policies to more personal or individual provision depending on the political, socio-economic contexts, referred to as policy-determined tensions (Sugrue, 2009).

Liu Jing in describing the SBEP effectiveness cited the importance of strengthening both individual and institutional capacity in order to provide both support and sustainability to the teacher support system.

Policy recommendation: Therefore what is required is a balance of the two so that teachers are allowed to be influenced not only by systemic professional development which benefits whole school or group development but also by their personal drivers, for example, life histories, personal circumstance and their career choices. Therefore rural teachers need support systems that not only centre on the curriculum and student learning outcomes but also systems that are able to reflect on their own practices, experiments and new approaches. This also links to extrinsic and intrinsic motivation in CPD.

Resources

Inevitably, funding is a key factor to the success and sustainability of teacher support systems as has been pointed out in the case studies. Commonly, there are no budget lines for teacher professional development at school-base level and this tends to be more prevalent in more rural and remote contexts.

Indeed, as Christie, Harley and Penny (2009) point out, '[w]here there is a lack of funding for basic education, CPD is readily displaced as a priority area, and is more likely to be narrowly targeted', which often means returning to the deficit model of CPD, filling in the gaps of knowledge or mass training on new education reforms and curriculum.

The CPD systems and activities described in this book have been proved to be cost effective but do require time and commitment. 'Time', as mentioned in many of the case studies, plays a major factor in setting up teacher support systems. Time needs to be given to any teacher training, as evidence has shown, short-term inputs are seldom effective so what is needed are long term inputs with follow up systems integrated into the design. Teachers also need time for practice (of new methods, approaches and techniques); for reflection and to share experiences. Any training for teacher professional development should be led by quality trainers using relevant and accessible materials. The emphasis should be on the practical, that is, there should be time to practice new skills and apply new knowledge.

Policy recommendation: Funding for CPD should be made mandatory and be a separate budget line in all schools. CPD should be integrated and an integral part of School Development Plans. There should be CPD Action Plans developed before the start of a new school year.

A More Holistic and Humanistic Approach

Finally and perhaps most importantly, it is necessary to look more at the affective elements of a teacher's development. This has not been given much attention in the case studies. Indeed, in general there is not enough emphasis on the more affective areas of teacher development.

However, a teacher support system should consider the teacher as a whole person, someone who is multi-dimensional rather than as one-dimensional, for example, 'a teacher in a classroom'. A more humanistic rather than behavioural approach to CPD is needed so that teachers can consider how they behave in the classroom and what their attitudes and assumptions towards their students are. In this way some of the more negative traditional teacher behaviour can be eradicated, for example, slapping and harsh punishments for children. This is obviously an important and serious aspect of CPD and has direct impact not only on the quality of education but also on children's welfare.

Policy recommendation: Therefore when teacher support systems are being designed equal emphasis should be given to affective areas as well as to knowledge content and pedagogical skills. Not only should CPD curricula include modules, such as, Inclusive Education and Equity and Education but, more importantly, teacher educators should behave and educate in an empathetic and humanistic way. There should be a humanistic ethos to CPD.

It is envisaged that should these policy recommendations come to fruition, teacher support systems would create not only a highly skilled and committed teaching staff but also provide quality teaching and learning at all levels and produce well rounded, skillful and knowledgeable students. This would indeed be 'taking a stand for teachers'.

References

Christie, P., Harley, K., and Penny, A. (2009). Cast Studies from Sub-Saharan Africa. In C. Day and J. Sachs (eds), *International Handbook on the Continuing Professional Development of Teachers*, pp. 167–190. McGraw-Hill Education: Open University Press.

Ministry of Education of Ethiopia (MoE). (2010). *Project Documents on National Pilot Project for Strengthening Mathematics and Science Education in Ethiopia* (unpublished).

Villegas-Reimers, E. (2004). Teacher Professional Development: An International Review of the Literature. UNESCO: International Institute for Educational Planning: www.unesco.org/iiep

Webb, D. (2010). Providing Teachers in Kindergarten and Basic Schools and Other Sector Professionals with Pathways for Career Enhancement. Strategy Paper for the Government of Eritrea, Ministry of Education.

About the Editors and Contributors

Editors

Zhao Yuchi is Programme Specialist and Administration Officer of UNESCO International Research and Training Centre for Rural Education (INRULED) as well as a lecturer in Beijing Normal University. He designed and started the project on teacher education in INRULED. Before joining INRULED, he worked in the International Department of Ministry of Education of China for seven years, with two years on international cooperation and exchanges in education and five years as the project manager of China–UK Southwest Basic Education Project, with a grant of 23.7 million pounds from UK government. For three years from 2001 to 2004, he worked as a research assistant in Research and Training Centre for Literacy Education, Southwest University, China. He has a doctorate in education and he finished his post-doctoral study on Support System for Rural Teachers' Continuing Professional Development in 2013.

Liu Jing has been working as Programme Specialist in UNESCO INRULED since 2012, with the responsibility to lead the programme called 'Quality Teacher for Rural Schools'. She is also a lecturer in Beijing Normal University. She has had over seven years of experience in research and practice of teacher education in China. She worked as an education consultant from 2007 to 2012 and provided technical assistance to a number of basic education projects in rural contexts supported by Department for International Development (DFID), UNICEF, Save the Children and Plan International. She has extensive

About the Editors and Contributors   247

experience in training material development, in-service training programme design, delivery, monitoring and evaluation. Also, she has experience in school development planning and inspection training with a focus on rural school improvement. She holds a Master's degree in Comparative Education and a PhD. in History of Education from Beijing Normal University.

Awol Endris is Programme Officer in teacher education and curriculum development at the UNESCO International Institute for Capacity Building in Africa (IICBA) located in Addis Ababa, Ethiopia. IICBA is an institute established by the General Conference of UNESCO in 1999 with a mandate to assist the 54 African Member States of UNESCO in the areas of teacher education, curriculum development, distance education and educational planning. Dr Awol coordinates the teacher education programmes of IICBA. He also facilitates training sessions in school leadership and management, management of teacher education institutions, and teacher policy development and implementation in many sub-Saharan African countries.

Prior to joining IICBA in 2005, he was Assistant Professor and Chairman in the Department of Foreign Languages and Literature of the Addis Ababa University, Ethiopia. He had also served at the then Bahir Dar Teachers College as a teacher trainer for English language teaching.

He has a Masters of Arts Degree in the Teaching of English as a Foreign Language (TEFL) from the Addis Ababa University, an MEd in Teachers of English to Speakers of Other Languages (TESOL) from the University of Leeds, UK, and a joint PhD. in TEFL from the University of Lancaster, UK, and Addis Ababa University.

Contributors

Ajuda de Desenvolvimento de Povo para Povo (ADPP; Development Aid from People to People) is a Mozambican non-governmental organisation. It was established in 1982 and has grown steadily during its 32 years of existence. It currently implements over 80 projects across all provinces of the country, employs more than 2,500 staff members and benefits more than 3 million Mozambicans annually.

ADPP works within the following areas: education, integrated community development programmes, economic development, HIV/AIDS prevention and care, agriculture and renewable energy, scholarship programmes and sale of second-hand clothes and shoes.

ADPP has been working with the sector of education since its establishment and presently runs 4 schools for children and young people, 3 vocational schools, 11 teacher training colleges and 1 university (with courses in Pedagogy and Community Development). The teacher training colleges train 1,800 teacher trainees a year, 500 vocational school students, 3,000 primary/secondary school children and 250 students in the university. It reaches over 1,500 teachers with in-service training and 400 primary schools with enhancement programmes. It reaches 14,000 small farmers with sustainable farming techniques and 2,000,000 people through the HIV/AIDS prevention programmes. ADPP works in all the provinces of the country.

Theodros Shewarget Belew is working as the Head of the Minister's Office in the Ministry of Education of the Federal Democratic Republic of Ethiopia. He has had 27 years of experience in teaching and management of teacher education at the regional and federal levels. He has strong experience in teacher education management, and module and material development for pre-service and in-service teacher education programmes. He holds a Master's degree in Organizational Leadership from Azusa Pacific University and a BA degree in Ethiopian Language and Literature from Addis Ababa University.

F. Helen Drinan has been researching issues relating to the language of instruction in education and its impact on teaching and learning. She has had almost 30 years of experience in education from early years through to the tertiary level, in developing contexts. Twenty years of this experience has been in teacher education and management: methodology of teaching, trainer training (TOT) course management and institutional development. This has involved individual and institutional capacity building, and experience in the design, delivery, monitoring and evaluation of education programmes.

She has also strong experience in curriculum material writing for pre-service, in-service and continuing professional development (CPD).

Most of her work has been in developing contexts for rural and remote areas and post-conflict situations.

She holds a Master's degree in Applied Linguistics from Edinburgh University and a Master's degree in Education and International Development (first) from the Institute of Education, University of London.

Ana Maria Sandi is a consultant with an extensive experience in education. As a lead education specialist at the World Bank, she was the task team leader of a rural education project in Romania. The project supported, among other things, a mentoring system for the professional development of teachers. Her credentials include a PhD. from the University of Bucharest, Romania.

Index

ADPP. *See* Ajuda de Desenvolvimento de Povo para Povo (ADPP)
Aga Khan Foundation (AKF), 18b
Ajuda de Desenvolvimento de Povo para Povo (ADPP), 184
AKF. *See* Aga Khan Foundation (AKF)
Australia
    ABRA training, 27b
    innovative links-school networks, 19b

Brazil, school that counts, 24b

Cambodia, history and politics of, 145–147. *See also* School Cluster system, in Cambodia
capacity building, 239
    China–UK Southwest Basic Education Project (SBEP), 121, 123
    county trainers, SBEP, 112–114
    School Cluster system, in Cambodia, 157
China, SBEP, 32b
China–UK Southwest Basic Education Project (SBEP)
    capacity and confidence level, 130
    capacity building, 121, 123
    classroom action research, 114
    classroom observation and feedback, 103, 113
    concept map of, 108f
    Continuing Professional Development (CPD), 100
    county trainers, capacity building of, 112–114
    and county trainers' role, 113
    Dakar Conference in 2000, 93
    develop and manage resources, 118–119
    distance education (DE), 103–105
    end-of-project (EOP), 124
    generic description of, 95, 97
    in-service teacher training (INSET), 103, 114
    interventions conducted by, 96f
    key teachers, 102
    mentoring skills, 113–114
    national support team (NST), 106
    nine-year compulsory education, 93
    overview of, 97–100
    pre-service teacher education, 131–132
    problem solving skills and creativity, 94
    rural teachers, 101
    support offered, to local teachers, 102–103
    teachers' professional development, 101–102
    teacher support pre-SBEP, 100
    teacher training, details of, 122t
    teacher training modules, 131
    teacher training school, 101–102
    teaching and learning, positive changes in, 124–125
    teaching research office (TRO), 101

Index 251

training of trainers (TOT), 113
training through county TSS, 121
cluster-based support systems,
  15–17, 16b
cluster-based teacher supervision
  system, 155–157. *See also* School
  Cluster system, in Cambodia
Cluster Resource Centre (CRC),
  Ethiopia
  administrative purpose, 225
  concept and rationale, 223–227,
    226t
  economic purpose, 224
  effectiveness of, 232–233
  hierarchical model, 227–228
  horizontal model, 228
  hybrid model, 228, 230–231
  monitor and support of, 231–232
  organisational model of, 227–231,
    229f
  pedagogical purpose, 224
  political purpose, 224
  school visits, 232
  supervisors' role, 231
  teachers' motivation, 232
Continuing Professional Development
  (CPD)
  action research, 31–32
  China–UK Southwest Basic
    Education Project (SBEP), 100
  cluster-based support systems,
    15–17, 16b
  definition, 3, 3n1
  demoing/modelling, 33–34
  distance education/learning
    systems, 24–26, 25b
  on Education for All (EFA), 4–6
  education quality, 77
  Ethiopia, 206–207
  experiencing and reflecting, 34–36
  information and communication
    technology (ICT) systems,
    26–28, 27b
  and international context, 4

  and paradigm shifts, 8–9
  partnership systems, 22–24, 24b
  peer coaching and mentoring,
    29–31, 31b
  peer observation and feedback,
    32–33, 32b
  Romania, 53
  rural teachers, challenges for, 10,
    11t–12t, 12
  school-based support systems for,
    13–15, 14b
  school networks, 19–20, 19b
  systems, 12–13
  teacher network systems, 20–22, 21b
  Teacher Resource Centres (TRCs),
    17–19, 18b
  UNESCO, 6–8, 7t
County Education Bureau (CEB), 99,
  109, 111
CPD. *See* Continuing Professional
  Development (CPD)

Dakar Conference in 2000, 93
Decentralisation, 16
Distance education (DE), 103–105

Education for All (EFA), 4–6
Education Quality Improvement
  Project (EQIP), 158, 160
education reform processes, 172–173
Education Strategic Plans (ESPs), 143
EFA. *See* Education for All (EFA)
Escuela Nueva, Colombia, Peer-
  teaching, 31b
ESPs. *See* Education Strategic Plans
  (ESPs)
Ethiopia
  administrative and training
    structures, 216, 217t–222t, 223
  challenges and problems of CPD,
    207–208
  cluster-based CPD, 216
  Cluster Resource Centre (CRC),
    223–227

Continuous Professional
  Development (CPD), 206–207
Education and Training Policy
  (ETP), 206
federal level administrative
  structure, 217t
initiation of new CPD framework,
  208–211
regional level administrative
  structure, 217t–218t
school-based CPD, 211–216
Technical Vocational Education
  and Training (TVET), 206
Wereda level administrative
  structure, 218t–219t
Excellence in Classroom Education at
  the Local Level (EXCELL) project,
  39b
EXCELL project. See Excellence in
  Classroom Education at the Local
  Level (EXCELL) project

gross domestic product (GDP), 83
Guinea, West Africa, school-based
  CPD, 14b

holistic and humanistic approach,
  244–245
humana people to people (HPP), 189

ICF. See International Coaching
  Federation (ICF)
ICT. See Information and
  communication technology (ICT)
  systems
Improved Basic Education in
  Cambodia (IBEC), 152
information and communication
  technology (ICT) systems, 26–28,
  27b
initial teacher education (ITE), 5n3
in-service teacher training (INSET),
  103, 114
in-service training (INSET), 37

INSET. See In-service teacher training
  (INSET); In-service training (INSET)
institutional (systemic) and individual
  (personal) drivers, 243
International Coaching Federation
  (ICF), 29
International Organisations (IOs), 149
International Rescue Committee
  (IRC), 149
ITE. See Initial teacher education
  (ITE)

Kampuchean Action for Primary
  Education (KAPE), 151
Kenya, SPRED 3, 25b
Kerala, India, ICT projects, 27b
key teachers, 102

learning circles, 21b

mentor, 53n2, 54
mentoring programme
  certification programme, 65
  cost-effectiveness, 75–77
  monitoring and evaluation, 65–67,
    65f
  pilot phase of, 67–69
  problems solved, 69–72, 71t, 72t
  quality assurance, 80–81
  right incentives, 79
  in rural schools, 63–64
  selection, training and recruitment,
    59–62
  setting up mobile and fixed
    resource centres, 62–63
  stakeholders' involvement, 65
  strong organisation, 79–80
  sustainability, 73–75
  takes time and follow-up activities,
    80
  training curricula, 58–59
  training modules and teaching/
    learning materials, 58–59
  transportation issue, 79

Index   253

mid-term review (MTR), 97
Millennium Development Goals, 10
monitoring impact and evaluation,
    240–241
Mozambique
    challenges, 186–189
    constraints, 186–189
    demographics, 185–186
    education quality, 189–190
    Ministry of Education (MINED),
        187
    pedagogical workshops, 190–197
    problems, 186–189
    pupils to qualified teachers
        (PQTR), 188
    pupil-teacher ratio (PTR), 188
    school and community level,
        197–199, 198f
    zone of Pedagogic Influence (ZIPs),
        194

Namibia, School Improvement
    Program (SIP), 42b
National Medium and Long-
    term Educational Reform and
    Development Programme, 131
Nine-Year Compulsory Education,
    93

ownership and community
    development, 239

pedagogical workshops (PW)
    purposes and functioning,
        190–197
    scale up of, 199–201, 200t
    school and community level,
        197–199, 198f
peer coaching and mentoring, 29–31,
    31b
peer observation and feedback,
    32–33, 32b
pupil-teacher ratio (PTR), 188
PW. See pedagogical workshops (PW)

reflective model, 8
REP. See Rural Education Project (REP)
Romania
    Continuous Professional
        Development (CPD), 53
    education quality, 81–82
    Education Reform project, 51
    grassroots activities, 78
    mentoring system, development
        of, 81
    political changes, 50
    Rural Education Project (REP), 51
    school-based professional
        development, 78–79
    school-based teacher professional
        development approach, 83
    Teachers' Houses (THs), 52
rural contexts, school-based support
    systems for, 13–15, 14b
Rural Education Project (REP)
    mentoring programme in, 57–58
    objective of, 55–57
rural teacher support system
    community, 41–42
    development and content of
        training, 40–41
    meeting local needs, 37–38
    modes, 40–41
    role of leadership, 38–40, 39b, 40t

SBEP. See China–UK Southwest Basic
    Education Project (SBEP)
school-based, Distance Learning
    Teacher Development Programme,
    25b
school-based professional
    development approach, 54
school cluster system, in Cambodia
    accountability, 160–161
    background, 147–148
    Cambodian Ministry of Education,
        Youth and Sport (MoEYS),
        143–145
    capacity building, 157, 171

cluster-based teacher supervision
  system, 155–157
contract teachers, 175–176
and cost effectiveness, 167–168
and decentralisation, 169–172
decision-making and
  empowerment, 171
double shift systems, 175–176
and education reform processes,
  172–173
and equity, 164–167
ethnic minority areas, 175–176
functions, 154–155
history and politics of Cambodia,
  145–147
methodology and content,
  162–163
mismatch of education providers'
  expectations, 173
multi-sectoral classification
  scheme, 161
organisation, 152–154, 153f
perceptions, 174
piloting of system, 1993–1994,
  148–149
post 1998, 151–152
resource centres, 157
resource sharing, 155
scaling up, 1995–1997, 149–151
and school improvement planning,
  168–169
shortage of teachers, 175–176
streamlined absorption, 171–172
support, 162–163
and sustainability, 164
teacher educators/trainers, 176–177
teacher professional development,
  158–160
teacher training, 162–163
School Development Planning (SDP),
  112
School Improvement Program (SIP),
  42b

Singapore, teacher networks, 21b
SIP. *See* School Improvement
  Program (SIP)
sustainability, 238
  mentoring programme, 73–75
  School Cluster system, in
    Cambodia and, 164

Teacher Education and Development
  Policy, 237
teacher educators, role of, 241–242
teacher incentives, 242–243
Teacher Learning Resource Centres
  (TLRC), 99, 111–112, 117–118
  in project provinces, 121t
teacher-led workshops, 21b
teacher network conferences, 21b
teacher network website, 21b
Teacher Resource Centres (TRCs),
  17–19, 18b
Teacher Support System (TSS), 99,
  105, 105b, 106–107
  county trainers, 128
  effectiveness and outcomes, 120
  government policies, 125–126
  initiatives, 127
  monitoring and evaluation,
    129–130
  monitoring and evaluation of,
    119–120
  reliable funding, 128–129
  understanding and adequate
    support, 126–127
Teaching Learning Support Network
  (TLSN), 26
teaching research office (TRO), 101
TLSN. *See* Teaching Learning Support
  Network (TLSN)
training of trainers (TOT), 113
transferring wholesale systems and
  models, 240
TRCs. *See* Teacher Resource Centres
  (TRCs)

Index   255

Uganda, school cluster-based CPD, 16b
UNESCO. *See* United Nations Educational, Scientific and Cultural Organization (UNESCO)
United Nations Children's Fund (UNICEF), 148
United Nations Educational, Scientific and Cultural Organization (UNESCO), 6–8, 7t, 179

United Nations Transitional Authority in Cambodia (UNTAC), 148, 151
United States Aid (USAID), 150, 151, 152

well-being programme, 21b
World Bank's Implementation Completion Report, 178